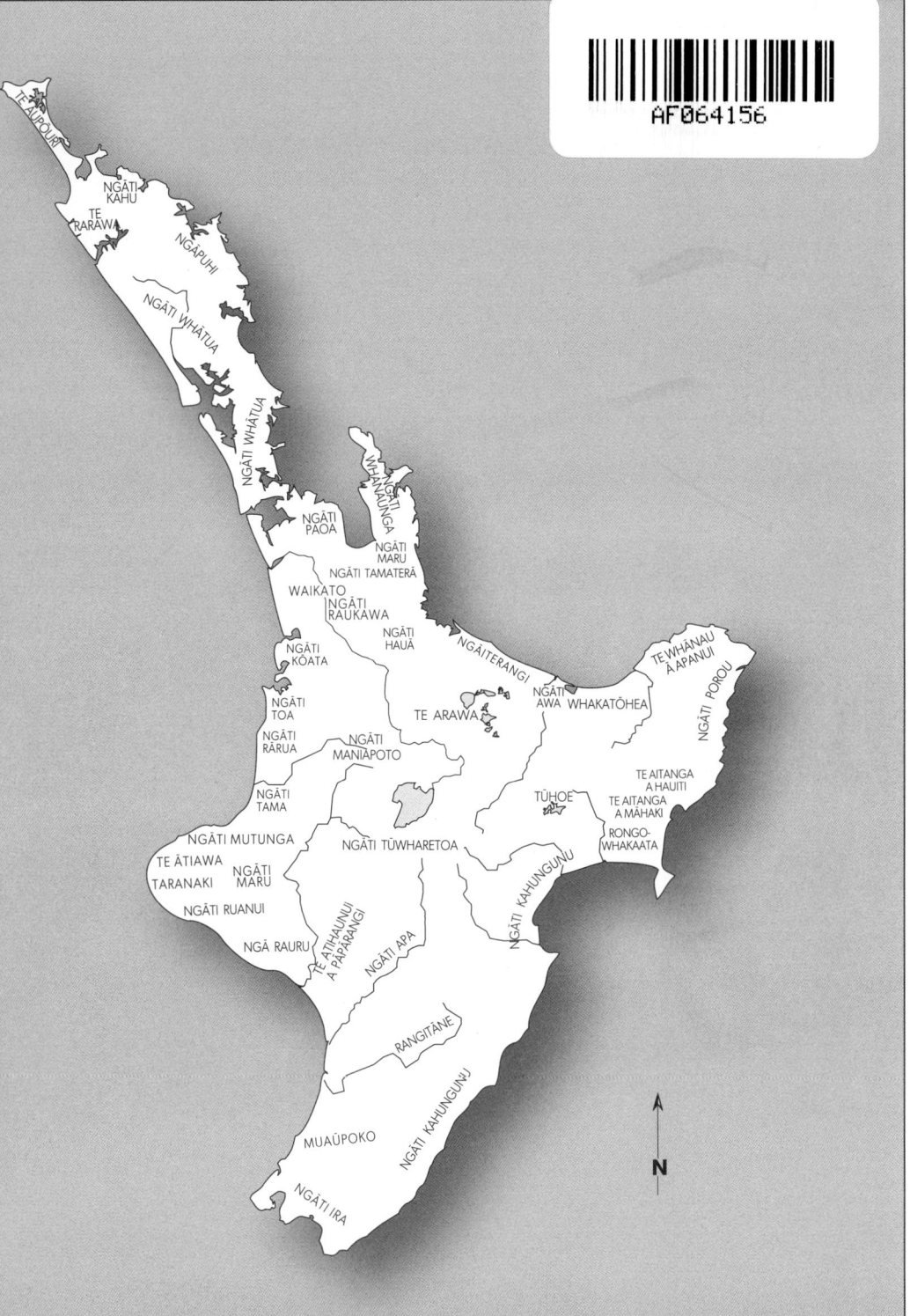

APPROXIMATE LOCATIONS OF MAIN IWI DISCUSSED IN THIS BOOK AS AT 1818

THE FORGOTTEN WARS

Why the Musket Wars matter today

RON CROSBY

Oratia

Front cover Mātāika, Nannette MacKenzie

Back cover PUBL-0034-2-355, Sainson, Louis Auguste de, 1800–, b. 1800: Flotte de guerre à la Nouvelle Zélande, Nargeon sc. [Paris, 1839]. Alexander Turnbull Library, Wellington, NZ

Published by Oratia Books, Oratia Media Ltd, 783 West Coast Road, Oratia, Auckland 0604, New Zealand (www.oratia.co.nz).

Copyright © 2020 Ron Crosby
Copyright © 2020 Oratia Books (published work)

The copyright holders assert their moral rights in the work.

This book is copyright. Except for the purposes of fair reviewing, no part of this publication may be reproduced or transmitted in any form or by any means, whether electronic, digital or mechanical, including photocopying, recording, any digital or computerised format, or any information storage and retrieval system, including by any means via the Internet, without permission in writing from the publisher. Infringers of copyright render themselves liable to prosecution.

ISBN 978-0-947506-79-7
Ebook ISBN 978-0-947506-83-4

First published 2020
Reprinted 2021 (twice)

Editor: Susan Brierley
Designer: Sarah Elworthy

ARTS COUNCIL OF NEW ZEALAND TOI AOTEAROA

The publisher acknowledges the generous support of Creative New Zealand for this publication.

Printed in China

CONTENTS

	Preface	6
	Acknowledgements	9
1	The significance of the Musket Wars	11
2	Features of the Musket Wars	20
3	The introduction of muskets and beginning of Ngāpuhi dominance	30
4	The peak and decline of Ngāpuhi dominance	47
5	Central North Island iwi react to musket power	72
6	Te Rauparaha's coalitions — heke, raupatu, disintegration	96
7	Impacts of the musket on Kāi Tahu and Moriori	131
8	Eastern iwi responses to musket power	148
9	The last conflicts	168
	Afterword	192
	Glossary	193
	Select bibliography	194
	Index	197
	About the author	207

PREFACE

In 1999, when I decided to write *The Musket Wars* as a history of inter-iwi conflict, one of the most challenging decisions was how to approach such a complex subject. The history could not be written neatly from the point of view of particular iwi, as most taua involved a combination of iwi or hapū, and similarly, each would commonly be engaged against a number of different iwi or hapū. Increasing the complexity of the situation, and the relationships between iwi, was the fact that as time passed it was common for alliances to change.

Nor could the history be written easily on a regional basis, as many taua traversed huge distances; further, repeated or reciprocal attacks might take place in different areas than the original raids. The most logical choice, then, was to endeavour to create a chronological record, moving between iwi and regions as events unfolded.

However, many readers in the general community, and particularly those with Māori whakapapa, have observed that it was too long and complex. A common concern was that they really only wanted to know about what had happened to their iwi or hapū, or in their region. Yet to gain that understanding they found themselves having to read the whole book.

Two aims, therefore, have led to the writing of this new book:

› First, a desire to respond to these concerns by presenting a more concise and accessible history of the Musket Wars era, while adopting a fresh thematic approach of cause, effect and response to the impacts of the era that more clearly explains the effects of the musket on specific iwi, hapū and regions, and their respective responses to those effects.

› Second, to endeavour to provide answers to questions about the significance of the Musket Wars era, not only to the history of Aotearoa (New Zealand), but also in terms of modern inter-iwi and inter-hapū relationships.

The latter point is particularly relevant at this time in our history, with the need for both Māori and Pākehā to understand the reasoning behind, and the implications of, such issues as the Treaty settlement process and ongoing customary rights. It is also fitting that the publication of this book coincides with the long-overdue introduction of a New Zealand history syllabus in our schools. It is to be hoped that the era of the Musket Wars receives recognition in its own right as a crucially important aspect of the history of Māori relationships — and not as some perceived minor aspect of 'initial contacts' with Europeans. Māori deserve to have their history taught as an important subject in its own right.

At the same time, I hope to answer questions that will inevitably be taxing the minds of younger readers in particular, as they grapple with being educated in their own nation's history at last. A crucial aspect for anyone struggling, or keen, to gain greater knowledge of the history of their iwi, hapū or region, is understanding the history that underlies contemporary relationships between iwi and hapū. This is not only vital to those who identify with a particular district or region; it is essential to anyone who is endeavouring to gain greater knowledge of our collective history.

For readers who would like additional information, the earlier book, *The Musket Wars: A History of Inter-iwi Conflict 1806–1845*, contains more detail, and includes a chronology, list of protagonists, appendices covering firearms of the era as well as logistics and tactics, a full bibliography and, in later editions, recommendations for further reading.

A NOTE ON THE USE OF TE REO

In general, Māori place names are used in the text, with their English-language equivalents provided when they are first encountered in each chapter. Similarly, translations of general terms in te reo are provided the first time they are used; in addition, there is a glossary on page 193. Macrons are used where they are commonly seen in current parlance, and where known for place names and iwi names, but not for the names of individuals.

As in any language, there are regional variations in both the meaning and the spelling of some terms in te reo. One notable example that occurs in this book is the name of the iwi that is known variously as Ngāi Tahu and Kāi Tahu. In the 1996 Act of Parliament that established the statutory entity Te Runanga o Ngai Tahu (now well-known as TRONT) 'Ngai Tahu' was used, with no tohutō (macron). By 1998, the statutory entity was being referred to as Te Rūnanga o Kāi Tahu. Currently, the spelling that is used on the iwi's website is generally Ngāi Tahu, although Kāi Tahu sometimes appears. On marae, and in more recent writing by Kāi Tahu people such as Hana O'Regan, who are seeking to re-establish their own original language style, the form Kāi Tahu is commonly used. While it seems, then, that both forms are acceptable today, at the time of the events described in this book the usage would undoubtedly have been Kāi Tahu. Respecting that fact, that is the form that has been used here.

ACKNOWLEDGEMENTS

Most books I have written have required so much intensive research, travel, accommodation, advice and assistance, whether physical or intellectual, that they have entailed a lengthy list of acknowledgements. This book is refreshing in that regard as I really only need to acknowledge a few individuals and groups, who have provided encouragement and support in a variety of important ways.

The first of these acknowledgements is very general. It is to readers who have made the constructive criticism that they would have preferred either a simpler book, or one in which it was easier to gain an appreciation of the effects of the Musket Wars era in relation to particular iwi, hapū, districts or regions.

The second is to two people who have enthusiastically supported this project right from the genesis of *The Musket Wars* and its publication in 1999, through a number of reprints of the original book, and latterly the development and publication of this book: I owe a particular vote of thanks to my wife Margy, and to publisher Peter Dowling, who was involved initially at Reed Publishing, and in recent years at Oratia Books.

I also need to acknowledge those teachers at Marlborough Boys' College, Marlborough Girls' College, and other Marlborough schools, and in more recent years at Burnside High in Christchurch, who have persuaded me to make regionally based presentations to their pupils on the effects of this era. Until I was compelled to reduce those presentations to a Powerpoint limited to the length of a school period, I had not believed such a task would be possible. As the pupils responded positively I gained confidence that a similar cause, effect and response approach was feasible for the whole era. So, many thanks to those enthusiastic and far-sighted teachers who requested those presentations, at a time when the subject matter was not part of an Aotearoa-wide syllabus. It is to be hoped that their foresight is recognised and reflected in the newly introduced New Zealand history syllabus.

A particularly special acknowledgement is owed to Nannette MacKenzie, whose drawing *Mātāika* is reproduced on the cover of the book. Nannette is an artist friend who lives in Kenepuru Sound in Marlborough with her husband Alistair MacKenzie, who is the author of books on military history. One day in 2012 Nannette arrived unannounced at our door carrying *Mātāika*, which she gifted to me with the following letter:

Ron,

My drawing "Mātāika" has been hanging in the wrong author's home! I feel the wairua flows directly to you to acknowledge your understanding, commitment and integrity around things Maori, so I'd be pleased if you would accept this gift.

The trade axe has two-coloured eyes to reflect that two cultures had input into the making (forged metal and carved bone), similarly the flint action has morphed into a manaia to reflect how both cultures were so involved with the muskets. The heart of the drawing has a fish hook searching for its mark.

All in all a good picture for a man who has taken time to learn and record our history.

Hope you enjoy "Mātāika".

Best Regards,
Nannette

I was delighted when publisher Peter Dowling agreed that Nannette's drawing captured the wairua of the Musket Wars era as she intended, and should grace the cover of a book on that subject. I also wish to thank designer Sarah Elworthy, who has utilised Mātāika and De Sainson's waka taua engraving so effectively. Thanks are also due to Mike Bradstock and Carolyn Lagahetau for their input.

Finally, I need to express my gratitude to the editor of this book, Susan Brierley, who has now edited a number of the books I have written. She invariably brings a level of clarity and directness of expression that I continually try to emulate, but need her support to achieve.

1

THE SIGNIFICANCE OF THE MUSKET WARS

The introduction of muskets to Aotearoa and their gradual spread and use throughout the country between 1807 and 1845 completely upset the natural balance of power between warring hapū or iwi engaged in customary Māori warfare. Prior to the availability of muskets, Māori toa (warriors) on each side of any conflict had been armed identically, using the same forms of traditional hand-held wooden, bone or stone weapons, coupled sometimes with limited use of short-range tao (spears). The advent of muskets enabled killing at a distance, and meant that those who first acquired them in large numbers could launch long-distance taua (raids), and dominate and decimate those who had only traditional hand-held weapons.

MAJOR PHASES OF THE MUSKET WARS

There were a number of identifiable phases to the Musket Wars, although these are not always clear-cut and frequently overlap.
› The first iwi to acquire muskets in large numbers and to launch aggressive taua were those in Te Tai Tokerau (Northland), predominantly Ngāpuhi. Between 1818 and 1825 they, and their closely related northern iwi,

swept aside all opposition in the top half of Te Ika a Māui (the North Island). Their wide-sweeping raids inflicted massive casualties, they took large numbers of slaves, and forced major migrations or temporary displacements, particularly of coastal iwi.

- The second phase was far more complex as, from 1821 to about 1834, iwi to their south desperately traded flax and other resources on an increasingly large scale to acquire muskets. When they had built up their own musket power, major central iwi such as the various Tainui iwi, Marutūahu iwi and Ngāti Tūwharetoa raided outwards. These raids were particularly to the west and south, into north and south Taranaki, and into Hawke's Bay and the Bay of Plenty. These taua also inflicted huge casualties and caused more migrations and temporary displacements from those areas as their victims sought refuge.
- The third phase was contemporaneous with the second as Ngāti Toa under Te Rauparaha, and his closely allied iwi, were compelled to migrate south from their Kawhia and north Taranaki homelands to avoid Tainui pressure. They based themselves on Kāpiti Island and in the adjacent Ōtaki area, from where they conquered in turn the local Horowhenua and Whanganui a Tara (Wellington) iwi.
- The next phase occurred from about 1827 to 1832 when Te Rauparaha's loose coalition embarked on a series of raids across Raukawa Moana (Cook Strait), and deep into Te Waipounamu (the South Island). These taua ventured well down both coasts of Te Waipounamu, although their initial impact was particularly devastating on Te Tau Ihu (Top of the South) iwi Rangitāne, Ngāti Kuia and Ngāti Apa ki te Rā Tō.
- Between 1829 and 1832, Kāi (Ngāi) Tahu suffered severely from Te Rauparaha and his allies in the Kaikōura and central Canterbury areas. The final raupatu (conquest) by some of these northern iwi occurred in 1835 when Ngāti Tama and Ngāti Mutunga invaded Rēkohu or Wharekauri (the Chatham Islands) and devastated the peaceful Moriori there.
- A reciprocal phase of response to these northern taua occurred in 1833 and 1834 when Kāi Tahu themselves launched two major long-distance taua from Murihiku (Southland), where they had access to muskets from trading with both sealers and whalers, as far north as Te Tau Ihu. In 1836 they followed up these aggressive taua with the total defeat of a very long-distance taua by Ngāti Tama, who travelled all the way from Mohua (Golden Bay; also often referred to as Te Tai Tapu or Te Taitapu) deep into Murihiku.

- The later phases of the Musket Wars taua were dominated by new areas of conflict. Ngāti Kahungunu initially had to defend themselves against repeated raids, but as they acquired muskets they conducted long-distance taua into the Taupō area. Between 1828 and 1834, warfare also broke out between eastern Bay of Plenty iwi and Ngāti Porou.
- The final phase occurred between 1836 and 1845 as reciprocal taua moved back and forth in the Bay of Plenty/Rotorua/Matamata areas. These wars were between an alliance of Ngāti Hauā and Ngāiterangi on the one hand, and Te Arawa on the other. The final taua involved a series of Ngāti Tūwharetoa raids into the Whanganui area.

THE END OF THE MUSKET WARS

There was no one factor that brought the Musket Wars to an end, and they did not end suddenly or dramatically because of any particular event or battle. Rather, a combination of developments, events and influences gradually brought Māori to the realisation that it was no longer possible to acquire or exercise power with impunity through the use of the musket.

- The primary factor in ending the wars was the widespread acquisition of muskets throughout the country. Ngāpuhi were the first to feel the impact of the new balance of firepower as their southern enemies turned the tables on them from 1826 to 1833. For other iwi, the realisation of the change in the balance of power took longer to accept, but as awareness grew the numbers of taua decreased steadily in the later years of the era. The final taua, a Ngāti Tūwharetoa incursion into the Whanganui area, took place in 1845.
- A more direct, but initially peaceful, influence in many areas was the sudden arrival of Pākehā colonists in large numbers at the end of the 1830s and in the early 1840s. They tended to settle in heavily contested areas that had become largely devoid of permanent Māori occupants as a result of the Musket Wars, such as Wellington, Nelson, Christchurch, Whanganui, New Plymouth, Napier and Auckland. In these areas rangatira suddenly had to face a new political and physical reality with the development of large settler communities, backed by a major European force in the form of the Crown, whose officials were supported by a standing military and naval power.
- The gradual conversion of many Māori to Christianity also had an impact, particularly in the late 1830s. Christian tenets of peace and good order

finally started to have a major effect, even tempering the desire to continue traditional customary practices such as the pursuit of utu for every slight, imagined or real, and curtailing the customary practices of slavery, the killing of captives and cannibalism.
- The impact of European diseases was also a localised factor in some areas. The classic example of the severe impact of disease occurred in the South Island in 1835. A major taua led by the Kāi Tahu rangatira Te Whakataupuka was heading north to attack Te Rauparaha, but stopped and dispersed after he and scores of his toa caught measles and died at what became known as Measley Beach, on the Otago coast. Similarly, Ngāti Hauā enthusiasm and drive was affected in 1837 when its imposing rangatira Te Waharoa died from disease at the height of his powers.
- The final influence in bringing the Musket Wars to an end was the Treaty of Waitangi. Regardless of what views rangatira held as to the effect of the Treaty (and recognising that many, particularly in inland or southern areas, had never read or signed it), the resultant creation of a national system of good order backed by Crown military force slowly spread across the nascent nation. In some cases, the presence of Crown military power was a new and persuasive influence.

SOME COMPARISONS AND LONG-TERM CONSEQUENCES OF THE MUSKET WARS

- Over a period of more than thirty years, from 1807 to 1845, the availability of muskets resulted in the most tumultuous period of warfare in our nation's history.
- During the Musket Wars era, there were more than a thousand conflicts, ranging from major taua, sieges and battles to more minor ambushes, skirmishes and other engagements.
- The casualty figures resulting from the Musket Wars greatly exceeded those of the later New Zealand Wars.
- The Musket Wars affected every iwi throughout the length of the country, either directly or indirectly.
- The numbers of people affected by the Musket Wars, whether through death, injuries, permanent migrations or temporary displacements, were massive — the lives of 50,000 people were affected over the 30-year span of the wars, against a background population of between 100,000 and 150,000.

- Major permanent migrations occurred, displacing or subjugating the original occupying iwi, and in one case effectively eliminating Ngāti Ira in the Whanganui a Tara area.
- As a result of migrations and displacements, large areas that were particularly vulnerable to raiding taua were depopulated and left vacant, sparsely populated or only intermittently occupied for the gathering of food or other resources.
- There were many temporary displacements of shorter duration, commonly causing strife in locations of refuge because of the ensuing pressures between those seeking refuge and the original occupiers.

THE SIGNIFICANCE OF THE MUSKET WARS FOR INTER-IWI RELATIONSHIPS

The main significance of the Musket Wars in both historical and contemporary terms is that their outcomes have laid the principal basis for inter-iwi relationships ever since. Consequently:
- Without some knowledge of the Musket Wars and their outcomes it is not possible to gain a proper understanding of contemporary inter-iwi relationships, or sometimes even inter-hapū relationships.
- Many of the relationship issues that affected iwi alliances and conflicts during the later New Zealand Wars can be attributed to events that occurred in the Musket Wars.
- The Musket Wars had substantial effects in terms of mana for those involved, which has had a continuing impact during the modern Treaty-settlement process.

EFFECTS ON THE MANA OF RANGATIRA AND INDIVIDUAL MĀORI

- A large number of rangatira gained exalted and nationwide reputations as a result of their exploits in leading long-distance or widespread taua during the Musket Wars.
- Other rangatira gained increased mana by playing significant leadership roles in defending their iwi's rohe (district).
- Some individuals, both men and women, were involved in amazing feats of endurance or courage that earned them widespread and enduring reputations in Māoridom.

IMPACTS ON MĀORI RELATIONSHIPS WITH EARLY COLONISTS AND THE CROWN

The devastation and depopulation of desirable areas as a result of the Musket Wars were apparent by 1839–40, around which time many land-hungry Pākehā colonists arrived, led initially by the New Zealand Company. Despite Crown guarantees to Māori in the Treaty of Waitangi, early settlers and later Crown purchase agents took advantage of the consequences of the Musket Wars to obtain land.

› Because many of the areas that were most heavily contested during the Musket Wars had largely been vacated, or were only intermittently occupied, they became the first locations to be purchased by the New Zealand Company and occupied by the early Pākehā settlers. This occurred with scant, if any, regard to the latent customary rights of Māori displaced from those areas.

› Some land was sold by particular hapū or iwi without the consent of all owners who held customary rights, and in some cases by non-occupying iwi. These sales subsequently became the cause of dissension and sometimes war between hapū or iwi, or later with the Crown.

THE CONTINUING SIGNIFICANCE OF THE MUSKET WARS TODAY

The consequences of the Musket Wars continue to reverberate today in a variety of ways, particularly in relation to customary rights and iwi/hapū relationships. These are issues that are relevant to all New Zealanders, particularly in the post Treaty-settlement world.

RELATIONSHIPS BETWEEN IWI AND/OR HAPŪ

One of the most significant consequences of the Musket Wars era is how it affected ongoing customary relationships between competing iwi and hapū.

Customary rights to acquire land interests by ringa kaha (i.e. by force of arms), in accordance with Māori lore, effectively came to an end shortly after the Treaty of Waitangi was signed. From that time on, British laws applied equally to all, and they did not allow for forcible acquisition of land. As a consequence, the rights of iwi and hapū under customary law, or Māori lore (which is increasingly recognised in our courts, and by Parliament during the Treaty-settlement process), are effectively those that existed as a result of the outcomes of the Musket Wars in about 1840.

Moreover, as tangata whenua entitlements and customary law become more widely respected and recognised by non-Māori, it is increasingly important and enriching for all New Zealanders to understand the events that underlie these complex historical relationships. Thus:

›   To understand who are the iwi who hold customary rights in any particular area — such as the holding of mana, or carrying the obligations of manaakitanga (hospitality) or kaitiakitanga (guardianship) — it is necessary to understand the inter-iwi relationships that resulted from the Musket Wars.
›   It should also be noted that in many areas throughout mainland New Zealand, and on Rēkohu/Wharekauri, these customary rights were still in turmoil or under challenge at the end of the Musket Wars era.
›   Differences over customary entitlements can still persist between competing iwi in various circumstances.

For example, and including:

›   in relation to entitlements from the Crown to compensate for Treaty breaches; fisheries and aquaculture settlement entitlements; customary rights to the foreshore and seabed; manaakitanga rights to conduct pōwhiri or host events; rights to declare rāhui (embargoes) or to exercise other kaitiaki obligations;
›   in terms of mana it is still common today for mana gained through the musket to be asserted in various localities, particularly in resource management issues. That results in disputed claims over the customary kaitiaki rights of iwi affected as to entire rohe, or parts of rohe, and whether those rights are exclusive or shared.

In other words, disputes over customary rights and entitlements can and still do arise over that most important Māori customary issue, mana — the rights to assert or exercise tangata whenua status in an area. The nature of those rights in the main rests on the outcome of the Musket Wars.

TREATY SETTLEMENTS AND THEIR AFTERMATH

As at 2020, New Zealanders as a nation had paid approximately $2.5 billion in settling claims for breach of the Treaty of Waitangi by the Crown, and much more will be paid out before final settlements are reached in all areas of the country. Yet through our lack of education in our country's history, and in particular the effects of the Musket Wars, most of us are unaware of who the recipient iwi of the Treaty settlements are. Most New Zealanders know even less about how, when or why the beneficiaries of these settlements came to enjoy tangata whenua status in any particular area.

In considering why these concerns matter in today's world, the following points are worth noting:

- The outcomes of the Treaty settlements have seen a substantial transfer of capital to iwi-owned Post Settlement Governance Entities (PSGEs), which have become major asset owners, development entities and employers in their rohe, and beyond.
- Unlike private or public companies, which can ebb and flow as entities, often ultimately fading and disappearing, entitlements for iwi members from their own entities such as PSGEs will endure, because they are bound by whakapapa to their resources.
- Among the most important of these benefits (which will increase in significance as the asset base of each PSGE grows) is the ability of iwi members and their children to access employment opportunities through the management and development of the PSGE assets, and crucial scholarship support for higher education.
- For these opportunities to be properly utilised, it is important to know which iwi have customary rights in each area, and how the iwi can support their members to achieve educational and employment goals.
- For the general community, who will increasingly be conducting business with PSGEs or other iwi entities, a knowledge of the background history of iwi and hapū relationships will make their interactions more meaningful and mutually respectful.

ENRICHING OUR KNOWLEDGE OF OUR OWN PLACES

The story of the Musket Wars has the potential to bring our countryside alive. Because taua ranged across the whole of the country, there are numerous sites where dramatic events, sometimes tragic, sometimes heroic, go unmarked or poorly signposted at best: sites such as Mokoia/Mauinaina pā in Auckland; Te Tōtara pā at Thames; Mātakitaki pā at Pirongia; Maungatapu and Te Papa pā at Tauranga; Pukerangiora pā on the Waitara in Taranaki; Te Whetumatarau pā at Te Araroa; Okurarenga pā at Mahia; Kapara Te Hau at Lake Grassmere; Kaikōura pā and Ōmihi south of Kaikōura; and Kaiapoi and Ōnawe pā in Canterbury.

With a background knowledge of the Musket Wars, supplemented with appropriate on-site interpretative material that enabled events to be envisaged on the ground, both the richness of the era's tales of endurance and courage and the depth of history in our country could be highlighted.

THE PLACE OF THE MUSKET WARS IN THE TEACHING OF OUR HISTORY

The lack of awareness of the significance of the Musket Wars era in both historical and contemporary terms was demonstrated as late as 2019, when the government announced that New Zealand history would finally become part of our national education curriculum. It was a very sound and long-overdue decision.

However, when the initial list of subject matter was revealed, there was a disappointing absence of specific recognition of the Musket Wars era and its long-term effects. Areas to be covered included:
- the arrival of Māori in Aotearoa;
- initial contacts with Europeans; and
- early colonial history;

then there was a leap forward to:
- the Treaty in 1840 and its history;
- colonisation, and immigration to New Zealand; and
- the New Zealand Wars;

followed by later events.

If the term 'initial contacts' was supposed to cover the 30-year Musket Wars era, this can only be described as a demonstration of classic Euro-centric thinking as to the 'real' history of our nation, given that the Musket Wars era involved minimal 'initial contacts' apart from the supply of actual muskets by Pākehā to Māori.

It is to be hoped that by the time this book is in print the curriculum will have been revised to include what was the longest period of continuous, tumultuous warfare throughout the length and breadth of Aotearoa, which in large part laid the basis of contemporary inter-iwi and inter-hapū relationships. Māori, and all New Zealanders, deserve to have that crucial period of our history identified and taught in our schools.

2

FEATURES OF THE MUSKET WARS

Over the more than thirty years of the Musket Wars, numerous taua, sieges, defences, migrations, displacements and acts of courage and endurance occurred throughout the country. In later chapters we will follow particular iwi; here, the focus is on some of the most notable features of the wars.

THE MOST TUMULTUOUS SHORT PERIOD IN OUR NATION'S HISTORY

Some things about the Musket Wars were not new. Prior to this, Māori customary warfare, particularly over the sixteenth, seventeenth and eighteenth centuries, had similar patterns of taua, forced tribal migrations, displacements and subjugation or amalgamation with other iwi.

The difference was that those events took place in relatively small stages, in an intermittent manner over hundreds of years. This was largely because there was an inherent balance of power between iwi or hapū who were similarly armed. With the arrival of muskets en masse, suddenly one side had unstoppable power. The possession of that power enabled taua to be far more wide-reaching, and far more devastating in their impacts.

Between 1816 and 1820, repeated taua by Ngāpuhi and their allies moved down the full length of the west coast of Te Ika a Māui (the North Island), and down the east coast into the Bay of Plenty. The greatest devastation, however, occurred in large portions of both islands during an intense period of some 12 years from 1820 to 1832, particularly by the Ngāti Toa-led coalitions. In addition, between 1828 and 1834 there were numerous taua from larger interior and southern groupings after they acquired muskets: for example, Tainui repeatedly headed into Taranaki or out to Hawke's Bay, often in alliance with Ngāti Tūwharetoa, who later also raided down into south Taranaki; Ngāti Maru raided heavily into the Bay of Plenty, and Kāi (Ngāi) Tahu raided north.

Just when that intense period seemed to be waning, in about the middle of the 1830s, fresh bouts of repetitive raiding broke out in the Bay of Plenty, East Coast, Taupō and south Taranaki areas. Heavy losses were inflicted as various taua raided over another intense five-to-seven-year period from 1835 onwards. And as if that was not enough extra devastation in a short period, 1835 also saw the advent of the most far-reaching taua, with the most severe effects, as Ngāti Mutunga and Ngāti Tama devastated Moriori on Rēkohu/Wharekauri (the Chatham Islands).

It was not until about 1845 that iwi and hapū throughout the country were able to draw a collective breath, as this maelstrom of brutal warfare finally settled down to an uneasy period of truce in the face of a widespread balance of musket power. In the same year of 1845, however, the new form of nation envisaged by the Treaty of Waitangi faced a different cause of war, as the new entity of the 'Crown' engaged in the first colonial war in the Bay of Islands.

CASUALTIES OF THE MUSKET WARS COMPARED WITH THE NEW ZEALAND WARS

The Musket Wars resulted in a huge number of casualties, many times more than the later New Zealand Wars. A few comparisons illustrate the point:

- In the Waikato, at the fall of Mātakitaki pā in 1822, and the following months-long occupation of the upper Waipa, Ngāpuhi killed several hundred Tainui (probably well in excess of a thousand), with hundreds more being taken back north as slaves. The losses far exceeded the total number of casualties inflicted or prisoners taken by Crown forces in the whole of the 1863–64 Waikato campaign during the New Zealand Wars.
- In the north, at the battle of Te Ika a Ranganui in 1825, and the extended pursuit, Hongi Hika and Tirarau inflicted hundreds of deaths on Ngāti Whātua, forcing them to seek refuge at Nohoawatea in Waikato where they were pursued by Ngāpuhi. Once again, the losses suffered in these two battles alone far exceeded the total inflicted by the Crown and kūpapa

Māori (who, for their own reasons, were fighting in alliance with the Crown) in all the battles of the later Northern Wars of 1845–46.
- In Tauranga, at Te Papa pā in 1828, Te Rohu of Ngāti Maru wiped out virtually all of the many hundreds of Ngāiterangi occupants of the great pā. The same rangatira later devastated the Ōpōtiki area. Again the casualties inflicted by those taua (which followed many earlier ones by Ngāpuhi) significantly exceeded the losses inflicted by the Crown in 1864 at nearby Pukehinahina (Gate Pā), and even the total when these are added to the much heavier losses at Te Ranga, and the later losses inflicted at Ōpōtiki in 1865.
- In north Taranaki in 1832, after the fall of Pukerangiora pā to Waikato, the slaughter of Te Ātiawa prisoners alone by Tainui, let alone the losses inflicted during the siege, was far greater than the total of all casualties inflicted by the Crown in the north Taranaki campaigns from 1860 to 1863.
- In Wellington, as a result of repeated taua from the north between 1819 and about 1827, the resident iwi of Whanganui a Tara, Ngāti Ira, were either killed, subsumed in slavery, or forced to migrate and be absorbed within other iwi, effectively wiping them out. These effects massively exceeded any impact of the casualties inflicted by the Crown and kūpapa in 1846 in the Hutt/Horowhenua fighting.

In summary, the human casualties inflicted in these localities during the Musket Wars were the heaviest in New Zealand's history, because of the imbalance of power that the musket provided. Yet these are only a few examples of the events that occurred during the Musket Wars era.

THE MUSKET WARS AFFECTED EVERY IWI IN THE COUNTRY DIRECTLY OR INDIRECTLY

The first of the major musket-armed taua predominantly spread from north to south from about 1816 to 1825, throughout the upper half of the North Island. But as muskets became available to central North Island iwi, they too raided in predominantly southerly directions from the late 1820s. In addition, in the north, Ngāpuhi taua had serious impacts in 1824–25 in the Kaipara and Te Oneroa (Ninety Mile Beach) areas, which were followed by the oft-overlooked Waikato taua into Whangarei Harbour and Ngunguru in 1828 and 1832.

As a result of all these taua, there were both major temporary displacements in the early years and later permanent migrations. Initially, particularly in the early and late 1820s, these migratory movements tended to be to more southerly areas of refuge. Some of those migrations led to worse outcomes as the former refugee iwi, such as Ngāti Toa and their allies, gained access to large numbers of muskets from about 1826 onwards. They then proceeded to launch repeated taua into Te Tau Ihu (The Top of the South) and right down the east and west coasts of Te Waipounamu (the South Island).

From the mid 1830s further major taua occurred repeatedly in the Bay of Plenty, East Coast, Taupō and Whanganui areas, continuing in a few limited locations even after the Treaty of Waitangi was signed. By 1835, the Musket Wars had even moved offshore to Rēkohu/Wharekauri, with devastating effects for Moriori there.

HUGE NUMBERS AFFECTED BY DEATH, PERMANENT MIGRATIONS AND TEMPORARY DISPLACEMENTS

In the absence of any reliable census data, population figures and casualty estimates will always be uncertain. However, a reasonable assessment would suggest that impacts from deaths, wounds, permanent migrations and temporary displacements could have affected over 50,000 people over the approximately 30-year course of the Musket Wars, out of a likely population of between 100,000 and 150,000.

Human impacts on such a level and rate were massively beyond those of any previous or subsequent warfare in Aotearoa over a similar time scale. In the later New Zealand Wars, while imbalances in forces and logistics existed, these were not as devastating in terms of direct human casualties as the effects of the imbalance in firepower provided by the musket. Any direct imbalance in the New Zealand Wars was principally limited to that created by artillery, and in the limited cases where it could be brought to bear, by the impact of massed bayonet use by well-drilled soldiers. Otherwise, the imbalance was far less direct, taking the form of much-higher-quality ammunition and more reliable food supply logistics.

MAJOR PERMANENT MIGRATIONS DISPLACED OR SUBJUGATED THE ORIGINAL OCCUPYING IWI

The major permanent migrations of the loose coalition led by Ngāti Toa occurred particularly from 1822 to 1832, when iwi from the areas around Kawhia down to north Taranaki, and the Matamata/Maungatautari (Cambridge) areas, headed south, settling in the Kāpiti, Horowhenua, and Whanganui a Tara (Wellington) areas.

From about 1827 to 1832, some of these iwi undertook massive and wide-ranging taua down south, some of which settled permanently in Te Tau Ihu, subjugating the Kurahaupō occupants.

Finally, from Whanganui a Tara, after conflict with their former allies of Ngāti Toa and Ngāti Raukawa, some Ngāti Tama and Ngāti Mutunga used a British sailing ship to migrate to Rēkohu/Wharekauri in 1835. Moriori suffered extremely, both from the initial killings and from a later long period of harsh slavery.

The effects on the original occupiers in all these areas of the arrival of thousands of migrants was devastating. Ngāti Apa and Rangitāne in both the North and South Islands suffered heavily, as did Ngāti Kuia in Te Tau Ihu; Muaūpoko suffered particularly badly in Horowhenua; and in the Whanganui a Tara area Ngāti Ira effectively disappeared entirely into captivity or were subsumed by surrounding iwi.

TEMPORARY DISPLACEMENTS OF HAPŪ OR IWI CAUSED FURTHER STRIFE

The first major temporary displacement was the almost entire depopulation of the greater Auckland isthmus area. The original Ngāti Whātua and Ngāti Paoa occupants fled after a series of devastating Ngāpuhi taua between 1818 and 1825, mostly to seek refuge with related iwi in various areas of the Waikato or upper Waipa.

Pressure from Ngāpuhi taua also led to major temporary displacements of Marutūahu iwi from Thames/Coromandel to the Matamata/Maungatautari areas. Those migrations placed pressure on Ngāti Raukawa and Ngāti Hauā, with the latter attacking the Marutūahu iwi in 1830, forcing them back to their own rohe.

In Hawke's Bay, Te Paraihe of Ngāti Kahungunu led a temporary withdrawal of his people from the Heretaunga (Napier/Hastings) area north to Mahia Peninsula. This was in response to successive attacks between about 1824 and 1828 from various inland taua of Waikato, Ngāti Tūwharetoa, Ngāti Raukawa, Tūhoe and Ngāti Awa. At Nukutaurua pā on Mahia Peninsula, a major irony occurred as Ngāpuhi muskets under Te Wera Hauraki protected Ngāti Kahungunu in a long siege known as Kaiuku, before the iwi later developed enough strength to reassert their mana in their own rohe.

In the eastern Bay of Plenty, repeated Ngāpuhi taua led to a temporary withdrawal south by Ngāti Awa into the refuge of the rugged Urewera ranges. These displacements in turn caused conflict with Tūhoe, who resented long-term Ngāti Awa occupation of the lower river valley reaches of their rohe.

The actions of Ngāpuhi and Ngāti Maru taua in the eastern Bay of Plenty in the 1820s led to a withdrawal by Whakatōhea inland, up and over the ranges from Ōpōtiki to the refuge pā of Kekeparoa in the inland Gisborne area. The final outcome there was an attack on Whakatōhea by the local Te Aitanga a Mahāki and others in 1832.

In 1825, in the north of the North Island, Te Aupōuri were temporarily displaced to the offshore Murimotu Island and Three Kings Islands under pressure from a joint Te Rarawa/Ngāpuhi taua.

Further south, on the lower Whanganui River Te Atihaunui a Pāpārangi faced repeated clashes with Ngāpuhi taua that passed through their rohe in 1818 and 1819, and again in 1821, and with Ngāti Toa-led heke (migrations) and Ngāti Raukawa heke from 1823 to 1832. The latter clashes led to a major retaliatory taua by Te Rauparaha in 1832, which attacked Putikiwharanui pā at the Whanganui River mouth. The result was a temporary withdrawal of Te Ati-Haunui hapū from the river-mouth area to the protection of their upper Whanganui whānaunga.

Meanwhile, the continual pressure of Tainui taua on the north Taranaki iwi of Ngāti Tama, Ngāti Mutunga and Te Ātiawa saw them depart in various heke from about 1823 to 1832 to the Horowhenua, Whanganui a Tara and Heretaunga (Hutt River) areas. There, they in turn came under increasing pressure as Ngāti Raukawa arrived later in growing numbers from Maungatautari in another series of heke. Major fighting broke out among these erstwhile allies in 1834 and again in 1839, leading many Te Ātiawa and Ngāti Tama to move to Te Tau Ihu, and other Ngāti Tama and Ngāti Mutunga to Rēkohu/Wharekauri.

By 1840, the year in which the Treaty of Waitangi was signed, all of the areas affected by these migrations were in a state of turmoil. The original occupiers still retained latent customary rights, and according to Māori customary lore they would have been entitled to reassert those rights by force as they acquired muskets — had it not been for the Treaty effectively bringing to an end those rights to re-establish mana by force.

DEPOPULATION LEFT AREAS VULNERABLE TO OCCUPATION AND PURCHASE

Following numerous successive Ngāpuhi taua, Ngāti Whātua and Ngāti Paoa occupiers of the Auckland isthmus and the surrounding islands headed south to refuges in the Waikato or pulled back into the Waitakere and Hunua ranges. In the 1830s, there was a strong move into southern parts of the isthmus by their

Tainui protectors after they had heavily defeated a series of Ngāpuhi taua from 1826 to 1832. However, the depopulation of a large part of the Auckland isthmus, around an excellent sheltered harbour, left it open to occupation and purchase by Pākehā colonists both before, and particularly after, the signing of the Treaty in 1840. It was a pattern that would recur in other depopulated areas further south, particularly those that were adjacent to a harbour.

› In north Taranaki, depopulation following the departure of the Ngāti Mutunga and Te Ātiawa occupants left areas that were seen as highly desirable, with good pastoral or agricultural potential, open to purchase by colonists. One early Pākehā purchase by the New Zealand Company led to the establishment of the New Plymouth settlement. In the Waitara area, as the original Te Ātiawa occupants returned in large numbers from 1848 onwards, conflict arose with the Crown as it sought to forcefully acquire more land, leading to a gross breach of the Treaty of Waitangi in 1860 and the outbreak of the major period of the New Zealand Wars.

› At the Whanganui River mouth, where much land was left sparsely occupied as a result of Te Rauparaha's heavy attack on Putikiwharanui in 1832, the New Zealand Company was able to purchase land in 1839 for the new Petre (Whanganui) town settlement. Once again, conflict with the Crown was to follow, in 1847.

› The area of Te Papa at Tauranga was devastated by the taua led by Te Rohu of Ngāti Maru in 1828 when almost all its hundreds of occupants were killed, with just a few escaping. As a consequence it was still mostly unoccupied when British troops landed there and set up a camp before commencing the Tauranga campaign. That resulted in the attack on Pukehinahina (Gate Pā) in 1864, which was disastrous for the British but was followed the next month by heavy losses by Ngāiterangi and Ngāti Ranginui at the incomplete pā defences at Te Ranga, inland from Tauranga.

› In the south of Te Ika a Māui, at the Heretaunga or Hutt River, the occupants at the beginning of the Musket Wars were Ngāti Ira and some pockets of their relatives from Ngāti Kahungunu. During the Musket Wars Ngāti Ira were pushed back onto their last island refuge pā at Taputeranga, where they were defeated by Te Ātiawa and Ngāti Mutunga. As a consequence of other taua from the north Ngāti Kahungunu pulled back out of the Heretaunga (Hutt) valley. However, after the northern coalition became embroiled in its own internal wars in 1834 and 1839, Ngāti Tama led by Te Kaeaea (also known as Taringakuri) formed an alliance with a small hapū of Whanganui called Ngāti Rangitahi, under Kaparatehau.

Together they occupied the central and upper Heretaunga river flats, with Te Ātiawa under Te Wharepouri and Te Puni occupying the lower flat areas. When the New Zealand Company purchased land in 1839 it did so only from Ngāti Toa and Te Ātiawa. Predictably, that led to war in 1846, when the Crown settled with Te Kaeaea, but not with Te Rangitahi who were supported in their ongoing occupation by Te Rangihaeata.

› In Te Tau Ihu large areas stretching over 100 kilometres in length on both the east and west coasts were left vacant as a result of repeated northern and southern iwi taua. From about 1827 to 1832 the northerners led by Te Rauparaha had dominated, but then, almost incredibly, in 1833 and 1834 Kāi Tahu responded with their two huge long-distance taua — Taua-iti and Taua-nui — which had travelled all the way up from their own musket sources at Ruapuke Island and Murihiku (Southland). Consequently, the risks of trying to occupy isolated locations like the coastline south of the Wairau on the east coast, or south of Whanganui Inlet on the west coast, were such that these areas were vacated and only intermittently occupied for food-gathering purposes.

Once again, the Crown purchasing officers were quick to take advantage in the late 1840s and 1850s. They 'purchased' initially from Ngāti Toa, paying them a token amount but only a pittance to other holders of customary rights over these vast areas of land.

FORTITUDE OF LONG-RANGING TAUA AND HEKE

The journeys undertaken by taua and by migratory heke, whether overland or by sea in waka, covered prodigious distances and lasted for many weeks, at times even months. They involved feats of endurance that would extend even the hardiest of modern-day long-distance athletes with their light, high-energy foods and specially designed clothing. Food for these journeys had to be foraged for or carried, and the most rudimentary clothing had to provide protection in all weathers.

One of the most important foods during these journeys was the humble potato, which had recently been introduced to Aotearoa. Readily available and transportable, it was also a food that lasted well, and hence was capable of sustaining taua over long periods of travel and fighting. High levels of energy were required, as both heke and taua had to traverse rugged, bush-covered terrain and cross numerous rivers; and at sea they faced strong, often unpredictable

> **The importance of the potato**
>
> Some idea of the increasing importance of the potato in this era, and its role in establishing confidence of food supply, can be found in records relating to the *Lord Rodney*. In 1835, when the vessel, under Captain Harwood, was compelled by Ngāti Mutunga and Ngāti Tama to convey about 900 people of those two iwi from Whanganui a Tara (Wellington) to Rēkohu/Wharekauri (the Chatham Islands), it was estimated that they loaded some 70 tonnes of seed potatoes on board.

offshore winds. Weather conditions could include extremely high or low temperatures, heavy rain, even sleet or snow. And as if the physical efforts of the day were not enough, they had to construct their own shelters at night.

EXTRAORDINARY ACTS OF COURAGE, ENDURANCE AND LEADERSHIP

Amid the widespread hardship, aggression, cruelty and injustice that took place during and as a result of the Musket Wars, there were acts of courage, endurance, wisdom and compassion that increased the mana of many rangatira and other individuals at all levels. The following are just a few examples of people whose acts earned them an enduring reputation in Māoridom, and convey the richness of the contribution they have made to the history of Aotearoa:

- The extraordinary courage of Te Waru of Ngāiterangi and Hikairo of Te Arawa, who in 1821 and 1823 respectively went back voluntarily into the victorious Ngāpuhi camps to seek relief for their surviving people, when umu (earth ovens) containing their relatives were still steaming.
- The almost unbelievable endurance of Ngawhakawa of Muaūpoko, a captive slave of Ngāti Tama: in 1837 he escaped from Kāi Tahu's attack at Tuturau in Southland, and on his own made it all the way back up the rugged

West Coast to Mohua (Golden Bay), to bring back to Ngāti Tama news of the loss of Te Puoho's taua.
- The dignity and courage of Te Aokapurangi of Ngāti Rangiwewehi (Te Arawa) as a captive slave wife of Te Wera Hauraki. She advocated for her Ngāti Rangiwewehi hapū, first during the advance of the invading Ngāpuhi taua into Te Arawa's rohe, and then during the actual events of the bitter Mokoia battle, saving many Te Arawa.
- The courage and endurance of Te Orahi (Manukorihi) of Tainui, who escaped from Pukerangiora in 1821 (when the Te Amiowhenua taua led by Tukorehu was besieged) and, fighting off his pursuers, carried the news to Te Wherowhero at Taupiri.

Sadly, the stories of many of these people have been lost through a lack of awareness in the broader community and the absence of resources to safeguard them. However, for iwi who have undertaken research in preparation for the hearing of their claims by the Waitangi Tribunal, many of these accounts have been uncovered and recorded — if not always at an individual level, then certainly at a hapū or iwi level.

3

THE INTRODUCTION OF MUSKETS AND BEGINNING OF NGĀPUHI DOMINANCE

Muskets were introduced to Aotearoa via three main sources: first, whalers and sealers; second, missionaries and timber traders; and third, traders in flax and general goods. The first Māori to gain the weapons, and the increased power that came with them, were those who had the advantage of being located in the area where safe haven could be obtained by visiting European vessels.

WHALERS AND SEALERS

Muskets were first acquired by Māori from about 1800 onwards as trade items from the crews of European sailing vessels engaged in two different activities at vastly separated locations, at the northern and southern ends of the country.

In the north were the whalers, principally on the northeastern coast and in particular at Pēwhairangi (the Bay of Islands), but also to a lesser extent in the Whangaroa Harbour and on the west coast in the Hokianga Harbour. These harbours provided safe anchorage after the long sea-journeys to reach New Zealand from North America or Europe, or nearer at hand from Australia. They also provided access to fresh water and food supplies from local Māori hapū. The hapū with the most regular and direct access to these keen European traders were those of the broader Ngāpuhi iwi, whose rohe encompassed the many desirable safe harbours on the northeastern coast.

At much the same time, but in far lesser numbers, European sealing vessels and later whalers were frequenting the southern waters of New Zealand, particularly around Southland, Fiordland and South Westland. They would drop off sealing gangs and return several months later to pick them up. Once again, muskets were traded for food supplies and flax, this time from Kāi (Ngāi) Tahu or Kāti (Ngāti) Māmoe hapū, particularly around Te Waewae Bay and Ruapuke Island. The numbers of muskets involved in the early trading with sealers were so small, however, that their spread and use even in limited inter-hapū fighting did not occur until the later 1820s.

From about 1828 many permanent shore-based whaling crews set up in various locations, such as at Te Awaiti and Port Underwood in the Marlborough Sounds, Wairewa at Horomaka (Akaroa Peninsula), Ōtākou (Otago), and Rakituma (Preservation Inlet in Fiordland), and at locations like Kāpiti Island and Ngāmotu (New Plymouth) in the North Island.

MISSIONARIES AND TIMBER TRADERS

From 1814, the missionary stations established by the Anglican Church Missionary Society (CMS) at Rangihoua, and later at Kerikeri in Pēwhairangi, provided a different, albeit disguised, source of muskets. Although Samuel Marsden had forbidden any dealing in muskets, the missionary Thomas Kendall demonstrated that, as in many other aspects of his life, he was willing to bend the rules to gain advantage with local rangatira. The need for this became particularly pressing when they were no longer providing food as readily as the missionaries required. Kendall's improper trade in muskets was dramatically revealed one day when a case marked for him fell and split open on the deck while being unloaded from a vessel, revealing its contents to be somewhat different from the innocent marking of 'Trade goods'.

Materials that were sought after for ship-building and repairs also became useful items of trade for northern hapū or their relatives at Pēwhairangi, Whangaroa and Hokianga harbours, and indeed as far south as the Hauraki Basin. Initial interest came from British naval or trade vessels seeking kauri timber, with muskets, powder and ammunition being the most valued trade currency. The large development of ship-building at Horeke in the upper Hokianga was part of this growth in the kauri trade, which was soon followed by demand for huge quantities of flax for rope-making.

Added to these market demands was the constant and growing demand for food supplies for the ships' crews, in the form of fish and later pigs and potatoes in large quantities. From the late 1820s onwards there were sometimes over a hundred vessels calling each year into Pēwhairangi alone, from where they fanned out around the coasts, trading in muskets as they went.

FLAX AND GENERAL TRADERS

As European knowledge of New Zealand trade goods such as flax increased during the later 1820s and early 1830s, the larger trading houses in Sydney, such as Montefiores, and other individual traders such as Hans Tapsell at Maketu and Captain Kent at Raglan/Kawhia, started to set up trading bases. Once again these individual trading stations soon spread widely. Growth was particularly marked around the North Island's east coast, with traders springing up in places like Auckland, the eastern Bay of Plenty, and south of East Cape.

These bases became sources of muskets, ball and powder to powerful iwi such as the Marutūahu confederation in the Thames area, and also predominantly inland iwi such as Tainui in the Waikato and Waipa basins, and Te Arawa and Ngāti Tūwharetoa on the Volcanic Plateau. In coastal areas other iwi including Ngāiterangi at Tauranga, Ngāti Awa at Whakatane, Whakatōhea at Ōpōtiki, and Whānau a Apanui, Ngāti Porou and Ngāti Kahungunu down the east coast were also able to trade for muskets. But while muskets were later to be acquired in very low numbers initially in various parts of the country, their worth would first be tested in battle in the north.

A TERRIBLE LEGACY

In 1806, an event occurred that was to have major effects in the decades to come for Coromandel and Bay of Plenty iwi. It began with the seizure of a small sailing vessel, the *Venus*, in Tasmanian waters by its mate, a man called Kelly, with the assistance of some convicts on board. The vessel was sailed to New Zealand by its captors and made landfall on the northeast coast, within the rohe of Te Aupōuri.

In a pattern that was to recur as the *Venus* made its way down the northern coastline, two Te Aupōuri women were enticed aboard in the far north and held as the vessel continued on south. The same occurred at Pēwhairangi, where another two women related to two senior Ngāpuhi rangatira were carried off; one was related to Hongi Hika, and the other was a sister of Te Morenga. At Whangarei Harbour two more women were seized and carried off, one of them

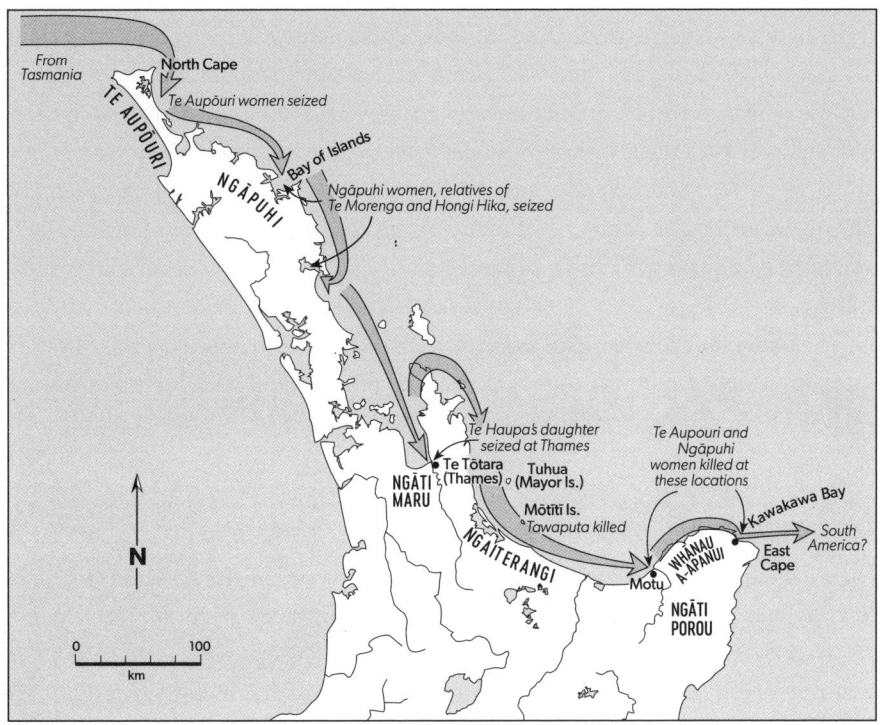

The presumed route of the Venus *in 1806.*

being another relative of Te Morenga — his high-ranking niece Tawaputa.

To compound matters, when the vessel called in at the head of the Hauraki Gulf, near the location of a Ngāti Maru pā, the leading rangatira Te Haupa was taken aboard with some of his family members. While onboard, Te Haupa noticed the sails billowing and realised the vessel was under way, leaving his waka (canoe) far behind. He and some members of his family managed to break free and dive overboard, where they were rescued, but his daughter was taken off as yet another captive.

Little is known now of the exact route the *Venus* took after leaving the Hauraki Gulf, but what has been handed down is that as the vessel progressed around Te Tara o te Ika a Māui (the barb of Māui's hook — the Coromandel Peninsula) and down the coast, it left various of the captive women at different locations in the Bay of Plenty.

Te Morenga's niece Tawaputa was left at Mōtītī Island, and tales came back to Ngāpuhi that her death had occurred at the hands of Ngāiterangi. Other accounts also made their way back over time to Ngāpuhi, and to Te Haupa of Ngāti Maru, about the grim fate of the other captive women, including Te Morenga's sister. They were reported to have been dropped off and killed, either at or near Maraenui at the mouth of the Motu River, or at Wharekahika Bay (Hicks Bay) near East Cape — places that fell within the respective rohe of Whānau a Apanui and Ngāti Porou. So those iwi, too, became objects for utu in Ngāpuhi and Ngāti Maru eyes in relation to the killings.

The *Venus* sailed away to an uncertain doom, which various accounts say befell it on the coast of South America. But in New Zealand it had left behind the seeds from which deadly utu obligations arose, which were to take a terrible toll.

THE FIRST MUSKET-ARMED TAUA

Their advantageous position close to the safe harbours in the north meant that Ngāpuhi were the first iwi to acquire muskets, but initially the numbers of weapons were low. It would be 12 years before they had enough muskets to launch taua that could confidently travel long distances, far beyond anything that had preceded them. In the meantime, efforts to obtain utu continued.

In 1807 a powerful Ngāpuhi taua of about 500 toa, under the leadership of Pōkaia, armed with a handful of muskets — believed to be only four or five at most — headed south to obtain utu from its near-neighbours Ngāti Whātua and Te Roroa; the latter shared whakapapa links with both Ngāti Whātua and Ngāpuhi. This was the first occasion on which muskets were used in warfare, and the taua was confident that, despite the small number of weapons, they would provide a crucial advantage. However, the taua was ambushed at Moremonui, just south of Maunganui Bluff, and was forced to retreat. The significant losses it suffered left a legacy of imbalance in terms of utu with Ngāti Whātua that was not resolved by Ngāpuhi until 1825.

THE BATTLE OF MOREMONUI

What became known as the battle of Moremonui took place on the beach at Ripiro (Bayley's Beach) just northwest of Dargaville, on the long ironsand coast. The battle commenced when the taua was taken by surprise at Moremonui Gully in an ambush that had been laid by Ngāti Whātua and Te Rōroa led by two experienced rangatira, Murupaenga of Ngāti Whātua and Tāoho of Te Rōroa. Scouts had reported that Ngāpuhi were intending to make camp at Moremonui after travelling down the beach from Maunganui Bluff overnight. Ngāti Whātua and Te Rōroa made sure they arrived earlier at Moremonui Gully, and waited in hiding among the flaxes, toetoe and coastal scrub until Ngāpuhi had stripped off their weapons belts. They then charged into the Ngāpuhi toa as they rested or ate a morning meal beside the freshwater stream.

The suddenness of the attack and the element of surprise meant that the ambushers were able to use their traditional hand-held weapons to great effect at close quarters. Moreover, as they saw Ngāpuhi about to fire their few muskets, Murupaenga urged his warriors to throw themselves flat on the ground and to leap up and take advantage of the delay in reloading the muzzle-loaded weapons. Any advantage that long-distance firing might have given the Ngāpuhi toa was thus lost. All those who survived the sudden onslaught had to flee for their lives, leaving about 150 of their compatriots' bodies on the beach.

So many Ngāpuhi men were lost in the sudden attack and the pursuit that followed, led by Tāoho, that the battle became known as Te Kai a te Karoro, the Feast of the Black-backed Gulls. The name arose because too many bodies were left on the beach to be consumed in the cannibal feasting that followed, and became the food of the gulls.

A monument in Moremonui Gully marks the location of the battle.
Photo courtesy Stuart Spicer

Among the Ngāpuhi losses were some of such high rank that utu was crucial in te ao Māori (the Māori world), and that rankled for decades. Among those lost was the senior rangatira Pōkaia, who was directly related to a young rangatira who was to dominate the events of the Musket Wars in the northern half of the North Island for the next twenty years. His name: Hongi Hika.

Hongi never forgot the debt in utu against Ngāti Whātua that Moremonui had caused. Not only had he lost his relative Pōkaia, but also his brother Houwawe and his sister Waitapu. He had seen Waitapu stop and turn to face their pursuers, to give him time to race away and save himself. He then had to watch from afar as she was killed, and see her body being mutilated by their enemies to symbolise the stopping of his line of descent.

Hongi Hika had to wait nearly twenty years, until 1825, to obtain full revenge for the losses inflicted on this day by Ngāti Whātua, both on Ngāpuhi and on himself personally.

NGĀPUHI TAUA HEAD SOUTH DOWN THE WEST COAST

Until about 1818, muskets were still only available to Māori even in the north in very limited numbers, in part perhaps because the number of whalers visiting during this period only grew relatively slowly. In traditional accounts the use of muskets is described as mainly occurring during inter-hapū clashes in the north, although in 1816 a long-distance taua to the Whanganui area was to find once more that the lessons of Moremonui remained real. Muskets undoubtedly provided a crucial tactical edge in battle — but they needed to be held in reasonable numbers.

Between 1816 and 1819, however, Ngāpuhi taua were demonstrating all around the North Island that not too many more muskets were needed to provide that crucial edge. Their experience soon became that even a small number of muskets enabled them to pick off leading rangatira from a distance, whether above pā palisading or in open battle, and thereby to cause a sense of despair among those under attack. These raids commenced in 1816 and 1817 when Ngāpuhi taua travelled down the west coast as far as south Taranaki and Whanganui, apparently motivated largely by a desire to obtain valued taonga — fine mats and cloaks — for which the various Taranaki iwi were famous. While these taua were mainly successful, they did suffer some losses of prominent rangatira and toa, creating fresh cause for utu and resulting in the almost immediate planning of further taua.

While the 1816 taua — the first that is known to have relied on the use of muskets to dominate in an extended southern foray — was initially successful

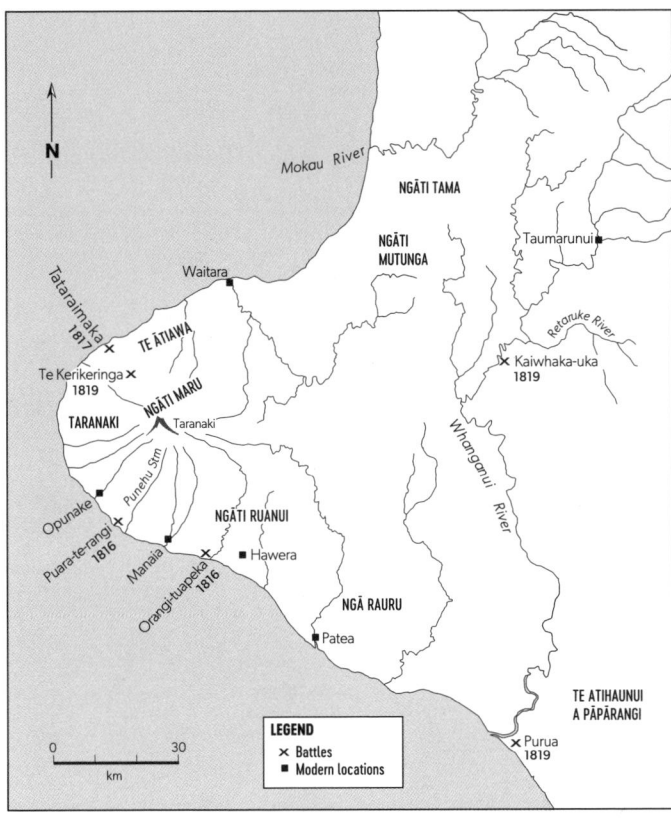

Localities affected by early Ngāpuhi, Ngāti Whātua and Ngāti Toa raids on Taranaki, 1816-19.

in north Taranaki, it failed in the end in south Taranaki. This was because the numbers of muskets were too small to overcome the large opposing forces that finally gathered in south Taranaki to repel the taua.

An intriguing and ultimately significant aspect of the 1817 taua led by Tuwhare was that it called at Kawhia, where it was joined by another young rangatira. This was Te Rauparaha of Ngāti Toa, whose name was to become feared in more southerly regions in decades to come.

Te Rauparaha was distantly related to Ngāti Whātua and had sent messages requesting their assistance on a taua to seek utu against the Ngāti Rāhiri hapū of Te Ātiawa. As it turned out, peace was made with Ngāti Rāhiri, but the taua moved further south to attack the Taranaki iwi pā of Tataramaika. There the few muskets possessed by the taua proved the crucial tipping point, enabling the toa to pick off

Te Rauparaha. This portrait of the Ngāti Toa rangatira shows him in an almost pensive pose.
Edward Immyns Abbot, 17??–1849, Te Rauparaha, 1845, 191 x 155 mm (corners trimmed), Dr Hocken's original collection, Accession 11,471. Hocken Collections Uare Taoka o Hākena

the leading Taranaki rangatira on the palisading before the pā fell. This demonstration of the power of the musket left a deep impression on Te Rauparaha.

The taua then returned north, and when it left Kawhia Tuwhare invited Te Rauparaha to join him in another major taua he was planning to launch in about a year. This time he intended to travel even further, beyond south Taranaki.

NGĀPUHI MUSKET POWER UNLEASHED IN THE EAST

In 1818, after a series of indeterminate inter-hapū conflicts in the north, Ngāpuhi focused on a common goal with Ngāti Maru beyond their own territories.

In large part these plans were triggered by the desire to seek utu for the hurt inflicted by the actions of those on the

Venus in 1806. Te Haupa of Ngāti Maru had repeatedly sent messengers north seeking Ngāpuhi muskets to join a taua he wished to send into the Bay of Plenty to avenge the loss of his daughter. Hongi Hika, whose hapū were from the Taiamai/Kerikeri area at the northwest head of Pēwhairangi, agreed to raise a taua to join with Te Haupa. Around the same time, but quite independently, Te Morenga and another Ngāpuhi rangatira, Korokoro, had been gathering a taua to head south, involving hapū from eastern Pēwhairangi to Whangarei. The two taua were both about the same size, each estimated by the missionaries to be about four hundred strong.

When Te Morenga arrived at Mōtītī Island he attacked and took the strong Ngāiterangi pā of Matarehua. However, Te Waru, one of the leading rangatira, escaped, meaning that Te Morenga's desire for utu against him and Ngāiterangi remained unrequited, in spite of the heavy slaughter that is said to have occurred when the pā fell.

Te Morenga and Korokoro carried on to Whakatane, where they attacked the Ngāti Pukeko who were then occupying the area. In the face of the Ngāpuhi muskets Ngāti Pukeko pulled back to join with their Ngāti Awa relatives around Te Teko. From there Ngāti Awa and Ngāti Pukeko withdrew further up the Rangitaiki valley, where they defended themselves at Okahukura pā, on a spur of the northwestern Urewera ranges.

During a prolonged attack Ngāpuhi succeeded in killing some of the leading rangatira, but the defenders of the pā were able to hold out until more support arrived. When Ngāpuhi saw even more defenders arriving they decided to withdraw so as to avoid being cut off from their waka, but many men were lost as they were harried through the broken bush country.

Once again, this successful defence by Ngāti Awa and Ngāti Pukeko, and other similar events during this period, demonstrated to Ngāpuhi that they needed more muskets to overcome determined and numerous defenders. This setback did not, however, deter Te Morenga, who continued on to attack Ngāti Porou, although the details of where are lost in time. What was recorded by the missionaries on his return home in early 1819 was that he came back with two rangatira captives and many other Ngāti Porou prisoners and many heads.

For the Bay of Plenty iwi there was to be no respite when Te Morenga moved on, as within less than a month they were assailed again, this time by the combined taua of Hongi Hika's Ngāpuhi and Te Haupa's Ngāti Maru. Once more the details of the battles they engaged in are lost in time, and the only accounts are those recorded by the missionaries on the return of the taua to Pēwhairangi. These accounts relate that Ngāti Pukenga, who at that time occupied Maketu, were the first to feel the effects of this far more powerful taua, which was partially armed with muskets. The taua also captured a large pā occupied by Te Whānau a Apanui at Maraenui at the mouth of the Motu, where Ngāpuhi believed some of their relatives, the women captives from the *Venus*, had been killed.

The taua then moved on to attack pā of Ngāti Porou at Wharekahika Bay (Hicks Bay) but seems to have had limited success there, possibly because Te Haupa was killed in a skirmish. However, Hongi Hika told Samuel Marsden that the taua had killed large numbers of their opponents, and had brought back many heads, and he also asserted that they had captured over two thousand people.

Even if some licence is allowed for in those numbers, it is plain from the duration of the taua, its size and Hongi's accounts, coupled with the number of captives and preserved heads that the missionaries did see, that these two taua had inflicted devastating blows on most of the Bay of Plenty's iwi, and on Ngāti Porou. Yet these raids were but a portent of what was to come over the next ten years from Ngāpuhi and, much later, Ngāti Maru.

INCREASING NUMBERS OF MUSKETS RAISE THE INTENSITY OF NGĀPUHI TAUA ON BOTH COASTS

Following closely on the heels of these two taua down the eastern coast, and particularly from 1819 on, the major effects of the musket started to be felt down both coasts. This began with the acquisition of larger numbers of muskets by Ngāpuhi rangatira such as Patuone and his brother Tamati Waka Nene in the Hokianga Harbour area on the west coast, and others such as Korokoro, Te Morenga, Tareha and Pomare on the east coast.

In 1819 another very large taua down the west coast, led by Patuone and Tamati Waka Nene, had major repercussions. One of the most significant of these stemmed from their invitation to Te Rauparaha to join the taua as he had done in 1817. This particular taua must have had a reasonable number of muskets as it caused devastating losses everywhere it travelled. Its impacts were particularly heavily felt in the Whanganui a Tara (Wellington) area, and the Heretaunga (Hutt) river valley, where the taua stayed for an extended period and inflicted heavy losses on Ngāti Ira.

Another major new development was that Te Rauparaha also plainly tucked away Kāpiti Island in his memory. It stood out to him as a very strong place of potential refuge if he ever needed it, with the added benefit of the potential to trade for muskets with whaling vessels. The association in his mind of sailing

Patuone. This photograph of the Ngāpuhi rangatira shows him in his later years, holding a tupara or double-barrelled musket.
E-452-f-003-2, Crombie, John Nicol, 1827–1878. Alexander Turnbull Library, Wellington, NZ

vessels with that area had become fixed when the taua saw a large sailing vessel offshore in Raukawa Moana (Cook Strait). (In a later account recorded by Te Rauparaha's son Tamihana, the taua saw the vessel from the cliffs above Omere, or Cape Terawhiti.)

In mid May 1820 the physically imposing rangatira Tareha of the Ngāti Rēhia hapū of Ngāpuhi led yet another taua with an unknown number of muskets southwest to seek utu once more against Ngāti Whātua in the Kaipara area, particularly in the Mangakahia and Kaihu valleys to the northeast and northwest of Dargaville. The taua then headed further south, attacking Tauhara pā near modern-day Pouto on the north head of the harbour. However, in retaliation for Tareha's raid Ngāti Whātua under Murupaenga launched their own attack on the Taiamai area, just to the west of Kerikeri Inlet, and captured two Ngāpuhi pā. Once again these defeats demonstrated to Ngāpuhi that large numbers of muskets were needed to ensure an irresistible swing in the balance of power. And once again, they increased the burning Ngāpuhi desire to obtain more comprehensive utu against Ngāti Whātua.

> **Sailing vessels in Raukawa Moana**
>
> It seems highly possible that the ship sighted by Patuone's taua was part of the Russian explorer Fabian Gottlieb von Bellingshausen's expedition to New Zealand. Von Bellingshausen's own log for 9 June 1820 describes seeing a huge fire lit onshore, most probably by this taua, as he traversed the southern shore of the North Island on his way home. He interpreted the fire as an invitation to go ashore, and a later Ngāti Toa account confirmed that a huge fire had been lit with that purpose in mind. While the Russians did not attempt to land, Te Rauparaha was to take back home with him an impression of Raukawa Moana that was associated with sailing vessels, and the potential access to muskets that offered.

THE INTENSITY LIFTS IN THE EAST

The earlier pattern of taua heading south towards the Hauraki Gulf and Tauranga was to recommence in the summer of 1819–20, with mixed results. Korokoro led another taua to the Hauraki, this time with some fifty muskets; Te Morenga led another shorter taua to Tauranga with about thirty-five muskets; Pomare and Te Wera Hauraki led a very long taua to the East Coast and beyond; and late in 1820 Korowhai led another taua down to Mahurangi to attack Ngāti Whātua.

Te Morenga was highly successful at Tauranga with his huge taua, which comprised nearly fifty waka gathered both from Pēwhairangi and the Whangarei Harbour area. Following its arrival at Mount Maunganui, Te Waru of Ngāiterangi made the fatal error, two days in a row, of opening his defensive battle with a charge across open ground with mau rākau (traditional Māori weapons), into the face of Te Morenga's assembled muskets. The taua soon managed to overcome the defences of Te Waru's pā, but once again Te Waru himself escaped. On the return of the taua to Pēwhairangi the toa told the missionaries they had killed over 400 Ngāiterangi, and they were seen to bring back hundreds of heads, even after leaving large numbers of both heads and slaves with the Whangarei contingent. Many Ngāiterangi waka were also brought back to Pēwhairangi, paddled by some of the 200 slaves who were brought north.

Te Waru's wife and children had been captured on the fall of his pā, and one day he stealthily approached the Ngāpuhi encampment near the mouth of the Wairoa River in Tauranga Harbour, where he managed to disarm the Ngāpuhi rangatira Te Whareumu. Te Waru then handed over his weapons to Te Whareumu and asked him to bind him and take him into the encampment. Once there he asked for the release of his whānau.

Te Morenga and Ngāpuhi were so impressed by Te Waru's sparing of Te Whareumu and his courage in allowing himself to be led into their encampment that they acceded to his request. Moreover, peace was made, and to mark that peace Te Morenga made a gift of a musket to Te Waru before the taua departed for home. That peace was to have unexpected consequences for Te Arawa three years later when Ngāiterangi guided Ngāpuhi into Te Arawa's rohe.

Korokoro's taua in 1819 experienced a very different outcome. It returned from the Hauraki area with the news that Korokoro had been killed as Ngāpuhi were repulsed in an attack on Te Tōtara pā, on the steep bluff above Kopu, just south of modern-day Thames. It is significant that Korokoro was killed and Ngāpuhi failed to capture Te Tōtara despite the taua having about fifty muskets. That outcome demonstrated that even a reasonably substantial number of muskets did not always completely alter the balance of power, particularly if the pā defences, as at Te Tōtara, involved massive entrenchments and strong palisading. Nonetheless, the news of Korokoro's death inevitably led to the gathering of

Hongi Hika

Te Morenga's taua arrived back at the Bay of Islands on 2 March 1820, the very day on which Hongi Hika left with his relative, the rangatira Waikato, and the missionary Thomas Kendall on the *New Zealander* en route for England. While Kendall's aim in taking Hongi Hika was so that he could assist in the preparation of the first Māori dictionary, Hongi Hika plainly had other motivations for making the trip. The sight of what a limited number of muskets could achieve, as Te Morenga's numerous waka passed their ship with the rangatira holding up dried heads as trophies, must have left a powerful impression on Hongi Hika.

Sauvages de la Nouvelle-Zélande. The title of this work by the French artist Emile Rouargue translates as 'Savages of New Zealand'. It depicts a scene that must have been commonplace during evenings on a taua.
PUBL-0040-01, Rouargue, Emile, 1795?–1865, Sauvages de la Nouvelle Zelande/ Rouargue del. Paris, Furne [1859], Alexander Turnbull Library, Wellington, NZ

yet another taua in January 1820, which headed south down the eastern coastline under the leadership of Pomare and Te Wera Hauraki to seek utu for this and previous causes. This taua lasted for over a year, and Pomare would not return to Pēwhairangi until April 1821.

People in several areas of the Bay of Plenty were to suffer heavily from this powerful taua. In the Maketu area, a prominent Te Arawa rangatira was killed and his head was severed and dried. His daughter Te Aokapurangi was taken captive and became a prominent slave wife of Te Wera, with the missionaries recording that when the taua returned and held up in triumph her father's preserved head, she covered her head with a mat in sorrow.

But Ngāiterangi were not the only ones to feel the impacts of this taua — it soon moved on, and Ngāti Awa, Ngāti Porou and Ngāti Kahungunu in turn felt its blows. For Ngāti Porou those blows fell heavily at Te Araroa, near East Cape, while Rongowhakaata felt the effects at the Waipaoa River just south of Tūranganui (Gisborne). Ngāti Kahungunu were also to initially suffer heavily during the passage of this taua.

News of the taua's progress towards Te Araroa sped ahead of it and Ngāti Porou pulled back into two pā on either side of the Awatere River. When Pomare and Te Wera Hauraki arrived they first took the smaller pā, Okauwharetoa, on the eastern side of the mouth of the Awatere. Initially, however, they found that Te Whetumatarau was not such easy plucking. This pā is located on top of a high hill above the Awatere, surrounded on most sides by precipitous cliffs with only a very few access points, all of which were heavily defended. However, while its defences were very difficult to overcome it had one major drawback in an extended siege: the gardens on which the Ngāti Porou occupants relied for food were the lower fan slopes well below the defended pā.

After a long siege, Ngāpuhi seemed to have accepted that they could not take the pā, and the famished Ngāti Porou were delighted when they saw that the Ngāpuhi waka were all loaded up and their besiegers were heading off into the distance. Cautiously, they waited before descending to seek food until they could see the last of the waka round Matakoa Point about ten kilometres away to the west as they headed home. Unknown to them, however, Ngāpuhi only travelled far enough to round the next major point to the west, Wakatiri (Lottin Point), where they pulled ashore at the small beach and camped for the next two nights. On the third night the waka were launched and the taua silently paddled back to land immediately before daybreak. They fell on the unsuspecting Ngāti Porou in their garden wharau (temporary sheds), killing large numbers and taking many captive. The surviving Ngāti Porou at Te Araroa and nearby coastal locations pulled back into the hinterland Taitai mountains in the face of these musket-carrying foes who they could not match.

At this stage Pomare turned for home, satisfied with the outcome, but Te Wera Hauraki decided to carry on around East Cape and head south with his section of the taua. He is said to have carried out major massacres of even more Ngāti Porou hapū on the fall of pā in the Waiapu River area, then at Whareponga Bay. Further south at Poverty Bay the large Rongowhakaata pā under Te Kani a Takirau fell after a fierce defence, with Te Kani a Takirau barely escaping by waka.

Even after this victory Te Wera continued on south to attack Ngāti Kahungunu at Mahia Peninsula. He is said to have taken a number of pā on the peninsula, but the most significant outcome for the long term was his capture of the prominent Ngāti Kahungunu rangatira Te Whareumu and his sister. The latter became yet another wife of Te Wera, and over time Te Whareumu became his close friend.

Finally, in early 1821, Te Wera turned for home. He arrived back in Pēwhairangi in April with a large number of prisoners and preserved heads from Ngāti Porou, Rongowhakaata and Ngāti Kahungunu.

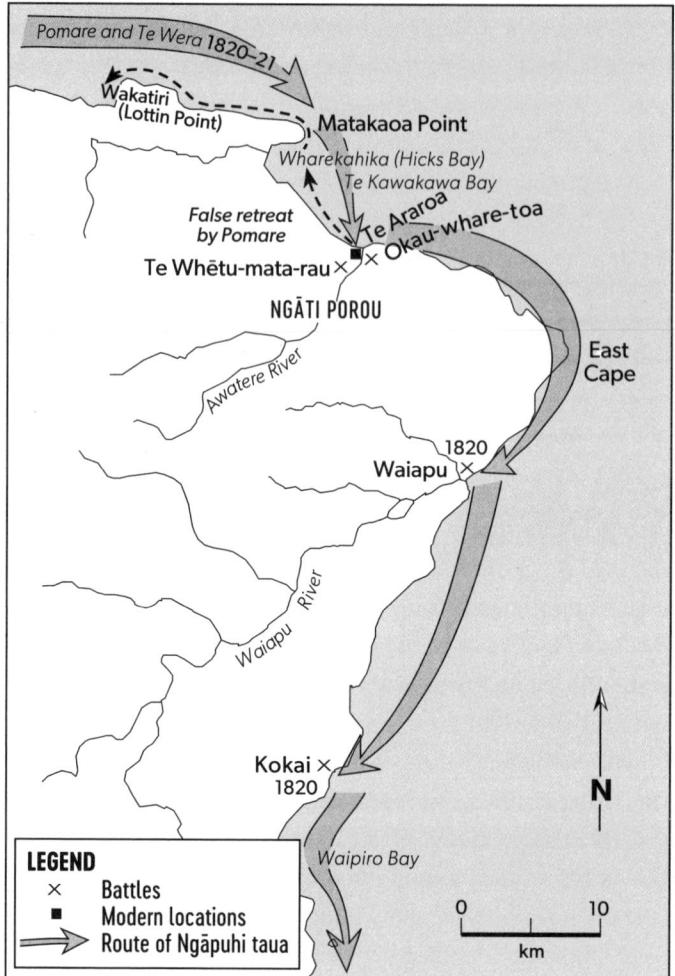

Pomare's siege of Te Whetu-matarau, 1820.

At the end of 1820, however, Ngāpuhi had suffered a considerable loss when a taua led by Korowhai against Ngāti Whātua was itself cut off by a combined Ngāti Whātua and Ngāti Paoa taua somewhere between the Pakiri River and Mahurangi Inlet, with Korowhai being killed. As he was related to the Ngāpuhi rangatira Te Whareumu — the prominent leader who had been captured temporarily by Te Waru earlier in the year at Mount Maunganui — that killing was to deepen even further in Ngāpuhi minds the desire to obtain utu against Ngāti Whātua.

4

THE PEAK AND DECLINE OF NGĀPUHI DOMINANCE

In 1821 Hongi Hika and Waikato finally returned home to Pēwhairangi (the Bay of Islands) after their visit to England. While staying on the return voyage in Sydney, Hongi acquired a large number of muskets. It has generally been thought that he exchanged most of the gifts he had received from his English hosts for these muskets, as well as ball and powder. A later theory, with some weight to it, suggests he may have reached agreement on a land sale with Baron de Thierry in London in return for many hundreds of muskets, which he was to uplift in Sydney as he passed through.

Regardless of how he in fact sourced his supply, the incontrovertible and chilling fact is that Hongi brought home from Sydney many hundreds of muskets. Thus armed, he was determined to lead taua that would finally achieve long-due utu for Ngāpuhi against their enemies. Between 1821 and 1825, Hongi Hika led numerous taua throughout the northern half of Te Ika a Māui (the North Island), devastating his opposition as the power of his musketry prevailed over even those iwi who were most strongly armed with traditional weaponry.

Hongi Hika, the famous Ngāpuhi rangatira who dominated all other iwi as far south as Taupō until his death in 1828 from the effects of a musket wound.
PUBL-0067-154, Robley, Horatio Gordon, 1840–1930: Hongi Hika, 1923. Alexander Turnbull Library, Wellington, NZ

TĀMAKI (AUCKLAND) AND HAURAKI (THAMES)

Ngāpuhi taua, led particularly by Hongi Hika and Pomare, began their onslaughts against Ngāti Pāoa in the Tāmaki isthmus in July 1821, and followed that up with heavy attacks on Ngāti Maru in the Hauraki. As over 2000 toa gathered and the waka taua practised in the Kerikeri River, the CMS missionaries watched in horror. Hongi Hika himself was resplendent in a red scarlet coat that had been given to him in England. The missionaries estimated that 50 waka left Pēwhairangi, each capable of carrying 40 to 70 men. The taua

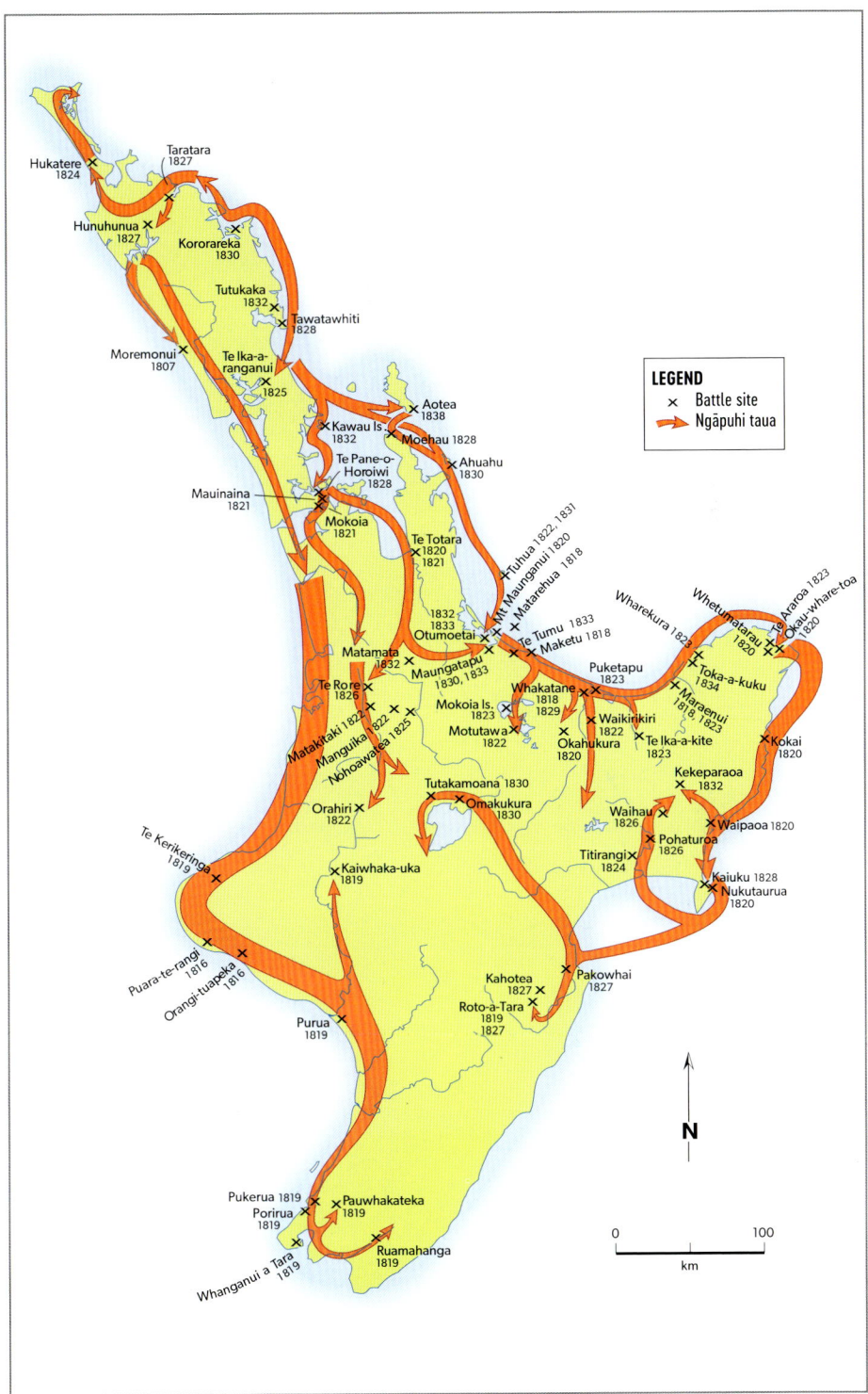

Battle sites and taua routes of Ngāpuhi and allies.

Tainui iwi and Ngāti Whātua: battle sites, and routes of taua and migrations.

RIGHT *Tamati Waka Nene. The renowned Ngāpuhi rangatira, a fearless warrior, who played a leading role in taua during the Musket Wars. Yet in 1840 he was also instrumental in persuading other rangatira to sign the Treaty of Waitangi.*

Gottfried Lindauer, Tamati Waka Nene, 1890, oil on canvas, Auckland Art Gallery Toi o Tāmaki, gift of Mr H.E. Partridge, 1915

BELOW *A famous portrait of Hongi Hika (centre) and his fellow Ngāpuhi rangatira Waikato with the missionary Thomas Kendall at the time of their trip to England in 1820.*

G-618, Barry, James, active 1818–1846: [The Rev. Thomas Kendall and the Maori chiefs Hongi and Waikato]. Alexander Turnbull Library, Wellington, NZ

Te Rauparaha. A portrait by John Gilfillan, dated 1842, of the Ngāti Toa rangatira who with his allies dominated the lower half of the North Island and northern half of the South Island from 1824 to 1840.

A-114-023, Gilfillan, John Alexander, 1793–1863: [Te Rauparaha] [1842]. Alexander Turnbull Library, Wellington, NZ

Te Rangituke. Leader of the 1828 Ngāpuhi taua that was destroyed by Ngāti Tipa (Waikato) and Ngāti Paoa at Te Pane o Horoiwi. Rangituke was among those killed, shortly after this portrait was painted.

G-634, Earle, Augustus, 1793–1838. Alexander Turnbull Library, Wellington, NZ

grew even larger when it assembled at Whangarei, where it was joined by toa from the Te Parawhau hapū and other southern Ngāpuhi hapū before it finally headed south.

Two major pā were attacked beside the Tāmaki River at Tāmaki Makaurau (modern-day Auckland), just north of the Panmure Basin. Thousands of Ngāti Paoa had been observed living there by missionaries during a visit just a few months earlier, when they had met with Te Hinaki, the principal Ngāti Paoa rangatira. They described Ngāti Paoa as occupying more than twenty kāinga, with massive gardens near two defensive pā sites. However, in contrast to the many hundreds of muskets available to Ngāpuhi, it is believed Ngāti Paoa had fewer than ten muskets at that time.

Mokoia, the pā immediately to the north of Panmure Basin, was the first to fall. Ngāti Paoa suffered massive loss of life, including the rangatira Te Hinaki. Mauinaina pā was assaulted next, and fell soon after. Some later accounts asserted that more than a thousand Ngāti Paoa were killed during these two sieges. The Ngāpuhi toa finally left after a long-running cannibal feast, but instead of returning home the taua moved south to attack Ngāti Maru, under their leader Te Puhi, at Te Tōtara pā just south of modern-day Thames.

After a siege at Te Tōtara lasting two days the strong defences still held Ngāpuhi at bay, so Hongi Hika resorted to a devious kōhuru (stratagem). He began by sending in some senior rangatira bearing valuable gifts; one of the rangatira was Te Morenga, another the huge, physically impressive Tareha. Their approaches were accepted as genuine by Te Puhi

Hongi Hika's helmet

Hongi Hika himself had cause to be grateful for the gift of a helmet that he received in England and wore during the siege of Mokoia pā. During one assault it saved his life when one of the few musket balls fired by Ngāti Paoa hit the helmet.

54 THE FORGOTTEN WARS

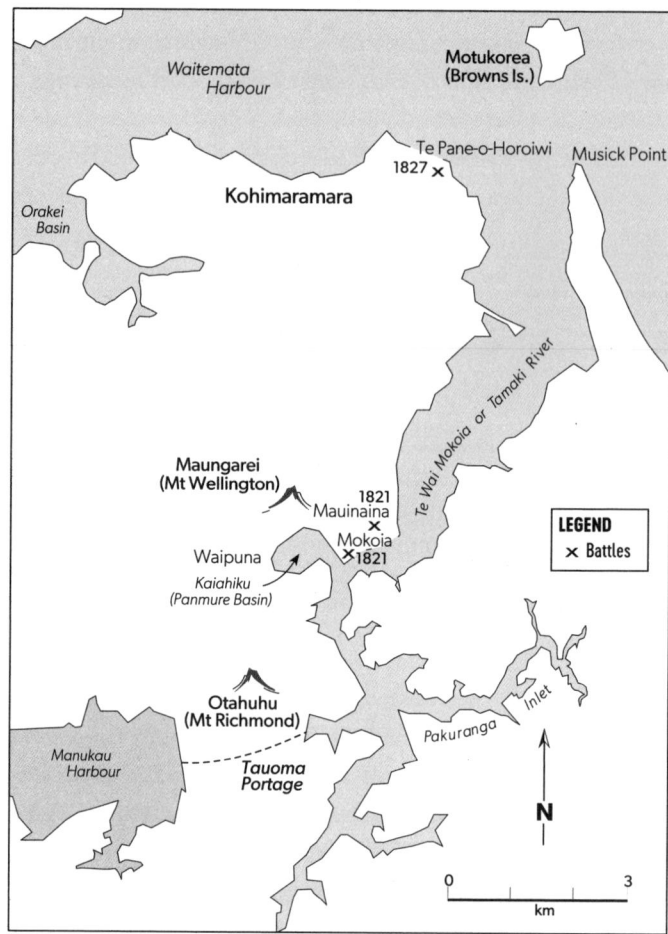

Mokoia/Mauinaina pā locations at Auckland, 1821.

and his rangatira, who in turn gave back valuable mere (short, flat clubs). After these exchanges and promises of peace, they were relieved to see Ngāpuhi launch their waka and head north, disappearing out of sight.

Sadly for Ngāti Maru, their relief was misplaced. After the Ngāpuhi waka had rounded the point at Tararu, about five kilometres north of Thames, they pulled into shore and awaited nightfall. Later, under cover of darkness, the waka were relaunched and, in a repeat of the strategy used by Pomare at Te Whetumatarau the previous year, they slid as quietly as possible through the waters of the gulf and up the mouth of the Waihou River to land beside the pā. The occupants of the pā being asleep, and having failed to set sentries, it was quickly seized amid heavy slaughter of those inside, who included some visiting Waikato, Ngāti Raukawa and Te Arawa. After that success Hongi's taua headed home with its trophies.

Although Hongi Hika's kōhuru emulated that of Pomare in 1820, Pomare and Te Wera Hauraki are said to have refused to be part of it, and they moved on to attack other iwi in the Bay of Plenty in an expedition that lasted well into 1822. They first attacked Whakatane to seek utu for the losses suffered there by Te Morenga in 1818. The progress of their large taua was noticed from the shore, and as a result Tūhoe pulled back from the coastal areas of their rohe into the mountainous and heavily bushed Urewera ranges, their refuge.

After their recent bitter experiences of musket-armed Ngāpuhi taua, Ngāti Awa and Ngāti Pukeko also pulled back from the coast and occupied some of the Tūhoe pā sites in and around Ruatoki. Ngāpuhi are said to have attacked and captured five of those pā near or in the foothills south of Whakatane, before the survivors fled up the Whakatane Valley led by their rangatira Te Mautaranui, who had whakapapa links to both Tūhoe and Ngāti Awa. The pursuit almost reached Ruatāhuna, about seventy kilometres south of Whakatane. At that stage, satisfied with the devastation they had inflicted around Whakatane, Pomare and Te Wera returned to Te Tai Tokerau (Northland).

MĀTAKITAKI — WAIKATO/TAINUI UNDER ATTACK IN THE WAIPA

In the west of the central North Island, 1822 saw Waikato/Tainui facing attack by a massive taua, once again led by Hongi Hika. Its aim was to attack deep into the Waipa catchment, a branch of the Waikato River where the huge Mātakitaki pā base of Tainui power lay.

Scores of Ngāpuhi waka were portaged over from the Waitemata Harbour at Otahuhu to the Manukau Harbour, then paddled right up the Waiuku River and portaged over to and down the Awaroa Stream into the Waikato. Tainui became aware of the onrush of the great taua and made desperate efforts to slow its progress by felling huge trees across the Awaroa Stream. That achieved a lull of some weeks, which was extended because the stream bed of the Awaroa was so narrow and twisty that in places tight bends had to be cut through for the very long waka taua (war canoes). The subsequent delay enabled most Waikato hapū to gather at Mātakitaki pā at Pirongia. According to Tainui accounts, there were between 4000 and 5000 people occupying the pā — principally of Tainui descent, but also comprising some Ngāti Paoa and Ngāti Maru survivors of the fall of the Mokoia/Mauinaina pā, and Te Tōtara pā.

One can only imagine the intense anxiety felt by the occupants of the pā as scores of waka taua swept around the last bend of the Waipa at its junction with the Mangapiko Stream. As they watched, the waka taua were dragged up onto the opposite bank and some 3000 toa, heavily armed with muskets, poured forth and drew up in serried lines. They then roared out a thunderous haka on the riverside, before some opened fire on the pā while others set up their main camp opposite the river junction. Other Ngāpuhi crossed the Waipa and started to set up camps on the northern side of the Mangapiko.

The broad and deep Waipa, and the deeply incised Mangapiko Stream, provided natural defences for the southern and northern sides of the pā, which occupied the plateau between them. The eastern end of the pā was heavily palisaded across a narrow neck between the Waipa and the Mangapiko, with a deep defensive ditch outside the palisading. The pā itself was divided by three sets of internal palisading with adjacent deep ditches. In the context of customary Māori warfare it was an immensely strong defensive pā site, and defended by several thousand experienced Tainui toa led by Te Wherowhero.

The siege did not begin well for Ngāpuhi in all areas. They had quickly occupied the northern side of the Mangapiko and their skirmishers had spread around the easternmost palisading, from where any Tainui breakout could be expected to occur. From the northern side of the Mangapiko Stream they directed fire south into the northern side of the pā, but as their lines extended east their numbers thinned. Te Wherowhero quickly recognised the opportunity for a surprise attack by Waikato — if a strong ope (group) was able to slip out of the pā it would be able to surprise the Ngāpuhi skirmishers by coming in behind them.

The constant roar from their thousands of muskets at the far western end, coupled with their activities in making shelters for their camp at the eastern end of the pā, diverted Ngāpuhi attention. Te Wherowhero's ope seized the moment to leave the pā unnoticed. Having got behind Ngāpuhi they were able to close in unseen and successfully launch their attack with traditional hand-held weapons. The surprise assault caused a desperate retreat by Ngāpuhi down into the Mangapiko, where for the moment greater Waikato numbers overwhelmed them at close quarters. Some 150 Ngāpuhi were killed during this localised rout. Over a hundred muskets were captured, and the Tainui ope triumphantly returned to the eastern end of the pā.

This triumph, however, was the only success Tainui were to enjoy at Mātakitaki, and it was dreadfully short-lived. On their return the gleeful Waikato climbed up onto the palisading on the northern side of the pā to jeer at the Ngāpuhi rout.

THE PEAK AND DECLINE OF NGĀPUHI DOMINANCE 57

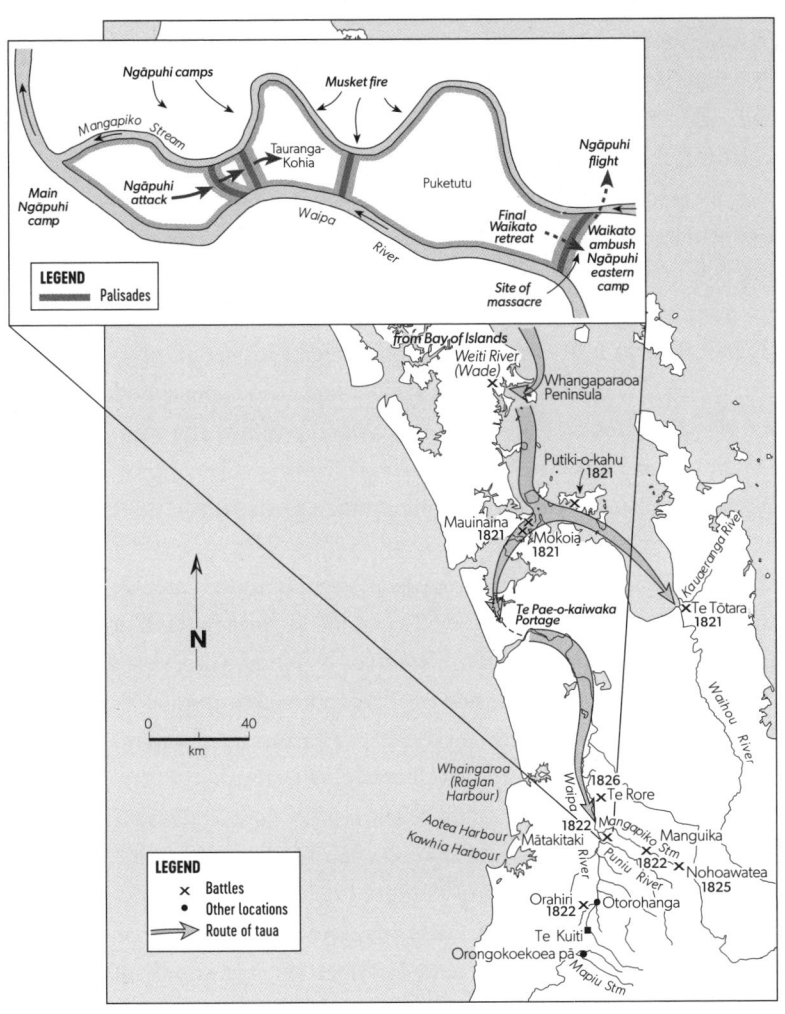

Ngāpuhi taua to Mokoia, Te Tōtara and Waikato, 1821-26.
INSET: Matakitaki pā, 1822.

The response was a series of accurate massed volleys across the Mangapiko, and large numbers of Waikato fell back killed or wounded, with the usual horrendous wounds made by large musket balls. The shock of these casualties, and their severity and scale, seems to have created mass panic within the pā. Large numbers of the terrified occupants rushed to the eastern end to avoid the mayhem. Te Wherowhero's men responded as well as they could at the western end, but Ngāpuhi could hear and see the panic, and they rushed the palisading all around that end of the pā. The roar of musketry from these assaults caused further terror within the pā, the panic increased like wildfire, and all reason seemed to disappear.

The gates at the eastern end of the pā were flung open. Literally thousands of people rushed forward and tried to cross the steep-sided ditch outside the palisading, which had only a few logs thrown across it. Within minutes masses of people had fallen into the ditch and were crushed as they struggled to get out, with more and more people falling in on top of them. By now Ngāpuhi were starting to arrive and fire into the seething mass of bodies, increasing the horror of the Waikato trapped in the ditch by the weight of numbers.

The only exception to this calamitous rout was the fighting retreat from west to east staged by Te Wherowhero's brave ope as Ngāpuhi scaled each set of internal defences, and in the end the Tainui defenders simply had to escape as best they could. The slaughter by Ngāpuhi was said to be colossal, even by the standards of those times when there was a heavy imbalance of power. Even Tainui sources put the number killed as 1500, with many more taken as slaves.

After the fall of Mātakitaki Ngāpuhi stayed in the upper Waipa area for several months, taking a number of other pā. However, some months later Te Wherowhero was able to mount a crucial and well-planned surprise attack at Orahiri pā, just west of Ōtorohanga, where a large group of Ngāpuhi were wiped out and their muskets captured. The total number of weapons captured by Te Wherowhero at Mātakitaki and now at Orahiri meant that Tainui were well on the road to being able to assemble a sizable taua well armed with muskets.

On leaving Mātakitaki Hongi Hika had made a peace offering by releasing some of the high-ranking Waikato women, and that was soon followed by some marriages being arranged between Waikato and Hongi's line of Ngāpuhi hapū. Pomare, however, was not a party to these peace accords, and within four years he would lead another taua up the Waipa. By then, Te Wherowhero's supply of muskets had been further increased by urgent trading.

ROTORUA AND TE ARAWA

In 1823 Ngāpuhi taua under Hongi and Pomare returned to the Bay of Plenty, where they carried out an even greater feat of portage and took Te Arawa by surprise as the waka fleet swept down the Ōhau Channel from Lake Rotoiti and into Lake Rotorua. This was an epic achievement, as dozens of waka were dragged up from the headwaters of the Pongakawa Stream, across into the waters of Lake Rotoehu, and again from that lake to Lake Rotoiti. Achieved with guiding assistance from Ngāiterangi, with whom Ngāpuhi had made peace three years earlier, this amazing physical effort enabled Ngāpuhi to launch an attack on the otherwise impregnable island refuge of Mokoia.

The reason for the assault was the need to obtain utu for the killing of a number of members of a limited exploratory Ngāpuhi taua under Te Pae-o-te-Rangi, which comprised about 200 men armed with muskets. The killings had occurred at Lake Rotokākahi (Green Lake) southeast of Rotorua in 1822. The taua had no waka and had been enticed onto the Motutawa Island pā at Rotokākahi by Tūhourangi of Te Arawa. At the suggestion of Te Rauparaha, who happened to be there while trying to persuade his Te Arawa relatives to join his heke south to Kāpiti, about 130 members of the taua were ferried out in small groups to different parts of the island. Each small group was then set upon and the toa killed, including Te Pae-o-te-Rangi. The balance of the rest fired on the island ineffectually, then had no other option than to head home to Te Tai Tokerau with news of the treacherous

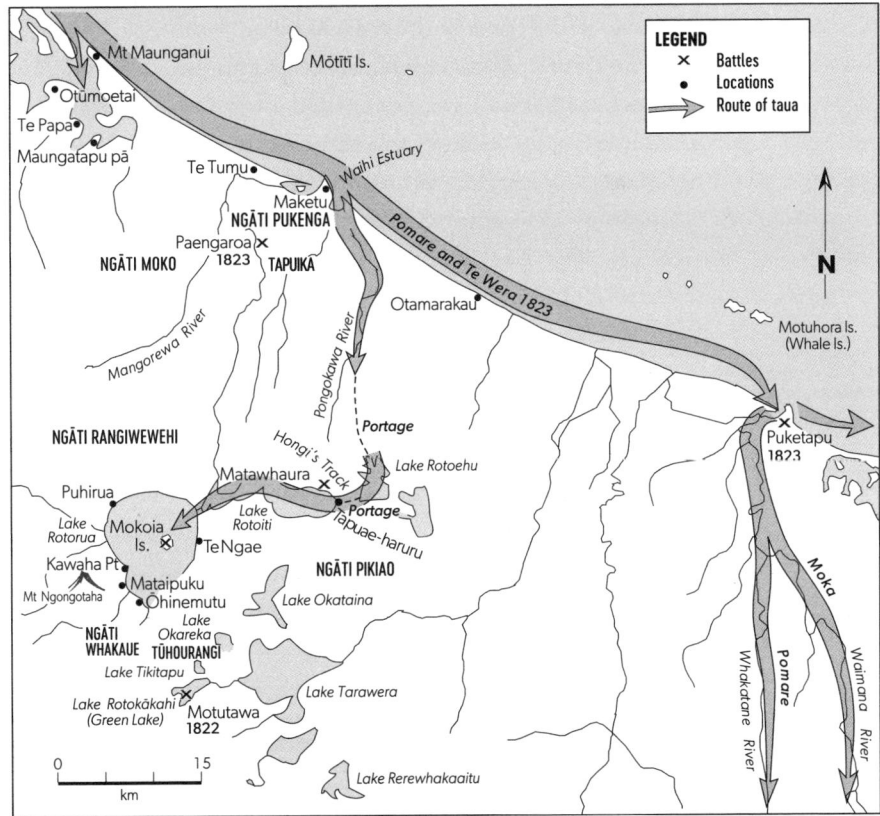

Ngāpuhi taua to Mokoia Island, 1823.

> **Te Aokapurangi**
>
> The losses at Mokoia would have been even greater had it not been for the courage of Te Aokapurangi, the captive Ngāti Rangiwewehi wife of Te Wera Hauraki, who had got Ngāpuhi to agree that all who passed through her thighs would be spared. She climbed onto the main wharenui Tamatekapua, straddling its entrance, and called out during the heavy fighting to Ngāti Rangiwewehi to seek refuge between her thighs. All who made it into Tamatekapua were spared.

attack. In urging Tūhourangi to attack, Te Rauparaha had been motivated by news that Ngāpuhi had killed some of his Te Arawa and Ngāti Raukawa relatives, or possibly his wife Te Akau, at Te Tōtara pā the previous year.

Despite desperate Te Arawa resistance the later Ngāpuhi attack on Mokoia was a one-sided affair in which Te Arawa suffered badly, an inevitable result as they had only one musket, which they had captured in a night raid on a Ngāpuhi ope a few days before at Rotoiti. Large numbers were killed on the island by the heavy musket volleys of Ngāpuhi, and many more were killed from waka as they desperately swam for the mainland. After the fighting had ended, Hikairo of Ngāti Rangiwewehi courageously engaged in negotiations with Ngāpuhi, who were so impressed by his oratory that Hongi announced they would soon be leaving.

After the return from Rotorua, again involving prodigious efforts of portage, but this time assisted by the hundreds of slaves they had captured, the Ngāpuhi taua divided. Hongi Hika led raids around Paengaroa and took two more pā, held by Ngāti Pukenga and Tapuika, then headed back up north. But Pomare and several other rangatira, including Te Wera Hauraki, turned east.

POMARE AND TE WERA HAURAKI HEAD EAST

One reason the still major taua under Pomare and Te Wera headed east was to launch further attacks on Bay of Plenty iwi in Whakatane and Ōpōtiki areas. Another reason was more unusual. Both Pomare and Te Wera had agreed to return wives who had been taken captive on earlier taua. Pomare returned Rangi-i-paea of Ngāti Porou, who had been captured at Te Araroa, to Kawakawa Bay, while Te Wera took his captive Ngāti Kahungunu wife and her brother Te Whareumu all the way back to Mahia Peninsula.

After attacking Ngāti Pukeko and Ngāti Awa at Whakatane, the Ngāpuhi taua divided into a number of ope that pursued the fleeing members of these iwi into the Urewera, as well as Ngāi Tūhoe, who they had increasingly started to encounter. These ope moved up the north-flowing rivers draining the Urewera, including the Whakatane, Waimana, Waiotahi, Waioeka and Otara. It was a massive assault on the rohe of Whakatōhea and Tūhoe, with Tūhoe adopting their traditional tactic of staging fighting withdrawals up each mountainous, bush-clad valley back towards Ruatāhuna and Maungapōhatu.

But at Ōhauā, in the upper Whakatane just north of Ruatāhuna, Pomare was approached by Te Mautaranui, a prominent rangatira of both Ngāti Awa and Tūhoe descent. He proposed peace terms, which Pomare agreed to, and a famous formal peace between Ngāpuhi and Tūhoe was made. Pomare travelled on with Te Mautaranui to Maungapōhatu to ensure the peace was observed by other Ngāpuhi rangatira, then Te Mautaranui returned with Pomare to the coast to ensure the peace was observed there between Ngāpuhi and Ngāti Awa. It was a peace and a personal friendship that Pomare was to honour in years to come.

Events were not peaceful at all, however, to the east of Whakatane. In the Otara Valley south of Ōpōtiki, Te Wera's ope had attacked a number of Whakatōhea pā and been met with strong resistance. Although the pā were taken, it was not without loss to the taua.

Reuniting, the taua then moved further east to attack Maraenui pā at the mouth of the Motu River, where Ngāpuhi understood some of their women who had been taken captive by the crew of the *Venus* have been killed. Further similarly motivated attacks were then launched against Te Whānau a Apanui at Te Kaha, and at Whangaparaoa Bay to the east. Once again the taua suffered losses in these attacks, including Te Wera's high-ranking nephew Marino, who was killed at Wharekura pā, Te Kaha.

When the taua landed at Te Araroa, Pomare sent out emissaries to contact Ngāti Porou, intending to return Rangi-i-paea. The initial result was a furious charge in the open by thousands of Ngāti Porou, who believed they would be

> **The first Ngāti Porou preachers**
>
> The longer-term consequence of the peace accord between Ngāti Porou and Ngāpuhi was that several years later, in about 1828, some Ngāti Porou rangatira were able to travel north in safety and seek the return of rangatira who had been taken as slaves, the most prominent being Piripi Taumata a Kura. During their captivity they had been trained in mission work by the missionaries at Pēwhairangi, and on their release in 1834 they brought back Christian principles and teachings to Ngāti Porou, and became their first preachers.

unstoppable against the much smaller taua. The deadly effects of the hundreds of massed Ngāpuhi muskets quickly brought home the reality of the power imbalance created by the new weapons. This time Ngāti Porou withdrew right back into the mountainous Taitai ranges around Mt Hikurangi.

A tremendously courageous rangatira, Taotaoriri, was now sent by Pomare to open negotiations. Ngāti Porou, impressed by his courage, agreed to negotiate, and a peace accord was achieved between these two major iwi. To cement the peace, Ngāti Porou gave a high-ranking woman, Hikupoto, to Taotaoriri as a wife.

Te Wera Hauraki, meanwhile, carried on south with his one great waka taua, *Herua*, and about fifty musket-armed toa to return his Ngāti Kahungunu wife and his brother-in-law Te Whareumu to Mahia Peninsula. Again, peace terms were agreed. Te Wera was persuaded to remain and, ironically, he and his musket-armed men were to become the protectors of Ngāti Kahungunu for the next 15 years, until his return north in about 1838.

TE HIKU O TE IKA — HONGI HIKA ATTACKS TE AUPŌURI IN THE NORTH WHILE POMARE HEADS SOUTH TO WAIROA

In 1824 Hongi Hika responded to a long-standing request from Poroa of Te Rarawa to take a Ngāpuhi taua north and attack Te Aupōuri, who occupied Te Hiku o Te Ika. While all three iwi had interrelationships in their whakapapa, and had jointly engaged on taua to the south in the past, both Te Rarawa and Ngāpuhi also had a history of conflict with Te Aupōuri. (In mythological terms Te Hiku o Te Ika was the top of the North Island — named as the hiku [tail] of the ika [fish] that Māui pulled up as he fished from his waka, Te Waipounamu [the South Island]. The top of the South Island was called Te Tau Ihu o te Waka ā Māui, being the prow [tip of the nose] of Māui's waka.)

The primary target was the rangatira Te Houtaewa of Te Aupōuri, who had frequently been a thorn in the side of Te Rarawa. In the past Te Houtaewa had famously relied on his speed and endurance to outstrip his pursuers, but this was a different situation. Te Aupōuri had only limited numbers of muskets and they were facing a large taua that was heavily armed with the new weapons. Coming under attack, Te Houtaewa and his people sought to defend the palisaded Hukatere pā, about 25 kilometres north of Kaitaia. For a time they held off their besiegers by lighting the grasses and scrub that surrounded the lower portions of the hill pā, while Te Houtaewa and other toa moved about, appearing in and out of the smoke to give the impression of large numbers of defenders. Finally, they used the cover of the dense smoke to break out and try to escape. Te Houtaewa had been shot in the thigh early in the siege, and after a long chase he was run down and killed near Houhora.

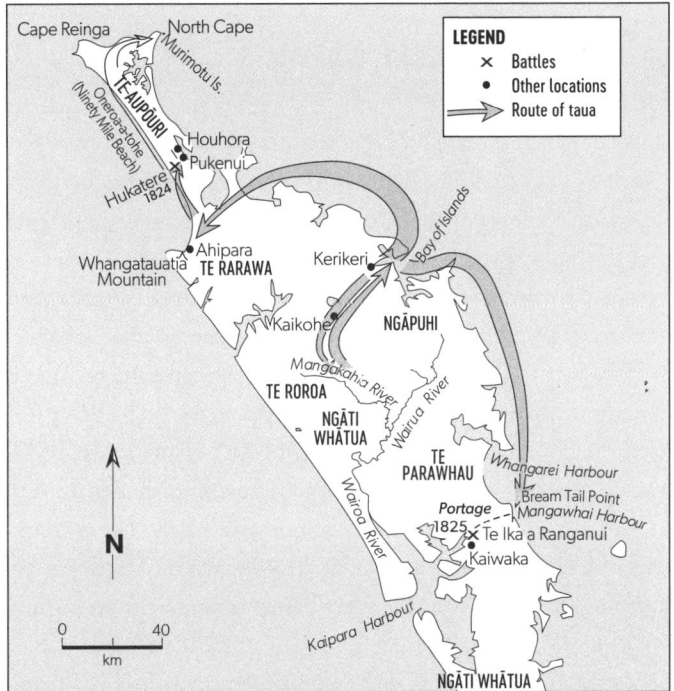

Hongi Hika's taua to Hukatere in 1824 and Te Ika a Ranganui in 1825.

The loss of Hukatere pā resulted in a long, ruthless pursuit that forced most Te Aupōuri to retreat to the far north and at last to seek refuge on Murimotu Island, off North Cape, and even, according to some accounts, on the Three Kings Islands. The effects on the iwi were devastating.

Meanwhile, in mid April 1824, in response to repeated urgings from the Tūhoe rangatira Te Mautaranui, Pomare had led another more limited Ngāpuhi taua all the way back to the Bay of Plenty. They were to join an alliance that included elements of Ngāti Whātua, Ngāti Maru, Ngāti Tamaterā, Ngāiterangi, Ngāti Awa, Whakatōhea and Ngāi Tūhoe, gathering at Ruatāhuna. The objective of the combined taua was to seek utu against Ngāti Kahungunu for the killing of a prominent Tūhoe rangatira, Te Rangiwaitatao, in the upper Wairoa.

For the third time in five years, then, Pomare travelled with an ope of his taua up the Whakatane, on this occasion as far as Ruatāhuna. This time, however, he was joining members of iwi, including Tūhoe, who he had raided ruthlessly each year for the last five years. Meanwhile, the balance of his taua travelled around East Cape by waka to Wairoa and attacked the prime objective of the alliance's various taua — Titirangi pā on the Waiau River, not far inland from Wairoa. Here their long-distance musket power was used to effect heavy losses, and this major Ngāti Kahungunu pā fell.

TE IKA A RANGANUI — KAIPARA AND NGĀTI WHĀTUA

In 1825 it was at last the turn of Ngāti Whātua — the enemy iwi closest to Ngāpuhi. The proximity between the iwi had led to a history of clashes between Ngāti Whātua and various Ngāpuhi hapū, including at Moremonui in 1807. The consequence was that, in terms of the utu ledger, Ngāpuhi regarded Ngāti Whātua as the iwi that probably owed them the most.

Another massive taua formed under Hongi Hika's leadership, and this time the scores of waka were taken into the head of the Mangawhai estuary, just south of Bream Bay, before beginning the long portage west toward the Kaipara Harbour. During this process they were intercepted by Ngāti Whātua, but decisively defeated their opponents after heavy fighting at the battle of Te Ika a Ranganui. Ngāti Whātua then had to undergo a particularly drawn-out and ruthless pursuit, during which even Murupaenga was killed. The pursuit carried on as far south as Nohoawatea pā, far up the Waikato/Waipa catchment, where large numbers of Ngāti Whātua were given refuge by their Tainui relatives.

Even there, the Ngāpuhi muskets enabled the pursuing taua to wreak savage revenge on Ngāti Whātua, but this was to be the last Ngāpuhi taua to experience unmitigated success.

A DEVASTATING FIRST DEFEAT AT TE RORE AND THE DEATH OF POMARE

Over the next seven years, from 1826 to 1833, the rapid acquisition of muskets by iwi who Ngāpuhi had previously attacked with impunity meant that the playing fields of battle became far more level. Ngāpuhi fortunes began to change, beginning with a shattering defeat and the death of one of their greatest rangatira.

In 1826 the prominent rangatira Pomare led a Ngāpuhi taua that again headed south into the Waikato. The precise aims of this particular taua are now lost to history, but the outcome was a decisive defeat for Ngāpuhi. Waikato, who had by now acquired even greater numbers of muskets to supplement those they had captured in 1822, set an ambush for the taua at Te Rore. Pomare himself was killed, along with other respected rangatira and almost all the members of his taua; only a handful of survivors made it back to the north.

Pomare had been one of the most courageous and highly regarded of the Ngāpuhi rangatira, probably only overshadowed in mana by Hongi Hika himself, and the news of his loss must have caused great concern in Te Tai Tokerau. But there was little outward sign of a loss of Ngāpuhi confidence. On the contrary, in 1827 they headed off in a number of taua, again in a variety of directions.

THE DEFEAT OF HONGI HIKA AND TE RANGITUKE, AND THE LAST MAJOR REVERSES OF THE DECADE FOR NGĀPUHI

In 1827 a further very heavy shadow fell on Ngāpuhi aims of supremacy with the loss of Hongi Hika. On this occasion Hongi was leading an inter-hapū taua

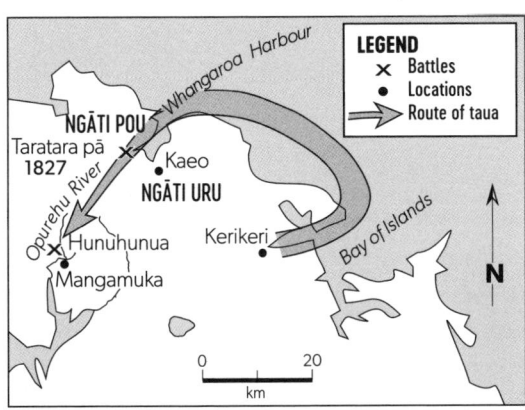

Hongi Hika's final taua, to Whangaroa and Hokianga, 1827.

Flotte de Guerre à la Nouvelle-Zélande. Although he did not make this engraving until the mid 1830s, the French artist de Sainson had seen taua at sea when with Dumont d'Urville in 1827. It is highly likely that this is an accurate impression of the large Ngāpuhi seagoing taua led by Te Rangituke at the entrance to Whangarei Harbour.
PUBL-0034-2-355, Sainson, Louis Auguste de, 1800–, b. 1800: Flotte de guerre à la Nouvelle Zélande, Nargeon sc. [Paris, 1839]. Alexander Turnbull Library, Wellington, NZ

against his relatives, but long-standing opponents, Ngāti Pou, from the area in and around Whangaroa Harbour. These northern Ngāpuhi were heavily armed with muskets, and Hongi was shot in the chest in a skirmish at Hunuhunua, near Mangamuka. His taua withdrew and brought him home, but he died a long, lingering death the following year.

Another powerful Ngāpuhi taua also headed south in 1827, this time under a younger rangatira, Te Rangituke. As it left Whangarei, the taua happened to encounter Dumont d'Urville's vessel *Astrolabe*, which carried south the news of its impending arrival. Thus forewarned, Waikato, in alliance with Ngāti Paoa, were able to plan a skilfully laid ambush, this time at the mouth of the Tāmaki River, on the Waitemata Harbour. The ensuing ambush was highly successful: Te Rangituke was killed, along with most of the men of his taua, and only a very few waka made it back to the north.

This time, however, the consequences were even worse for Ngāpuhi, as Te Wherowhero followed up the defeat of Te Rangituke's taua by invading the Whangarei area in early 1828. He inflicted heavy losses on the Te Parawhau hapū of Ngāpuhi, in what was the first invasion in decades of any part of the Ngāpuhi rohe by a southern grouping of iwi. The wheel of musket power had well and truly turned, even if it would still be some years before Ngāpuhi themselves recognised the change.

Later that same year a further Ngāpuhi taua travelled south, led by Rangitukia. This taua was intercepted by Ngāti Maru under Te Rohu and heavily defeated at Moehau, on the Coromandel Peninsula. Rangitukia was killed, and once more only remnants of the taua made it back home. It was also later in this year that the great Hongi Hika died from the wound he had suffered the previous year.

THE 'GIRLS' WAR' OF 1830 AND ILL-PLANNED CONSEQUENCES

It is probably not surprising, in view of these recent events, that for the first time in over ten years no Ngāpuhi taua headed south in 1829 or 1830. Instead, however, an outbreak of inter-hapū fighting occurred in 1830 at Pēwhairangi. This began with an incident that involved a physical fight between some high-born women of differing hapū — hence the name, the 'Girls' War', that was subsequently attached to these events — and grew in magnitude into a series of clashes led by

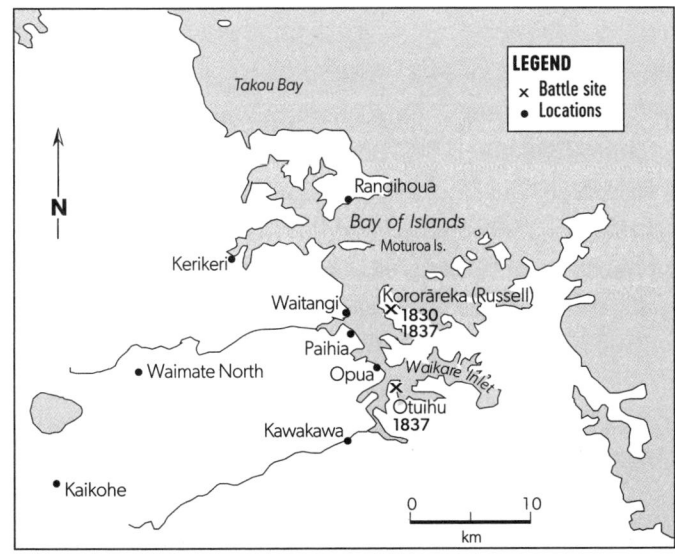

Sites of conflict in the Ngāpuhi civil wars, 1830 and 1837.

Titore and Pomare (II), respectively. Titore was from the northwest Kerikeri and Waimate North areas, and Pomare was from Otuihu, just southeast of Kororāreka (Russell). (Pomare was the nephew of the famous Whetoi Pomare who Tainui had killed in 1826 in the Waipa; originally called Whiria Pomare, the younger man later adopted the name of his illustrious uncle, also calling himself Whetoi Pomare.)

The real tragedy of this 'war' was that after a precarious peace was reached, utu was sought later in 1830 against other distant iwi not involved at all — an acknowledged step often taken in Māori customary warfare so as to avoid merely re-igniting a fragile peace between closely related hapū. This process of seeking utu in the south began when a relatively small northern Ngāpuhi taua, comprising mostly Ngāti Pou toa, attacked the occupants of Ahuahu (Great Mercury Island). The taua then moved even further south, and it was eventually repulsed with the loss of some of its own rangatira in an unsuccessful attack on Ngāiterangi at Maungatapu in Tauranga Harbour.

The losses at Maungatapu in 1830 led an old Ngāpuhi rangatira, Te Haramiti, to decide the following year to lead yet another surprisingly small taua of about 140 toa south to attack Ngāiterangi at Mōtītī Island. Te Haramiti and his small taua were wiped out on Mōtītī by a surprise joint attack by Ngāiterangi and Ngāti Hauā (an alliance that was to recur in later years). Believing that another ope of Ngāpuhi might be joining them, Te Haramiti and his men had made the mistake of going down to the shore to welcome waka they saw sweeping in, only to find themselves overcome by their bitter enemies.

TAREHA AND TITORE REBUFFED AND PUKERANGI KILLED

The losses of Ngāpuhi taua in the Waikato, and more recently of Te Haramiti's taua in the Bay of Plenty, continued to give rise to customary demands for utu. Those take (motivations) resulted in two major Ngāpuhi taua being launched in 1832.

One of these taua comprised two major ope, led by Tareha and Titore, that set out to attack the major home pā of Ngāti Hauā at Matamata and Ngāiterangi at Tauranga. The huge rangatira Tareha led the attack at Matamata, but again with little success as a consequence of Ngāti Hauā's acquisition of muskets. Tareha then withdrew to the Bay of Plenty coast to link with Titore for the attack on Ngāiterangi at Tauranga. Here Ngāpuhi found their Ngāiterangi adversaries had also armed themselves with muskets, and the taua withdrew after some time without achieving any success.

In the same year another Ngāpuhi taua, this one led by Pukerangi and Tirarau,

Titore's taua. A well-known drawing by the missionary Henry Williams of the Ngāpuhi taua led by Titore to attack Tauranga. Williams and other missionaries accompanied the taua and endeavoured unsuccessfully to dissuade its members from warfare. (An interesting feature is the use of sails by waka on a taua.)
PUBL-0031-1835-1, Williams, Henry, 1782–1867: New Zealand war expedition. [Engraving, London, Seely's 1835 & 1849.] Alexander Turnbull Library, Wellington, NZ

headed south once more into the Waikato to seek utu for repeated Ngāpuhi losses to Tainui. Yet again, their powerful taua encountered the now common outcome of Ngāpuhi taua into this region. They were repulsed by a resurgent Waikato, now heavily armed with muskets and led once more by Te Wherowhero.

Even more concerningly for Ngāpuhi, Te Wherowhero again pursued the fleeing taua all the way to the Tutukaka area, just north of Whangarei, where Ngāpuhi were heavily defeated. For the second time in four years, Te Wherowhero had shown that he could travel north to invade Ngāpuhi territory and inflict heavy casualties.

THE LAST GASP OF NGĀPUHI POWER REBUFFED

Despite these repeated setbacks, in 1833 a huge taua of Pēwhairangi Ngāpuhi led by Titore headed south to attack Ngāiterangi at Tauranga. Even though this time they were armed with some small cannon, had been joined by one waka with an ope of Ngāti Maru under Te Rohu, and had support from most Te Arawa hapū, the results were no different from those experienced the preceding year.

Against opponents who were themselves heavily armed

with muskets (including, unusually, support from the Ngāti Rangiwewehi hapū of Te Arawa), Ngāpuhi faced a balance of power they could not overcome. After some months of heavy but ineffectual expenditure of ammunition at long ranges, the taua returned with nothing of note achieved other than taking Te Tumu pā, from which Ngāiterangi withdrew for the time being after limited skirmishing there. Titore's taua was the last major long-distance Ngāpuhi taua of the Musket Wars era.

HE WHAKAPUTANGA – A STRATEGY SHIFT BY NGĀPUHI?

The succession of defeats and the heavy loss of rangatira and toa that they had suffered over the last seven years, coupled with Te Wherowhero's two successful attacks in the Whangarei area, meant Ngāpuhi were now well aware of the significant musket power that lay in the hands of southern iwi. Most concerning would have been the graphic demonstration provided by Te Wherowhero's invasions in 1828 and 1832, that powerfully armed southern iwi now had the capability to successfully invade the north. Moreover, Ngāpuhi rangatira would have been only too well aware of the deep desire for utu felt by all those southern iwi who they had devastated. It seems highly likely that this awareness would have influenced the strategic thinking of Ngāpuhi leaders. For after 1833 they suddenly ceased entirely any attempts to exercise power through musket-armed taua to the south.

As early as 1831 Ngāpuhi had written to request British Crown protection against external threat, and in 1835 a more formal approach for Crown protection of their 'statehood' was made in clause 4 of 'He Whakaputanga o te Rangatiratanga o Nu Tireni' (A Declaration of Independence by the Chiefs of New Zealand), now commonly referred to as He Whakaputanga. The 1835 Declaration was initially signed by 34 Ngāpuhi rangatira at the Waitangi home of the British Resident James Busby, for the purpose of asserting that sovereignty lay with rangatira, and that only they had the power to make laws in Aotearoa. The Declaration included, however, the request in clause 4 that the Crown extend its protection over their combined statehood against external threats. While modern historians commonly address these threats to Ngāpuhi as emanating solely from France, clause 3 of He Whakaputanga expresses an often overlooked invitation, or request, to southern iwi: 'kia wakarererea te wawai', which can be translated as either 'to set aside their animosities' or 'to desist from fighting'.

It seems logical in terms of Māori tikanga that an obvious and real threat felt by Ngāpuhi lay in their exposure to the deep-seated urge for utu from other iwi to the south. The customary force of utu was still undiminished among Māori in 1835, and Ngāpuhi knew all too well how strong these urges could be. Ngāpuhi rangatira also knew only too well how recently those utu obligations among southern iwi had been created. They had arisen from the widespread man-killing Ngāpuhi raids that had been almost continuous from 1817 right through to 1833. They knew that the rangatira of southern iwi would be keen to exact their own revenge, and that this keenness would grow over time. It would only require strong southern rangatira to form strategic alliances, and heavily armed taua could be expected to head north.

FINAL NGĀPUHI INVOLVEMENTS IN THE MUSKET WARS

By this time the missionaries were actively involved in trying to secure peace between iwi, which they finally achieved. Ironically, one of the last heavy engagements Ngāpuhi were involved in during the Musket Wars was at Pēwhairangi in 1837, when serious extended inter-hapū warfare broke out again between Titore's people and those who supported Pomare at Otuihu pā. Despite the large numbers of toa and the heavy expenditure of ammunition, casualties were now few because of the balance in musket power.

One of the least-known Ngāpuhi taua of 1838 saw the swansong of their involvement in the wars, when once more a small taua of about 120 men from Pomare's hapū headed south. Even the purpose of the taua seems to have become lost in time, although it may have been limited to the actions at Aotea (Great Barrier Island) that led to its demise. For it is known that the taua attacked the Ngāti Rehua hapū of Ngāti Wai and some Ngāti Maru people there, some of whom escaped to seek assistance from their Hauraki whānaunga. A Ngāti Maru taua was quickly launched and inflicted a heavy defeat on the Ngāpuhi, few of whom were said to have escaped.

It was an ignominious end to Ngāpuhi taua, and a graphic demonstration that their dominance had been eclipsed. The acquisition of muskets by other iwi meant that after 1825 the balance in power had been gradually restored, and Ngāpuhi hegemony had been brought to an end.

5

CENTRAL NORTH ISLAND IWI REACT TO MUSKET POWER

In addition to the shock of repeated and extensive raids by musket-armed Ngāpuhi, two other events marked the opening of the third decade of the century for iwi further south. Both were to prove very significant, and they were to end up being interconnected.

TE RAUPARAHA COMPELLED TO ABANDON KAWHIA
The first of these events resulted from a major onslaught in 1821 by central Tainui Waikato, Ngāti Hauā and Ngāti Maniapoto hapū against the coastal Ngāti Toa and their closely allied iwi Ngāti Kōata and Ngāti Rārua. The latter iwi occupied rohe to the north and south respectively of the Kawhia rohe occupied by Te Rauparaha's Ngāti Toa. The inland Tainui hapū were led by some of the greatest Tainui rangatira, among them Tukorehu, Te Rauangaanga, his son Te Wherowhero, Te Hiakai, Mama, Te Waharoa and Te Awaitaia. Their hapū had been engaged in long-running conflicts with Te Rauparaha, and had finally decided to mount a massive invasion of the rohe of Ngāti Toa and their allies Ngāti Kōata and Ngāti Rārua.

The outcome was a major defeat for Te Rauparaha and his allies, who had no option but to abandon their homeland rohe and head south to the refuge of the Kāpiti area. The huge heke involved all of the people in those iwi, and some Ngāti Tama as it moved south through their rohe. The need to cater for everyone from the oldest kaumātua and kuia to the youngest tamariki meant it moved slowly.

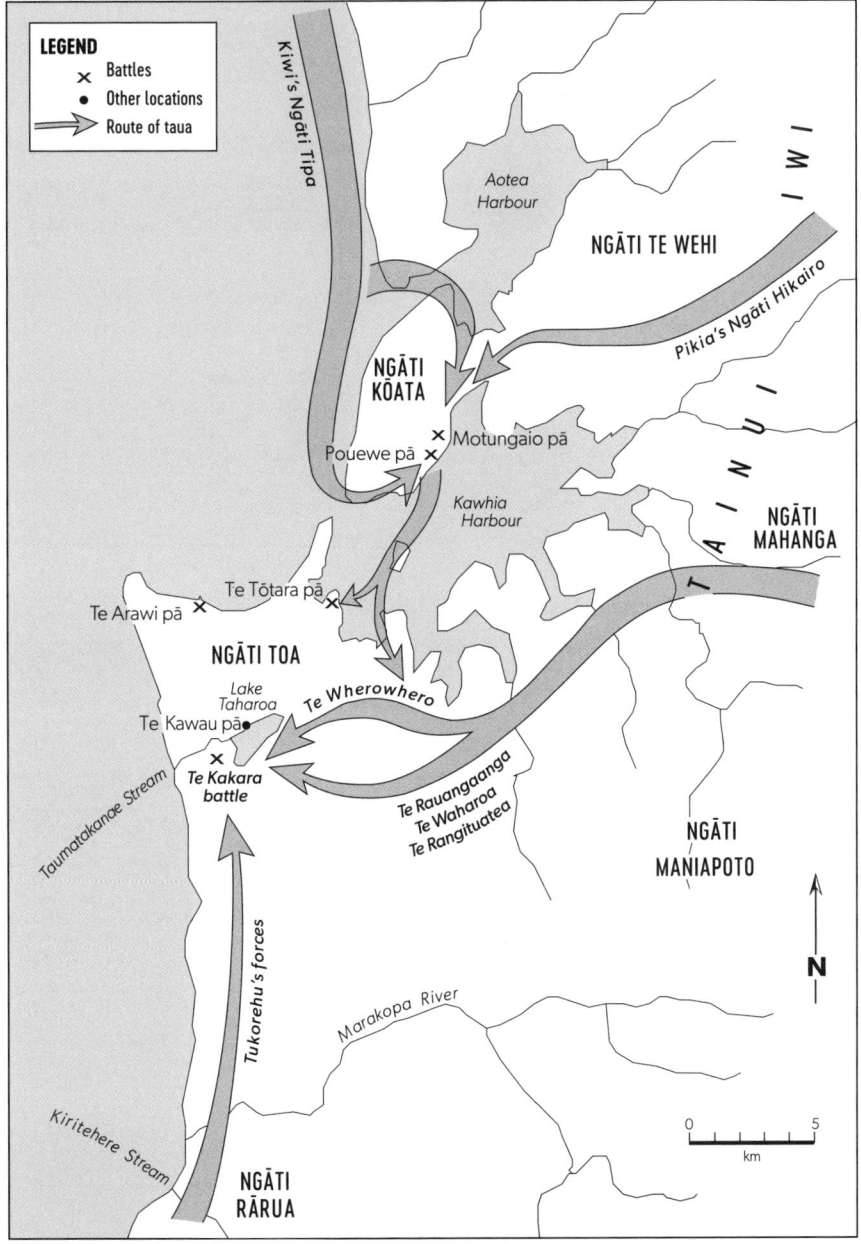

The Waikato attack on Ngāti Toa at Kawhia, 1821.

74 THE FORGOTTEN WARS

That necessitated an extended winter stayover with their Ngāti Mutunga and Te Ātiawa supporters at the famous Okoki pā, located on the north bank of the Urenui River, just north of the Waitara area.

The heke took almost two years to reach Horowhenua, and it was joined by some Ngāti Tama and Ngāti Mutunga as it headed south through their rohe.

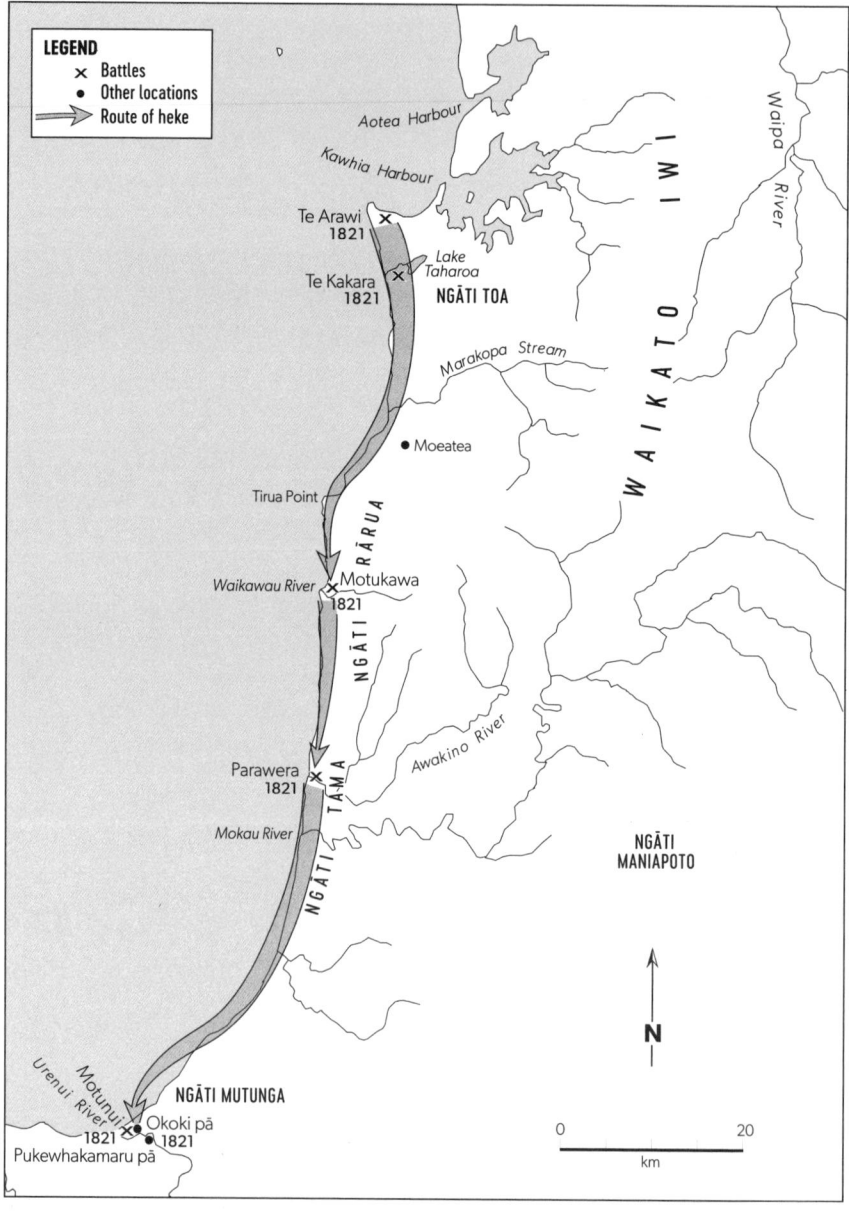

Te Heke Tahutahuahi: Te Rauparaha heads south from Kawhia, 1821.

In total it is believed that somewhere between two and three thousand people were involved as these iwi moved en masse. All were relying on Te Rauparaha's judgement that Kāpiti Island in particular offered a major refuge. Te Rauparaha had seen the advantages offered by the island while he was on the 1819 taua with the Ngāti Whātua rangatira Tuwhare and Tamati Waka Nene and Patuone of Ngāpuhi. These advantages lay not only in its qualities as a refuge, distant from Tainui threat, but also as a location where it would be possible to trade for muskets with passing European sailing vessels.

TE AMIOWHENUA — THE ENCIRCLING OF THE LOWER NORTH ISLAND

The second significant event was the launch later in 1821 of a large Ngāti Whātua and Tainui taua that came to be called Te Amiowhenua — the encircling of the land. The name derived from the fact that while the taua emanated from the southern Kaipara area, its travels took it around most of the southern and western parts of Te Ika a Māui (the North Island). Te Amiowhenua was notable not only because of its length, but also because of the identities of those who allied to form it, the limited number of muskets with which it was armed, and the high drama of its concluding months.

Initially Te Amiowhenua was completely independent of the Ngāti Toa-led heke toward Kāpiti, but they became entangled when Te Amiowhenua's return home through northern Taranaki brought them close to Okoki pā, where Te Rauparaha's heke was wintering over.

The taua had originally been formed by Ngāti Whātua, led by rangatira such as Apihai Te Kawau from the Taoū hapū in the Muriwai area, north of the Auckland isthmus. Whakapapa links with Tainui iwi were reflected when Ngāti Tipa from the lower Waikato, under Kukutai, joined the taua as it moved south through the Waikato, where it was also joined by a group of 140 Ngāti Maniapoto under Tukorehu and Te Kanawa from the upper Waipa. The taua was said to number about 600 men as it entered the Rotorua area, from where it headed over the Kaingaroa Plains and traversed the ranges to descend into the area around Hawke's Bay. From then on Ngāti Kahungunu were to feel its effects. The taua captured the island pā of Roto-a-Tara, south of modern-day Hastings, but only after it had been abandoned by Te Pareihe, its Ngāti Kahungunu rangatira, in the face of the taua's overwhelming strength. From there it moved south into the Wairarapa, capturing the very strong pā at Hakikino on the Wainuioru River, although once again most of its defenders, led by Potangaroa, managed to escape before the pā fell.

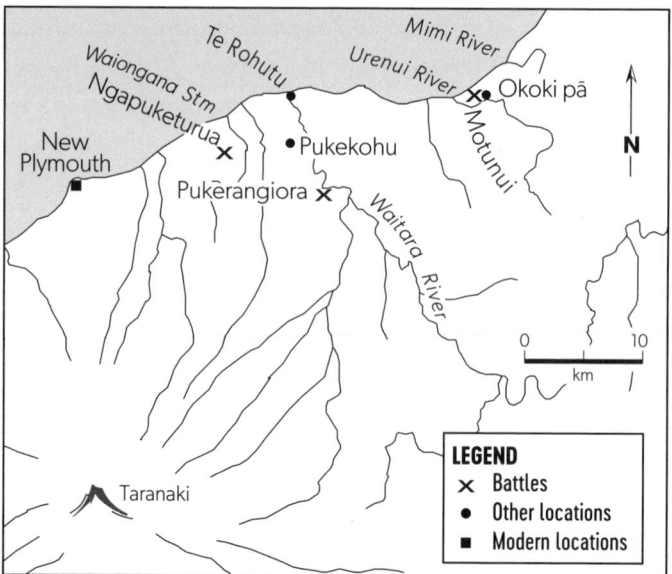

Pukerangiora and Okoki, 1821–22.

The taua then continued south to arrive at Te Whanganui a Tara (Wellington) where the unfortunate Ngāti Ira, who had suffered so badly from the ravages of the 1819 taua led by Tuwhare, Patuone and Waka Nene, once again suffered when Te Amiowhenua attacked and captured the island pā of Taputeranga. Turning and heading north along the coast, the taua found that the inhabitants of these areas had pulled back to Kāpiti Island, the island pā on Lake Horowhenua, or into refuges in the Tararua Ranges. It was not until it reached Whanganui and north Taranaki that the taua encountered serious opposition. At Mangatoa, a considerable distance up the Whanganui River, a major attack by Te Atihaunui led the taua to withdraw, although a small number of its Ngāti Raukawa members made their escape upriver. (They later sought refuge at Lake Rotoaira, where their killing by Te Wharerangi at the island pā of Motuopihi was to rebound on him in later years.)

Worse was to come for Te Amiowhenua in north Taranaki. The opposition hit hard as Te Ātiawa from north of the Waitara repeatedly attacked in a running series of clashes, during which the taua was surprised to come under fire from the few muskets held by some Te Ātiawa rangatira. The final outcome of these clashes was the besieging of Te Amiowhenua by some hapū of Te Ātiawa at Pukerangiora, a large pā located above high cliffs on the Waitara River. This siege, in which the attackers constructed a double row of palisading outside the original pā palisading, was so effective that Te Ātiawa called it 'Raihe-poaka' — the battle of the penned-up pigs.

THE CLASH BETWEEN TE RAUPARAHA AND TE WHEROWHERO

The entrapment of Te Amiowhenua so near to Ngāti Maniapoto territory led to a number of attempts by courageous members of the taua to break out and carry news of the siege to Tainui. Only one of these toa, Te Orahi, finally managed to escape. Despite a long and determined pursuit he was eventually able to carry the news to Te Wherowhero at Te Kaitote pā, at Taupiri on the Waikato River.

The Ngāti Maniapoto rangatira Tukorehu was the father of one of Te Wherowhero's wives, and Te Wherowhero lost no time in gathering a powerful Tainui taua to head south to break the siege and rescue Te Amiowhenua. However, the route to Pukerangiora took the Tainui taua directly past Okoki pā, where Te Rauparaha and his alliance of Ngāti Toa, Ngāti Kōata and Ngāti Rārua, now supplemented by Ngāti Tama, were temporarily based. The resultant clash between

---

Te Orahi's courage

The tale of Te Orahi's courage and endurance is one of the most stirring of the Musket Wars era. After a pursuit over some of the most rugged coastline in Te Ika a Māui he managed to evade, and later kill, the most dogged of his pursuers at Marakopa Beach, some 120 kilometres north of Pukerangiora. He later took the name Manukorihi, after the hapū to the west of the Waitara, as a mark of the mana he gained from these events involving that hapū.

the Tainui taua and Te Rauparaha's heke ended with the execution of a kōhuru (stratagem) by Te Rauparaha that involved the classic feigned panic retreat leading to an ambush site. The successful ambush, which has become known as the battle of Motunui, resulted in the slaying of large numbers of Tainui, including the prominent rangatira Te Hiakai and Mama.

From Motunui Te Wherowhero moved south to the Waitara, and he managed to raise the siege at Pukerangiora by negotiating a temporary peace with Te Ātiawa. Te Amiowhenua and their Tainui allies then headed north by inland routes, receiving news on the way of a huge taua of 3000 Ngāpuhi toa under Hongi Hika that was heading up the Waipa toward Mātakitaki pā. The combined force seems to have separated at that point, as Te Wherowhero and the Tainui cohort moved off rapidly and assisted strongly in the defence of Mātakitaki, while Apihai Te Kawau and his Ngāti Whātua carried on toward their home rohe.

Te Wherowhero's only weapon

During the ambush at Motunui, Te Wherowhero himself exhibited his prowess in an extraordinary series of personal confrontations. These occurred in a ritualised manner, with both sides holding back and watching as individual Taranaki rangatira stepped forward to challenge Te Wherowhero, armed with their rakau Māori (Māori weapons). In contrast, Te Wherowhero's only weapon was his kō (digging stick), which he had been using to clear some ground for his bed when the false pursuit began. He had taken the kō with him as he rushed after his men to call them back, and now faced attackers who were armed with carefully crafted hand-held weapons. Notwithstanding the imbalance in terms of weaponry, Te Wherowhero demonstrated his exceptional physical skills, strength and dexterity by killing or disabling the leading Taranaki rangatira, who he engaged one after the other. It was a display of martial might that established Te Wherowhero's mana as one of the leading rangatira of his era.

TAINUI ACT ON LESSONS LEARNT AT MĀTAKITAKI

The devastating Tainui losses at, and following, the fall of Mātakitaki in mid 1822 are described in detail on pages 55–58. The events that occurred at Mātakitaki then, and during the Te Amiowhenua taua, brought home grimly to Tainui the massive effects of the imbalances resulting from uneven musket power. The vital need to acquire muskets thus became the driving force of Tainui endeavours over the next few years. Despite their losses at Mātakitaki they had managed to capture a large number of Ngāpuhi muskets there and later at Orahiri. Their efforts to gain more weapons were later assisted significantly when, in 1828, a permanent trading post was established at Kawhia by an enterprising Pākehā trader, Captain Kent, who soon married Tiria, one of Te Wherowhero's daughters. However, as the defeat of Pomare at Te Rore demonstrated, even by 1826 Tainui had enough musket power to successfully defend themselves against foes plentifully supplied with firearms.

The successful defeat of Ngāpuhi at Te Rore was repeated against the Ngāpuhi rangatira Te Rangituke at the Tāmaki River mouth in the summer of 1827–28. By that time Te Wherowhero felt confident enough in his musket power to follow up the Ngāpuhi Te Parawhau hapū, leading a musket-armed taua to attack them in their own rohe at Whangarei Harbour.

TAINUI LAUNCH AGGRESSIVE TAUA

The losses Tainui and their allies suffered at the hands of Taranaki iwi at Pukerangiora and Motunui in 1822 had also given rise to the fiercely strong customary urge for utu. In 1826, a request came in the surprising form of a tau (a traditional type of song) from Te Wharepouri of the Ngāmotu hapū of Te Ātiawa, from the north Taranaki area. The tau told of the death of two young high-ranking Te Ātiawa at the hands of Ngāti Ruanui from south Taranaki, and Ngāmotu sought Waikato support for a taua to exact utu. It was accepted in customary Māori warfare that opportunities to exact utu were not always directed against the iwi who had created the take (cause), and that was the case here, where another hapū of Te Ātiawa had inflicted the take for utu at Pukerangiora in particular.

Te Wherowhero, Tukorehu and Te Kanawa responded with a call to assemble a Tainui taua. The desire to exact utu after the bitter experiences of recent years received an enormous response, with up to three thousand toa gathering to join the Ngāmotu Te Ātiawa. This powerful taua raided extensively throughout the rohe of Ngāti Ruanui and their related iwi of Taranaki and Ngāti Maru. The major Ngāti Ruanui pā of Te Ruaki on the Tangahoe River was sacked, as were all

Waimate pā. The twin pā of Orangi-tuapeka on the left or north side of Kapuni Stream, and Ngā Teko pā on the right or south side, were known jointly as Waimate. They were most famous for the successful defence, under Wiremu Kingi Te Matakatea, against Waikato under Te Wherowhero in 1834.
A65.889, Puke Ariki

ten of the high-altitude refuge pā of Ngāti Maru on the slopes of Mount Taranaki. The twin pā known as Waimate on either side of the mouth of the Kapuni Stream, southeast of Manaia, were also besieged. For these southern and central Taranaki iwi the all-too-familiar imbalance of musket power was devastating. Many Taranaki iwi members sought sanctuary by heading for Horowhenua to join Te Rauparaha's coalition, while other members of all these iwi sought refuge with Wiremu Te Moki at Te Namu pā on the coast by Opunake.

The boldest Tainui taua, however, were launched against adversaries who also had access to muskets — in 1830 against the Marutūahu iwi in the Maungatautari/Matamata area, and in 1832 against Ngāpuhi themselves in the Whangarei/Tutukaka areas.

The 1830 assault on Ngāti Maru and Ngāti Paoa resulted from other Tainui iwi such as Ngāti Hauā also building up their musket power to cope with threats they perceived from closer at hand. In their case the most immediate threat, given the repeated rebuffs of Ngāpuhi that had by then occurred, now lay in the huge numbers of Ngāti Maru and Ngāti Paoa who were still living in their midst. Their occupation had arisen after they sought refuge with Ngāti Hauā from Ngāpuhi, particularly after the fall of Mauinaina/Mokoia in 1820 and Te Tōtara pā in 1821.

Over time Ngāti Hauā had become increasingly concerned as Ngāti Maru and Ngāti Paoa built some 15 pā in the area, the principal ones being Haowhenua pā near Maungatautari (Cambridge), and Kaipaka pā under the Ngāti Maru ranga-tira Takarua; the latter was located on the bush-clad peak Maungakawa, which was close to Te Waharoa's own pā,

Kaweheitiki, on the same peak. By 1827–28 Marutūahu iwi under Te Rohu and Tuterangianini (of Ngāti Tamaterā) had themselves acquired considerable numbers of muskets and they had undertaken raids into the Bay of Plenty and south into the Taupō area.

In 1827 relationships between Ngāti Hauā and Ngāti Maru broke down when Takarua's pā Kaipaka was sacked by Ngāti Hauā one night when Te Waharoa was ostensibly away in Tauranga visiting Ngāiterangi relatives. Takarua and about two hundred of his people were killed, and general fighting broke out between the two iwi over the next few years, with Marutūahu pulling back into Haowhenua pā.

In 1830 Te Waharoa entered into an alliance with Ngāiterangi of Tauranga, one of the Bay of Plenty iwi that had been attacked earlier that year by Ngāti Maru. Ngāiterangi sent a taua of about a thousand toa to assist Te Waharoa in his attack on Ngāti Maru in the Matamata and Maungatautari areas. A major battle occurred at Taumatawiwi, near Maungatautari, in which both sides suffered heavy losses before a truce was arranged, under which Marutūahu left the Waikato and returned to their own coastal rohe.

The alliance of Ngāti Hauā and Ngāiterangi also played a major role in 1831 in wiping out the Ngāpuhi taua to Mōtītī led by Te Haramiti. By this time Captain Kent's trading post was well established, and providing a steady supply of muskets to Tainui. The result of Tainui's increased musket power was demonstrated in the summer of 1831–32 when Te Wherowhero led a huge taua to attack the pā at Pukerangiora, where Te Ātiawa had inflicted such indignities on Te Amiowhenua ten years earlier. After a long siege the pā fell, with heavy loss of life and large numbers being taken captive and ruthlessly killed.

From Pukerangiora the taua moved on to besiege the remaining Ngāmotu Te Ātiawa in Otaka pā and other offshore island pā at modern-day New Plymouth. During this siege Te Ātiawa largely owed their survival to the firepower of the

The killing of Pukerangiora's captives

The brutal killing of about 350 captives following the fall of Pukerangiora was carried out personally, first by Te Wherowhero, then by Te Awaitaia, who took over when Te Wherowhero became too tired to continue the grim task. Te Wherowhero is said to have used the famed Waikato mere, Whakarewa.

carronades (short, large-calibre cannon) of a small group of Pākehā whalers who had taken Te Ātiawa wives. In yet another grim example of the flexibility of customary Māori warfare, the leading Te Ātiawa rangatira at Otaka was Te Wharepouri — the very man who had invited Tainui to join his proposed taua to attack Ngāti Ruanui just six years earlier. Now, at the end of February 1832, his iwi were saved in a last desperate assault by the extra firepower of the whalers' heavier guns. Waikato finally withdrew, but they were now burning for fresh utu for their losses at Ngāmotu.

Other unrelated events in northern Waikato areas in 1832 ensured Te Ātiawa would have some breathing space in which to consider their future. They realised Waikato would eventually return in even greater force, so they decided to take advantage of the Waikato withdrawal to head south in a major heke to join their compatriots in the southern Horowhenua area. They were also joined on the heke by Ngāti Tama, who after Ngāmotu had launched a taua against Ngāti Maniapoto at Motutawa pā at the Mokau River mouth. While they had inflicted considerable losses the pā did not fall, and Ngāti Tama also knew that retribution would soon follow for the losses they had caused. The heke came to be known as Te Heke o Tama Te Uaua ('uaua' denoting the difficulties the heke faced).

The other events of 1832 that were diverting Waikato were the activities of two major Ngāpuhi taua. One of these, led by Tareha, attacked Te Waharoa at Matamata, but after a siege lasting many weeks it was unsuccessful and moved off overland to link with the taua led by Titore to attack Ngāiterangi at Tauranga.

News of the advance of the other Ngāpuhi taua that year had spurred the return of Te Wherowhero from Ngāmotu. This taua was led by Pukerangi and Tirarau of the Te Parawhau hapū at Whangarei. It was a large taua numbering more than three thousand toa, but Pukerangi realised when he reached the Whangape/Waikare lakes area that it was equalled by the opposing Waikato — both in numbers and, more concerningly, in musket power.

Pukerangi's fighting retreat in fact turned into a rout, and the taua was followed north all the way back to Kawau Island, where Pukerangi himself was killed. The pursuit was then continued by Te Wherowhero with a second invasion of Ngāpuhi's southern rohe, as he successfully attacked the Whangarei and Tutukaka areas.

TAINUI EXPERIENCE BOTH DOMINATION AND REBUFF IN TARANAKI

In 1833 and 1834 Te Wherowhero once more returned to Taranaki, with an even greater taua than in each of the previous years. In 1833 he and Kaihau took the small island pā of Mikotahi at New Plymouth, where remnant Te Ātiawa had

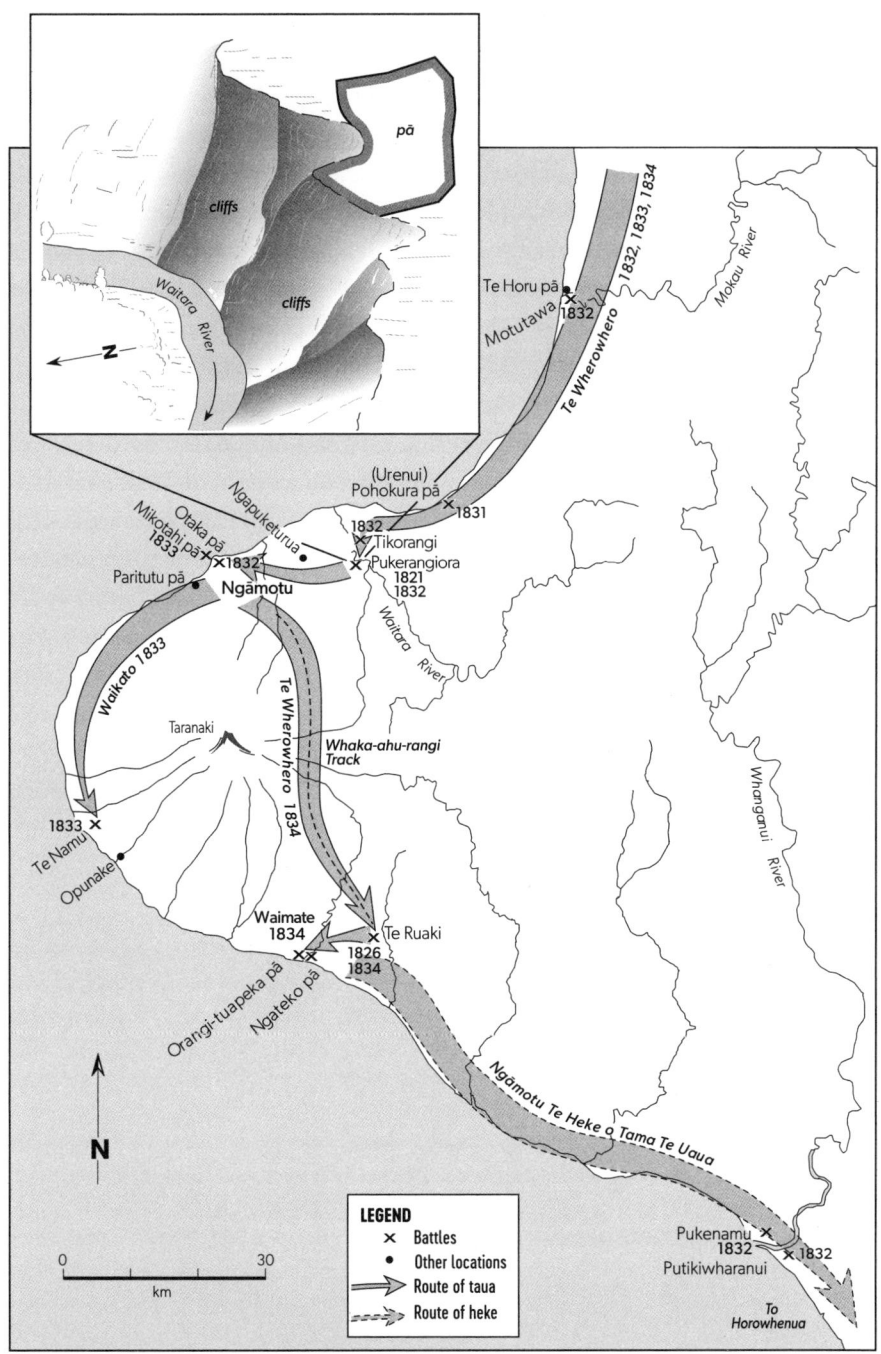

Tainui taua to Taranaki 1832–34, with the battle sites at Whanganui 1832. **INSET:** *Pukerangiora pā.*

sought refuge, then moved south around the coast to attack Te Namu pā just north of Opunake.

The defenders of Te Namu were a mixture of the Taranaki iwi under their rangatira Wiremu Kingi Te Moki, Te Ātiawa refugees, and Ngāti Ruanui, with whom many Taranaki iwi members were interrelated. While the pā itself had many natural defensive advantages as a steep-sided headland, and was strongly palisaded on the landward side, its defenders possessed only one musket. However, as the siege wore on Wiremu Kingi Te Moki earned such a reputation for his accurate shooting of large numbers of Waikato rangatira that he was given the name Te Matakatea — the far-sighted or sharp-eyed one. The name stuck, and he is known to history as Wiremu Kingi Te Matakatea.

The successful defence of Te Namu was a setback to Waikato, but the pā's defenders decided to withdraw south to link with Ngāti Ruanui in the defence of Ngā Teko pā on the northern side of the Kapuni Stream, one of the joint pā known as Waimate. The pā on the other side of the stream was called Orangituapeka. In 1834 both these pā came under attack from another taua led by Te Wherowhero, which traversed east of Mt Taranaki on the Whakaahurangi track to attack Te Ruaki pā. It was taken after a long siege, before the taua moved on to besiege the two Waimate pā.

Te Matakatea's accurate shooting once more played a major role in the siege

Te Matakatea, the great rangatira of the Taranaki iwi. He successfully defended south Taranaki at Te Namu pa in 1833 and Waimate pā in 1834 against massively superior Waikato forces. In 1840 he defeated Tauteka of Ngāti Tūwharetoa at Patoka pā, and faced the famous warrior Iwikau Te Heuheu on the Whanganui River in 1840.

PAColl-5800-31, Griffin, Erin Michael (Dr), 1903–1984. Wiremu Kingi Matakatea. Alexander Turnbull Library, Wellington, NZ

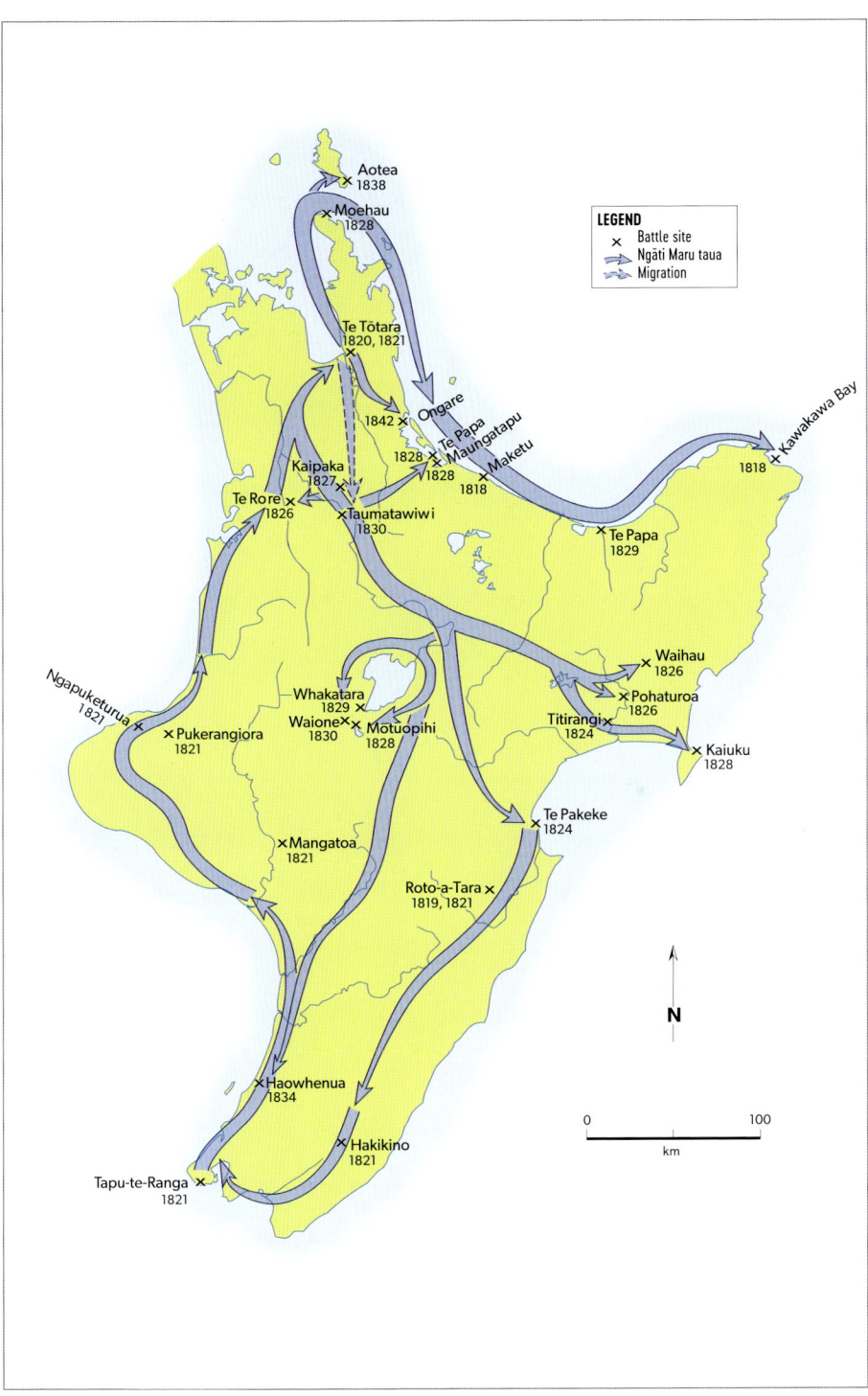

Ngāti Maru and related iwi: battle sites, and routes of taua and migrations.

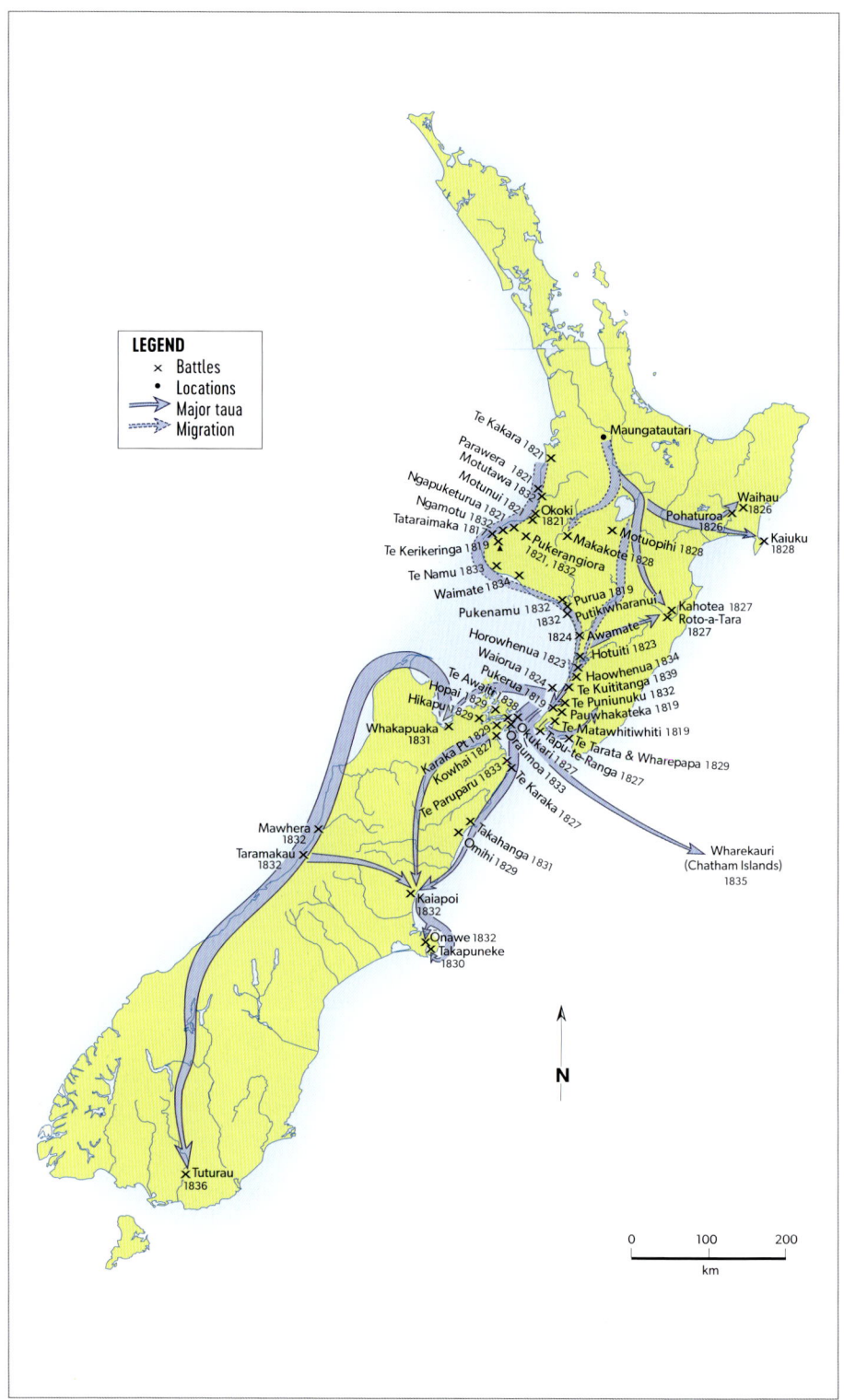

Ngāti Toa and allies: battle sites, and routes of taua and migrations.

ABOVE *Motuopihi pā. This Ngāti Tūwharetoa pā was captured by Ngāti Maru and Ngāti Raukawa in 1828 and its rangatira Te Wharerangi was killed. In earlier years, Te Rauparaha was said to have composed his version of the famous haka, Ka Mate, here.*

B-080-028, Angas, George French, 1822–1886: Motupoi Pah and Roto-aire Lake; Tongariro in the distance/George French Angas [del] J.W. Giles —[London; McLean, 1847]. Alexander Turnbull Library, Wellington, NZ

RIGHT *Pictured with his nephew Tamahiki (standing) is Apihai Te Kawau, the ruthless Ngāti Whātua rangatira who led Te Amiowhenua, the taua that encircled the lower North Island in 1821. In more mellow times, he greeted Governor Hobson when the seat of government was moved to Auckland in 1841.*

PUBL-0014-56-2, Giles, John West, 1801–1870: Te Kawaw & his nephew Orakai/George French Angas [delt]; J.W. Giles [lith]. Plate 56 [right side]. 1847. Angas, George French 1822–1886: *The New Zealanders Illustrated*, London, Thomas McLean, 1847. Alexander Turnbull Library, Wellington, NZ

Te Wherowhero (Pōtatau) was the pre-eminent Waikato rangatira in the Musket Wars. He led repeated raids through Taranaki in the late 1820s and early 1830s and was the only rangatira from the south to lead successful taua into Ngāpuhi territory. After the Musket Wars he became the first Māori king, under the name Pōtatau, in 1858.

PUBL-0014-44, Angas, George French, 1822–1886: Te Werowero, or Potatau the principal chief of all Waikato. George French Angas delt & lith. Plate 44, 1847. Alexander Turnbull Library, Wellington, NZ

Pomare was the rangatira who defended Otuihu in the Bay of Islands during the civil war between various Ngāpuhi hapu in 1837.

Gottfried Lindauer, Whetoi Pomare, 1896, oil on canvas, Auckland Art Gallery Toi o Tāmaki, gift of Mr H.E. Partridge, 1915

at Waimate, as did various counterattacks that he led. One of these enabled some of the Ngāti Ruanui captives from Te Ruaki to escape, including their principal rangatira, Te Rei Hanataua. In the end, in direct face-to-face negotiations that also involved other prominent Waikato rangatira such as Te Kanawa and Te Waharoa, Te Wherowhero recognised Te Matakatea's courage and the stand-off that had developed, and the siege was called off. A binding truce was agreed, and apart from one short taua into Ngāti Ruanui territory that Tukorehu led in the following months, both sides abided by the peace agreement. Waikato depredations against Taranaki iwi had finally ceased.

The pattern that had occurred for Ngāpuhi had in part recurred with Tainui. The sudden acquisition of musket power had enabled early domination of iwi in Taranaki, but as these iwi obtained more muskets, and became able to rely on the carronades of Pākehā whalers, as well as the extraordinary sharp-shooting skills of rangatira such as Te Matakatea, easy campaigning became a thing of the past. Despite this, it would be many years before those Taranaki who had migrated felt safe enough to return en masse, and in the case of Te Ātiawa that did not occur until 1848, under Wiremu Kingi Te Rangitake.

THE RESPONSE OF NGĀTI MARU AND THEIR RELATED IWI TO MUSKET POWER

As described in chapter 4, all the iwi related to Marutūahu, including Ngāti Maru, Ngāti Paoa, Ngāti Tamaterā, Ngāti Whanaunga and Ngāti Hei, suffered dreadfully under early Ngāpuhi attacks, and large numbers had pulled back into Waikato and particularly Ngāti Hauā's rohe for refuge. They had the advantage, however, that their coastal areas were still regularly visited by sailing vessels seeking spars, flax and food supplies. The items that were traded for these were muskets, powder and ammunition.

By 1828 the Ngāti Maru rangatira Te Rohu felt sufficiently strongly armed, despite having only a limited number of muskets, to launch the first of many taua seeking to gain utu for a range of grievances — particularly against Ngāpuhi, Ngāiterangi and other Bay of Plenty iwi. This initial taua, though, first sought utu against Ngāpuhi for their killing of a Ngāti Maru rangatira, Te Maunu, on Aotea (Great Barrier Island). The taua camped overnight at Port Jackson, near the tip of the Coromandel Peninsula, and its fires were seen by a heavily armed Ngāpuhi taua that had arrived at Aotea. The Ngāpuhi taua, which comprised about five hundred toa led by Rangitukia, immediately set out to cross the 20 kilometres to the peninsula and launch a night attack on Ngāti Maru. At first they achieved some success, but as day dawned they came under heavy musket fire from their well-armed and more numerous foe; soon Rangitukia was killed and his taua routed. Only one Ngāpuhi waka is said to have been able to get away.

Flushed with this unexpected success, and after their celebratory feasting, Ngāti Maru headed south confidently to attack Ngāiterangi. The overwhelming effect of Ngāpuhi muskets had been experienced by Ngāiterangi on a number of occasions before they had managed to negotiate a peace in 1820. Now, in 1828, they faced peril again, this time at the hands of Ngāti Maru at Te Papa pā (today part of Tauranga).

An accurate record of the severity of this attack is available thanks to the movement of the missionary vessel *Herald*, captained by Gilbert Mair senior. The *Herald* had called to visit Te Papa and the nearby pā of Maungatapu and Otūmoetai in 1827, and Mair had estimated then that the three pā were defended by about two and a half thousand toa. Large numbers of women, children and old people also resided in the pā, and hundreds of waka of all sizes were also seen.

When the *Herald* returned in early April 1828, after a visit to the Whakatane/Ōhiwa Harbour area, they found that while the other two pā had managed to withstand Te Rohu's attack, Te Papa lay silent and in burnt ruins, with no survivors. The remains of bodies cut up for the umu (earth oven) were found hanging in trees. The Europeans heard from other Ngāiterangi that only about twenty or thirty people had managed to escape death or capture, out of the many hundreds

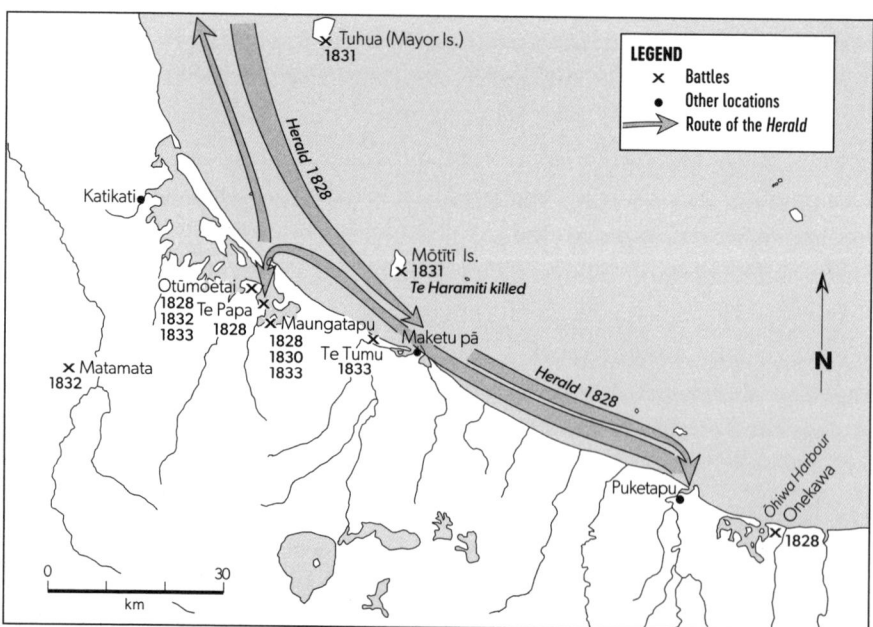

Battle sites of the Ngāti Maru and Ngāpuhi taua to Tauranga, 1828-33.

> **Te Raukaraka**
>
> During the 1828 visit to the Tauranga area the missionaries and the captain of the *Herald*, Gilbert Mair, had made friends with Koraurau, the leading rangatira at Te Papa. Mair had presented Koraurau's wife with the gift of a shirt to mark the birth of their baby, who they called Hohepa Te Mea in honour of the Mair name. Koraurau gave Mair a mere (a short, flat, sharp-edged clubbing weapon, in this case made of pounamu [greenstone]) called Te Raukaraka, which Mair asked him to hold until his return.
>
> Koraurau was killed during the 1828 attack and his wife was shot as she swam across the harbour with their young baby, but managed to make the other shore before she died. The baby, Te Mea, grew to manhood and later met with Mair's son, also called Gilbert, giving him the mere when it was discovered as graves were dug to bury the British bodies after the battle of Gate Pā in 1864. The mere had obviously been buried for safekeeping when the pā was attacked.

who were in the pā when it fell. Writing in 1839, Mair noted that he had estimated the number killed at Te Papa to be about 500. When coupled with his observation of between 50 and 70 Ngāti Awa and Whakatōhea bodies Mair saw lying on the beach at Ōhiwa, these figures lend considerable weight to reports of the very high casualty rates inflicted in the battles of this era.

Whakatōhea accounts also note that in 1830 another taua led by Tuterangianini and Te Rohu did not stop at Tauranga, but continued on to raid into Ngāti Awa and Whakatōhea areas in the eastern Bay of Plenty. Many Whakatōhea were captured on the fall of a pā also called Te Papa, on the Waioeka River just inland from modern-day Ōpōtiki. These Whakatōhea captives seem to have been left at Haowhenua pā when it passed back from Ngāti Maru into Ngāti Hauā hands after the battle of Taumatawiwi later in 1830. They were then present with Te Waharoa of Ngāti Hauā in alliance with Ngāiterangi against the Ngāpuhi taua led by Te Haramiti in 1831, during which they were led by their own rangatira, Titoko, who had arrived at Tauranga from Ōpōtiki seeking their release. The contribution of Titoko and his people to Ngāiterangi and Ngāti Hauā during those engagements was so valued that they were released to go home, together with a captured Ngāpuhi cannon that they called Te Haramiti after the slain Ngāpuhi rangatira.

NGĀTI MARU TAUA SEEK UTU AGAINST NGĀTI TŪWHARETOA

In both 1827 and 1828 Ngāti Maru had also sent taua south under Tuterangianini, armed with just one musket. Their aim seems to have been not only to seek utu against Ngāti Tūwharetoa, but at the same time to consider the potential of the large area of the central North Island volcanic plateau as a possible homeland. In each year the taua went as far south as Waihi, at the southern end of Lake Taupō.

In 1827, Ngāti Maru captured Whakatara pā at Waihi, using their one musket to pick off rangatira from a distance and routing Ngāti Tūwharetoa under their rangatira Te Heuheu.

The following year, another south-bound Ngāti Maru taua combined with a major heke of Ngāti Raukawa, who were now feeling under pressure from other Tainui hapū. A large section of this heke, under Te Whatanui, joined the Ngāti Maru taua in an attack on the prominent Motuopihi Island pā on Lake Rotoaira. The pā was captured and the renowned Ngāti Tūwharetoa rangatira Te Wharerangi was killed, but his wife Te Rangikoaea was spared. Te Wharerangi was the rangatira who with Te Rangikoaea had provided refuge for Te Rauparaha at Motuopihi at the time he composed the haka *Ka Mate*. Ngāti Raukawa's motivation for seeking utu against Te Wharerangi stemmed from his 1821 order that Ngāti Raukawa refugees from Te Amiowhenua be killed, when that taua was rebuffed by Te Atihaunui in the Whanganui River at Mangatoa.

Making the killing of Te Wharerangi even more significant was the fact that Te Whatanui had left his family as hostages with Te Heuheu, providing the assurance that the heke would not attack any Ngāti Tūwharetoa as it headed south. The arrangement was that when the heke left his rohe, Te Heuheu would release the hostages. Ngāti Tūwharetoa anger at the treachery involved in Te Wharerangi's killing made it seem likely that Te Whatanui's wife and whānau would also be killed. However, Te Whatanui had brought back Te Rangikoaea, and Te Heuheu intervened to allow her to be exchanged for Te Whatanui's wife and whānau. This magnanimous act by Te Heuheu cemented a long-standing bond between the two that would last well into the future.

In the summer of 1829–30 another Ngāti Maru taua besieged the rebuilt

Whakatara pā at Waihi. Initially the Ngāti Maru toa dominated events. Their one musket again provided a major advantage, until a prominent and courageous rangatira from the pā, Te Riupawhara, managed to enter the besiegers' camp and persuade a relative within it to steal the musket as its owner slept. When Ngāti Maru realised that the advantage now lay with their opponents, they abandoned the siege and headed home.

As 1830 progressed, both sides made efforts to become better armed with muskets. Unknown to Ngāti Maru, Te Heuheu led a trip to Maketu to acquire muskets, trading large amounts of dressed flax with Hans Tapsell, who had recently set up a trading post there. Despite this, northern Ngāti Tūwharetoa did not achieve immediate success, losing Piripekapeka pā, on the point opposite modern-day Taupō, to Ngāti Maru under Te Arakai. Soon after, however, in the south at Lake Rotoaira, Te Heuheu showed graphically that the tide had turned when with his newly acquired musket power he heavily defeated Ngāti Maru. Te Arakai was killed, and the surviving Ngāti Maru retreated rapidly from Ngāti Tūwharetoa's rohe for the last time.

Just as Ngāpuhi had found that they had lost their former dominance after 1825, Ngāti Maru now realised their fortunes had changed suddenly as their southern opponents had also acquired muskets. Any hopes they may have had of migrating and occupying Ngāti Hauā or Ngāti Tūwharetoa territory now had to be abandoned, and by the end of 1830 they had returned to their home rohe. But now, at least, they were powerfully

Utu

Part of the grim side of the utu ledger was the desecration of those who were killed, which was part of the tikanga (customary practice) of Māori warfare. A graphic demonstration of this occurred after the Ngāti Tūwharetoa success at Lake Rotoaira, when one of Te Arakai's hands was cut off, preserved and sent to Te Wharerangi's son as a receptacle for food.

armed and confident they could inflict defeat on any Ngāpuhi taua in the future, as Te Rohu had succeeded in doing when he defeated Rangitukia in 1828.

NGĀTI RAUKAWA'S RESPONSE TO MUSKET PRESSURES

Another iwi impacted by the growing strength of the Waikato iwi as their musket power grew was Ngāti Raukawa, whose rohe encompassed the area around Maungatautari and down toward Taupō.

Te Rauparaha was partly Ngāti Raukawa by descent, and Ngāti Toa and Ngāti Raukawa had often acted in alliance in battles against other Tainui iwi. After his heke to the Kāpiti area Te Rauparaha had sent messengers inviting Ngāti Raukawa to join him in the Horowhenua — he knew, as did they, that Tainui pressure would inevitably turn their way. Ngāti Raukawa rangatira such as Te Whatanui and Te Ahukaramu were aware of the growing Waikato musket power to their west, and after a preliminary exploratory visit to Horowhenua Te Ahukaramu led a limited heke south, known as Te Heke Whirinui. This was followed soon after by another of similar size.

Initially, Te Whatanui chose rather to respond to requests by Ngāti Te Upokoiri to move southeast and assist them in the Heretaunga (Hawke's Bay) area. After a period there, however, Te Whatanui and his people were repulsed by the Ngāti Kahungunu rangatira Te Pareihe, assisted by the muskets of the Ngāpuhi rangatira Te Wera, and were pursued as they withdrew up past Taupō. Te Whatanui then finally led a major heke south, called Te Heke Mai i Raro. It was this heke that in 1828 met up with Ngāti Maru at Te Rapa on the western side of Lake Taupō and there split in two. The larger part stayed under Te Whatanui and was involved in the Ngāti Maru attack on Motuopihi, where Te Wharerangi was killed, before it continued on south through the central volcanic plateau.

News of Te Wharerangi's killing reached his relatives among Te Atihaunui of the Whanganui River, with disastrous consequences for the other section of the heke under Te Ruamaioro, which had headed south by way of the headwaters of the Whanganui. It was cut off at Makakote pā, at the junction of the Whanganui and Retaruke rivers, by the great Whanganui rangatira Te Pehi Turoa, and was almost totally destroyed. Those who were not killed at Makakote, or during the pursuit up the Ohura River, were taken captive as slaves and moved downriver to the area round the Whanganui River mouth.

When Te Whatanui's heke arrived in Horowhenua in about 1829 it placed great pressure for living space on the loose coalition under Te Rauparaha. Te Whatanui chose to settle between Lake Horowhenua and the Ōtaki area. His arrival was fortuitous for Muaūpoko in that area, who were being constantly harried by Te Rauparaha, as Te Whatanui provided them with some refuge at last. But over the next few years, at the interface in the south between Ngāti Raukawa and Te Ātiawa in the Ōtaki area, arguments and strife over gardening areas and other resources soon broke out. By 1834 these conflicts had erupted into open warfare in the bloody Haowhenua battles, and they were repeated five years later in 1839 in the series of conflicts known as Te Kuititanga.

To understand the settings for these later conflicts it is now necessary to understand the events that surrounded the arrival of Te Rauparaha's coalition in the area, and their extensive subsequent taua.

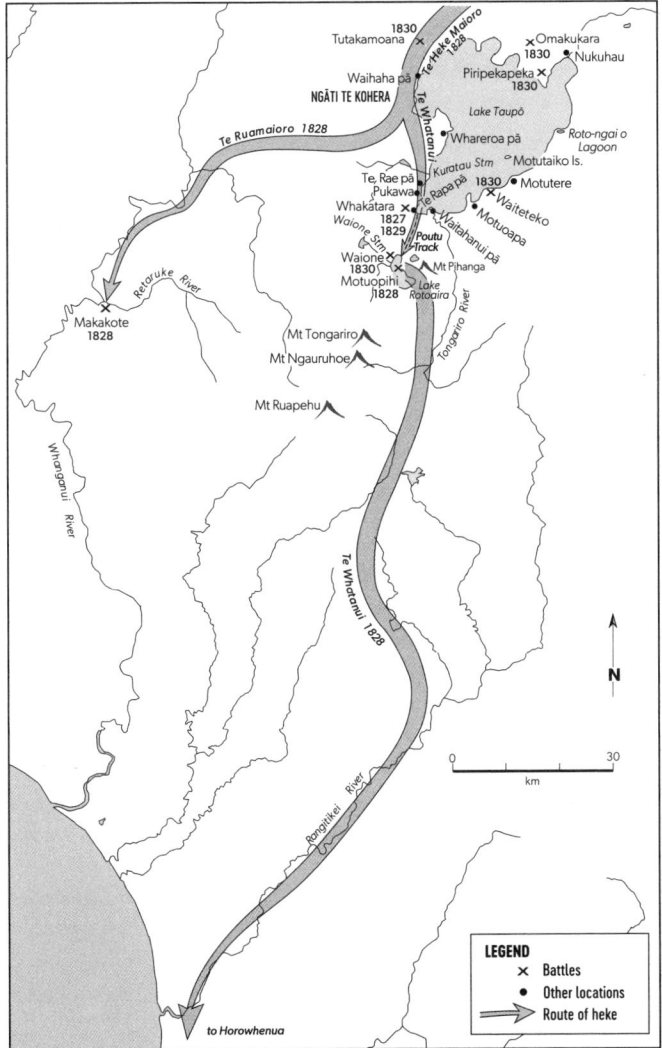

Ngāti Raukawa heke routes, 1828–29.

6

TE RAUPARAHA'S COALITIONS — HEKE, RAUPATU, DISINTEGRATION

The name given to the huge heke of Ngāti Toa, Ngāti Kōata, Ngāti Rārua, Ngāti Tama, Ngāti Mutunga and Te Ātiawa that left north Taranaki in 1822 was Te Heke Tātarāmoa. It was so-named after the hooks of the plant known as bush lawyer, reflecting the trials the heke faced as it passed through the rohe of iwi impacted by its passage.

Conflicts occurred frequently as it traversed the rohe of the south Taranaki, Whanganui and Manawatū iwi of Ngāti Ruanui, Ngā Rauru, Te Atihaunui a Pāpārangi, Ngāti Apa and Rangitāne before finally arriving in Horowhenua and Kāpiti. Particularly heavy fighting occurred with Ngā Rauru at the mouth of the Waitōtara River, where the heke captured a number of waka that some of its less active people were able to use as they headed down the coast.

For the Muaūpoko people of Lake Horowhenua and Ōtaki, the arrival of such a powerful alliance of so many iwi, led by aggressive rangatira, and their decision to settle within the Muaūpoko rohe was an unmitigated disaster. At this stage the heke still had relatively limited numbers of muskets, but the fact that they had any at all made them even more dangerous to the Muaūpoko, who had none. In a subsistence society, however, the really concerning matter was the strain this sudden influx of well over a thousand people would put on their food resources.

MUAŪPOKO REACT

To begin with, Muaūpoko feigned a formal welcome as the heke arrived at the mouth of the Waikawa Stream in late 1822 or early 1823, and they offered land for settlement on the flats of the stream, which at that time shared a common river mouth with the Ōhau River.

In reality, the warm welcome was intended to lull Te Rauparaha into a false sense of security, leaving him vulnerable so that he could be killed and the heke repelled. Surprisingly, despite warnings from Te Rangihaeata, Te Rauparaha accepted an invitation from Muaūpoko to attend a welcoming hākari (feast) of eels put on for him and his close family at Lake Papaitonga, between the Ōhau River and Lake Horowhenua. Accommodation was provided for Te Rauparaha's family in a number of whare, with Te Rauparaha himself sharing a whare with his host Toheriri. During the night, however, when all were asleep, Toheriri left the whare and launched an attack on the approximately twenty Ngāti Toa in the party. The whare containing Te Rauparaha was set alight, and although he managed to escape through its raupō walls he was forced to look on helplessly from a distance as his eldest son Rangihoungariri and his daughter Te Uira were killed.

The loss of his close whānau through this treacherous attack was a bitter blow for Te Rauparaha, who fiercely vowed to obtain the utmost in utu from Muaūpoko. It was a vow he never relented on, and one that led to huge losses for Muaūpoko as from then on he hunted them at every opportunity.

Most Muaūpoko withdrew to their island pā on Lake Horowhenua, where for a time they had at least some security. Others fled to seek refuge with surrounding iwi with whom they had long-standing interrelationships, such as Rangitāne and Ngāti Apa of the inland Horowhenua and Manawatū areas, Te Atihaunui of Whanganui, and Ngāti Ira and Ngāti Kahungunu in the Whanganui a Tara (Wellington) and Wairarapa areas.

TE RAUPARAHA'S RUTHLESS RAUPATU COMMENCES

In 1823 Te Rauparaha moved north from the Waikawa under the cover of darkness with a small fleet of waka. At the mouth of the Hokio Stream the waka were dragged across the beach into the deeper waters of the small stream, which emanates from Lake Horowhenua (near modern-day Levin). In what must have been a massive physical undertaking, the huge waka were paddled, pushed and dragged up around the twisting path of the gentle, narrow stream.

Finally, just as dawn broke, they were able to break out and paddle into the waters of the lake. So thick was the mist on the lake that Muaūpoko on their

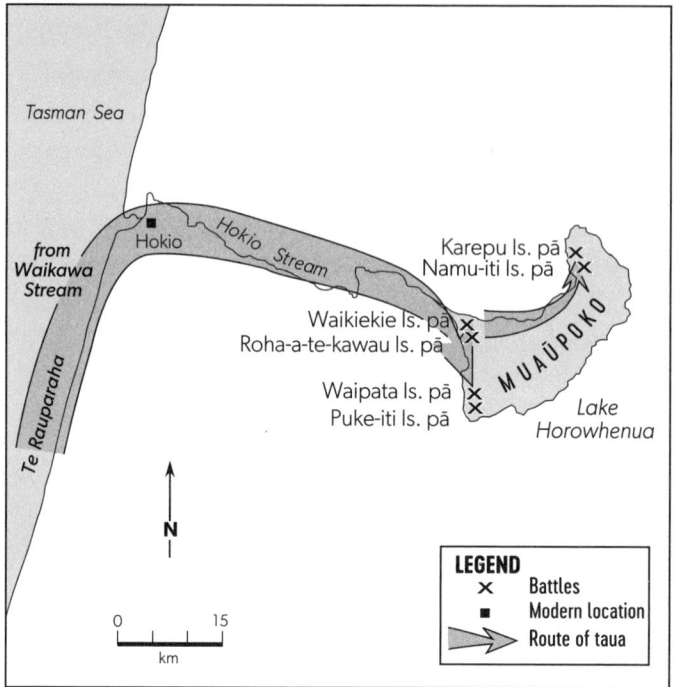

Te Rauparaha's attack on the island pā on Lake Horowhenua, 1823.

island pā were completely unaware of what was about to strike them. These pā had been built on islands laboriously constructed by driving tree trunks into the lake bed then filling the enclosure they made with soil and sand. When the lake waka were pulled up onto the islands the occupants felt secure in the belief that the Hokio Stream was too small for waka taua to traverse up it.

Now, these hopes of security were dashed in a moment as the roar of musketry lashed the pā from the Ngāti Toa waka. Having no defence against the musket balls, those who survived desperately tried to swim ashore. In the main their attempts at escape were fruitless, as they were chased and killed from the waka, or attacked by Ngāti Toa and their allies lining the banks of the small lake. The scale of the killing was said to be horrendous, but some did survive and carried news of the attack to nearby iwi, who gave them refuge, while others headed south to a Muaūpoko pā at Paekākāriki.

Among the survivors were some from related iwi in Te Tau Ihu (the Top of the South Island), including Te Ratu (or Te

TE RAUPARAHA'S COALITIONS – HEKE, RAUPATU, DISINTEGRATION

Raki) from Ngāti Apa, and two Ngāti Kuia men, Pakauere and Maihi, who were from Rangitoto (D'Urville Island) and Te Hoiere (Pelorus Sound) respectively. To all the surrounding iwi, the slaughter of Muaūpoko seemed a portent of what they all faced if the heke was not repulsed and forced out of their general area.

That anxiety grew as Te Rauparaha's forces then attacked and took the Paekākāriki pā, again with a ruthlessness that stemmed from Te Rauparaha's personal desire for utu against Muaūpoko. On this occasion, however, an ope of Ngāti Ira and Ngāti Kahungunu responded to a call for help from Muaūpoko, and inflicted significant casualties on Ngāti Toa as they were celebrating the fall of the pā.

The losses suffered at Paekākāriki by Ngāti Toa reinforced Te Rauparaha's awareness that they and their allies needed a safer refuge from these new enemies who surrounded them. His response was carefully planned. Te Rauparaha himself led a powerful taua inland to attack the Rangitāne pā at Hotuiti, north of Waikanae, which at the time was occupied by some Ngāti Apa as well as Rangitāne. Soon after, Te Pehi Kupe, who was Te Rauparaha's uncle, staged another night raid by waka, this time landing unnoticed on Kāpiti Island. News that Te Rauparaha's taua was heading north had put the Ngāti Apa occupiers of Kāpiti off their guard, and Te Pehi Kupe's toa were

Roha-a-te-kawau and Waikiekie pā. Two of the artificial island pā constructed by Muaūpoko in Lake Horowhenua.
Gift of G.L. Adkin family estate, 1964. Te Papa (A.005860)

able to capture all its pā in turn. While the plan to capture Kāpiti succeeded, initially some of Te Rauparaha's coalition remained on the mainland.

However, Ngāti Toa suffered further losses when, in retaliation for the attack at Hotuiti, Ngāti Apa staged a return raid on Waikanae. Some sixty Ngāti Toa were killed there, and this, combined with the losses at Paekākāriki, made Te Rauparaha decide to leave the mainland entirely. The members of the heke now moved en masse across to Kāpiti Island to gain greater safety from surprise attack. At this stage Ngāti Tama under Te Puoho decided that, as the principal heke now appeared more secure, it was safe for them to return north to the Mokau area to defend their own rohe against Tainui. Reretawhangawhanga of Te Ātiawa also accompanied Te Puoho back with his hapū to north Taranaki.

MUAŪPOKO'S ALLIES GATHER

In response to the succession of attacks by the Ngāti Toa coalition, there was a rapid co-ordination of a large number of southern iwi determined to defeat the coalition and drive it out of Kāpiti and the Horowhenua. Many of these iwi were approached by the Ngāti Apa rangatira Te Ratu, who had managed to escape from Kāpiti.

Ope or contingents came from Te Tau Ihu in Te Waipounamu (the South Island), consisting of Ngāti Apa ki te Rā Tō, Ngāti Kuia and Rangitāne; from the north came Te Atihaunui of Whanganui, Rangitāne of Manawatū and Ngāti Apa

Te Pehi Kupe. The senior Ngāti Toa compatriot of Te Rauparaha. He was killed at Kaiapoi by Kāi Tahu in 1830, and his death sparked major onslaughts on that tribe by Te Rauparaha from 1830-32. This painting was completed when Te Pehi Kupe was in England, most likely in 1826.
John Sylvester, 1826, National Library of Australia, nla.obj-134562135

TE RAUPARAHA'S COALITIONS — HEKE, RAUPATU, DISINTEGRATION 101

of Rangitikei; and, from the south and east of Te Ika a Māui (the North Island), Ngāti Ira and Ngāti Kahungunu. All joined up with the surviving Muaūpoko. This massive force gathered over some weeks, with the increasing number of campfires along the coast at night visible to Te Rauparaha's people opposite on Kāpiti.

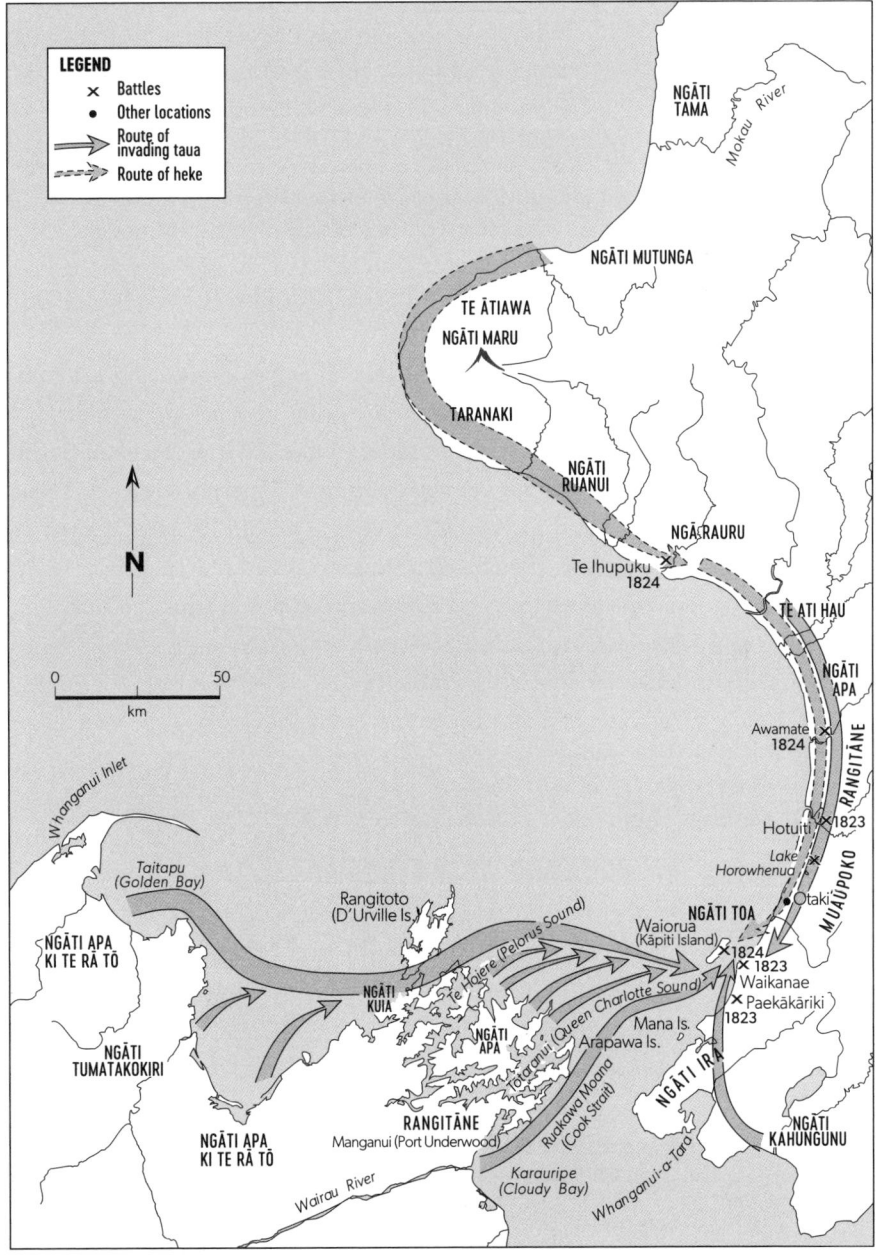

Waiorua invasion and the heke of west coast and Taranaki iwi, 1824.

> **Te Pehi Kupe**
>
> During this period, a highly significant event occurred that was to provide Ngāti Toa with a large source of muskets four years later, when they were desperately needed. As the whaling vessel *Urania* was passing Kāpiti Island, Te Pehi Kupe leapt aboard from his waka, managing to grab some of the ship's trailing ropes despite a large swell and attempts by the crew to dislodge him. He travelled in the end to England and, in a repeat of Hongi Hika's actions, while passing through Sydney on his return journey he seems to have traded valuable gifts he had received in England for large numbers of muskets.

Once the various ope had all arrived, a hui was called of the rangatira, two of the more prominent being Tutepourangi and Pouwhakarewarewa from Te Tau Ihu (the Top of the South Island), who were of Ngāti Kuia and Ngāti Apa descent. These two disagreed on the tactics that should be used against Te Rauparaha. Pouwhakarewarewa advocated staging a night attack to remove Ngāti Toa's musket power from the equation, while Tutepourangi insisted that a dawn attack would be as effective and still confer the required surprise. There was agreement about the initial target, however — this would be Waiorua pā, at the northeastern corner of the island.

WAIORUA AND ITS AFTERMATH

In the end Pouwhakarewarewa went ahead with his night attack at Waiorua pā, which was occupied by Te Ātiawa and Ngāti Kōata. The pā was about 2.5 kilometres north of Rangatira pā, and 6 kilometres from Taepiro pā, which was occupied by Te Rauparaha. Pou's attack was initially successful, but just as it seemed the pā was about to fall Te Rauparaha and Te Rangihaeata burst onto the scene with their muskets. The final outcome, after intense fighting, was a rout of the invaders, hundreds of whom were killed or captured as they sought to flee. They also left a valuable fleet of waka, both on the island and on the beaches on the mainland as they fled the closely pursuing Ngāti Toa forces. Significantly, among those who had been captured was Tutepourangi.

The stunningly successful outcome at Waiorua led to a number of consequences of strategic importance for Te Rauparaha. First was the creation of a take for even wider utu to be sought against the Kurahaupō iwi of Ngāti Apa, Ngāti Kuia and Rangitāne on both Te Ika a Māui and Te Waipounamu, providing space for the northern coalition as it expanded. Secondly, the captured waka provided Te Rauparaha with the means to seek utu in Te Waipounamu.

The third major consequence was that news of the impending invasion had reached Ngāti Raukawa and others such as Ngāti Tama in north Taranaki, and messages had been sent asking for reinforcements from those allies. A huge heke of about fifteen hundred people started from north Taranaki soon after the battle at Waiorua, as Te Puoho of Ngāti Tama brought down most of his people, as well as more Te Ātiawa and Ngāti Mutunga.

Finally, the capture of Tutepourangi by Ngāti Kōata gave them the opportunity to negotiate hard terms with Ngāti Kuia and Ngāti Apa for his return. During the initial attack on Waiorua a high-ranking young Ngāti Kōata named Tawhe had been captured by Ngāti Kuia and subsequently taken back to Rangitoto. He was able to be exchanged for Tutepourangi, but because of Tutepourangi's seniority an additional tuku (formal gift) was made of Rangitoto, and other areas to Ngāti Kōata. Ngāti Kōata then moved down and peacefully took possession of these areas as they returned Tutepourangi, whose Ngāti Kuia people now lived alongside their Ngāti Kōata protectors in the Marlborough Sounds, on Rangitoto and in Croisilles Harbour.

On the mainland opposite Kāpiti, the coalition now embarked on a widespread campaign of utu killing as it took possession of the Waikanae and Ōtaki areas, clearing most of the surrounding lands. Moreover, Ngāti Ira from Porirua pulled back under their rangatira Te Kekerengu onto their island pā Taputeranga at Whanganui a Tara, and Ngāti Apa and Rangitāne retreated from coastal areas into the inland Rangitikei and Manawatū.

For the time being at least, space and resources were being occupied, creating room for other heke from the north to settle.

SETTLEMENT PRESSURES

The first of the heke to arrive after Waiorua were Ngāti Tama, who were invited by Te Rauparaha to settle in the vacated areas in the south. Te Ahukaramu was next to arrive with his heke of Ngāti Raukawa, followed over the next few years by two other heke from that iwi, the last being that led by Te Whatanui in about 1829.

The arrival of these newcomers soon led to a build-up of pressure. Te Puoho decided to move with some of his Ngāti Tama people to Kāpiti Island itself, and in 1826 that resulted in an outbreak of fighting with Ngāti Toa on the island at Tokakawau. The conflict was only brought to an end through the negotiating skills of Topeora, the sister of Te Rangihaeata, and a young Ngāti Tama woman.

Ngāti Mutunga decided to head south to the Whanganui a Tara area, where they attacked Ngāti Ira on their island refuge of Taputeranga pā in 1827. The pā soon fell, with a large number of deaths and the enslavement of survivors. Among those captured was the prominent kuia Tamairangi and her son, the young rangatira Te Kekerengu. Tamairangi in particular so impressed Te Rangihaeata with her dignity that she and her son were taken to Kāpiti Island. While there, however, Te Kekerengu committed a sexual indiscretion with one of Te Rangihaeata's wives or sisters. When this became known he fled for his life, managing to get away on a small waka to Te Waipounamu, where he sought refuge with Kāi Tahu at Ōmihi, south of Kaikōura. Thus yet another take for utu against a South Island iwi had eventuated — this time against Kāi Tahu for sheltering Kekerengu.

Further east, Ngāti Tama had begun to apply what would be continued pressure on Ngāti Kahungunu as two pā were built at Lake Onoke in south Wairarapa. At first good relations were maintained, with trading between the two iwi leading Ngāti Kahungunu to provide the raupō for the whare in the two new Ngāti Tama pā, Te Tarata and Wharepapa. Before the pā were completed, however, the two sides had grown suspicious of each other, both fearing an attack. Each decided on a pre-emptive attack, with Ngāti Tama launching their assault after inviting the raupō workers to a hākari. The victors in the conflicts at the two pā, however, were the Ngāti Kahungunu rangatira Nukupewapewa and Tutepakihirangi, and a general slaughter of Ngāti Tama resulted. Knowing that an utu raid was certain to follow, Ngāti Kahungunu now pulled back to improve the defences of Pehikatea pā, near modern-day Greytown.

The following year, 1830, the Ngāti Tama rangatira Te Kaeaea (later called Taringakuri by Te Rauparaha), who was Te Puoho's brother, set out to seek utu at Pehikatea. He led a powerful taua of Ngāti Tama, Ngāti Mutunga and Te Ātiawa, totalling between six and seven hundred toa. This force overwhelmed the defences Tutepakihirangi had constructed at Pehikatea, and most of the women and children in the pā were captured, although Tutepakihirangi and many of the men managed to escape.

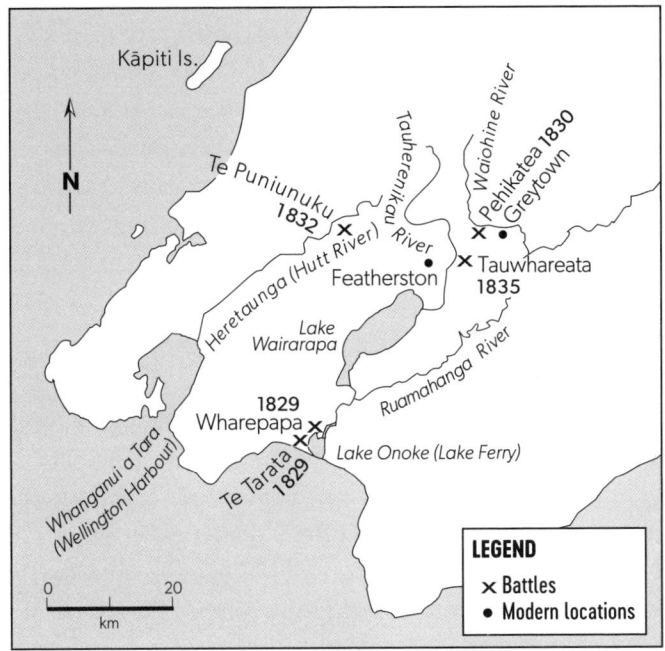

Wairarapa battle sites involving Ngāti Kahungungu, Ngāti Tama, Te Ātiawa and Ngāti Mutunga, 1829-35.

THE MUSKET WARS EXTEND INTO TE WAIPOUNAMU

Not long after the battle at Waiorua in 1824, Te Rauparaha heard that a Rangitāne rangatira, Te Ruaoneone, from the Wairau River area in Te Tau Ihu, had uttered a curse against him: if Te Rauparaha dared to come to the Wairau, he, Te Ruaoneone, would crush his head with a patu aruhe, a heavy stone tool that was used to beat the roots of ferns (aruhe) to soften them for cooking. The curse was Te Ruaoneone's response to the news that Te Rauparaha had killed Rangitāne rangatira to whom he was related at Awamate, in the Manawatū.

For a rangatira of Te Rauparaha's exalted status, whose head was highly tapu and must be protected from being defiled by items like food-preparing tools, such a base threat was extreme. It demanded utu. And by now Te Rauparaha had the waka that enabled him to cross Raukawa Moana (Cook Strait) and obtain that utu. The first of these waka had been captured during the heke south, but their numbers were increased significantly by those taken at Waiorua. Te Rauparaha had also had further waka built and these took some years to complete — in this he had the assistance of expert carvers from Te Arawa to whom he was distantly related.

Te Rauparaha launched his taua to attack Te Ruaoneone and the Rangitāne people of the Wairau in 1827 or 1828 — the exact date is unclear. It is known that

Te Pehi Kupe returned from his overseas travels in 1828, having acquired large numbers of muskets. Whether or not these were available to Te Rauparaha for this taua is in the end irrelevant, however, because what is clear is that Rangitāne and their boastful rangatira Te Ruaoneone had no muskets. They were about to experience a series of attacks that became known as Tukituki Patu Aruhe (the beating of the fern-root pounder) and with them the dreadful feelings of hopelessness that the victims of the Ngāpuhi taua had had to endure.

THE FIRST BLOWS OF TUKITUKI PATU ARUHE

The first powerful taua that Te Rauparaha launched entered Tōtaranui (Queen Charlotte Sound) by way of Te Kura Te Au (Tory Channel). Two Rangitāne pā were taken there: Okukari pā in the first bay on the northern side near the entrance to the sound, and another on the southern side. Smaller groups of whare were attacked as the taua progressed up the channel to enter Opua Bay, at the head of the larger Onapua Bay. From there the taua climbed the steep ridge to cross over into the Manganui (Port Underwood) area, from where it made its way across the steep, broken and heavily bushed country to descend onto the Wairau Plain at Rarangi.

A pā was taken at or near Rarangi before the taua arrived at Kōwhai pā, at the Wairau River mouth, where Te Ruaoneone had his base. Not surprisingly, Kōwhai pā was taken as the taua's muskets cut down the leading defenders from a distance, causing utter terror and loss of morale. The pā then fell to the massed assault and large numbers of its occupants were captured, among them Te Ruaoneone.

The taua continued on to take the Huataki pā at the foot of Parinui o Whiti, the huge white bluffs on the southern side of the Vernon Lagoons that they would have seen clearly as they crossed Raukawa Moana. The pursuit did not end there, however, as the taua continued south as far as Cape Campbell where the pā Te Karaka at Marfells Beach was taken with further slaughter.

Hundreds were taken captive during this major raid, many of whom were taken back to Kāpiti as slaves. Others were directed to remain in the Wairau and gather food in readiness for the return of Te Rauparaha the following year, taking advantage of the huge seasonal food resources in birds and eels at both the extensive Vernon Lagoons area and at Kapara Te Hau (Lake Grassmere). Te Ruaoneone, however, was taken back to Kāpiti, where he was killed.

While this massive blow devastated Rangitāne in the Wairau area, large numbers still survived in other areas of the Sounds, where they were commonly living intermingled with their Kurahaupō relatives of Ngāti Kuia and Ngāti

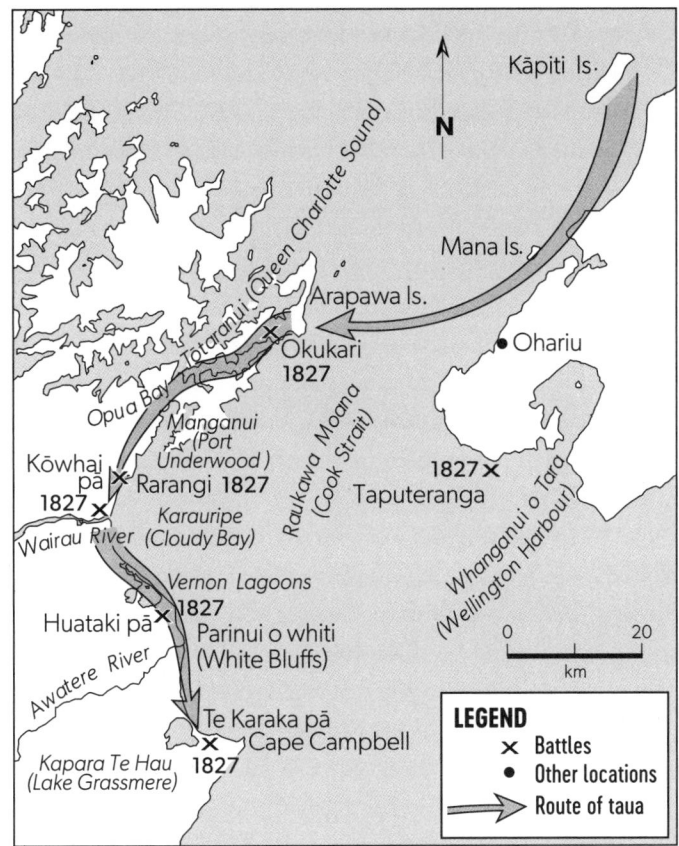

Te Rauparaha's Tukituki Patu Aruhe taua of 1827-28.

Apa. Their turn would inevitably come when Te Rauparaha decided to return. The escape from Waiorua to Te Tau Ihu of the Kurahaupō rangatira Te Ratu made that return even more certain, as utu was required for his activities in assembling the attack at Waiorua. And when Te Rauparaha did return the remaining iwi in Te Waipounamu would be faced with an extremely powerful foe, as by then Te Rauparaha's coalition had certainly received the huge boost in musket power from Te Pehi Kupe's additional hundreds of muskets.

A WIDER RAUPATU TAUA TO TE WAIPOUNAMU

Another curse uttered against Te Rauparaha was the immediate trigger for the massive taua that he led to Te Waipounamu in 1829. This curse was uttered by Rerewaka, the Kāi Tahu rangatira at Ōmihi, where Te Kekerengu had sought refuge after his narrow escape from Kāpiti. On hearing what had befallen Ngāti Ira, Rerewaka responded by saying that if Te Rauparaha dared to come south to Ōmihi he would rip open his belly with a niho mangā (a barracouta's tooth). Added to that take for utu was Te Rauparaha's ongoing desire to obtain utu for the involvement of the Kurahaupō iwi in the Waiorua battle.

However, an underlying desire to return to Te Waipounamu was sparked by its being the source of the most valuable of all taonga (treasures) for Māori — pounamu, or greenstone. It is not clear whether Te Rauparaha initially sought to obtain access to pounamu by trade or by raupatu (conquest). But as events were to turn out, the latter became the means, and these events were triggered by the responses of Kāi Tahu during this first major extensive series of raupatu raids beyond the Wairau.

The huge taua began by completing the conquest of the Kurahaupō throughout the extensive Sounds complex, which comprises over 1500 kilometres of coastline. In East Bay and Endeavour Inlet to the east and west respectively of the entry to Tōtaranui, large numbers of Rangitāne were killed or captured; at East Bay the name Umukuri was given to the bay where the umu steamed with the bodies of Rangitāne. Well up the sound at Karaka Point another Rangitāne pā, which today is still reasonably well preserved, also fell as heavy musket fire from the waka below resulted in a frantic rush to leave.

As the taua headed toward Te Hoiere (Pelorus Sound) Ngāti Kuia suffered heavily when their major pā at Alligator Head and Titirangi were taken, followed by further pā at Paruparu (Forsyth Island) and Wakatahuri. The taua then swept on to enter Te Hoiere itself.

The huge Te Hoiere complex was dominated by two Kurahaupō pā — one at Hopai Peninsula in Crail Bay and the other at Hikapu, opposite the junction of the main sound with Kenepuru Sound. They were believed to be predominantly occupied by Ngāti Kuia and Ngāti Apa. Once more heavy musket fire carried the day at Hopai, with many being killed and others captured. During this active stage of fighting large numbers of captives were more of a hindrance for the taua than an advantage, so they were taken offshore to nearby Ouokaha Island and left there under a few well-armed guards. The taua then pressed on into Te Hoiere and south to attack the major pā at Hikapu, again taking it easily from occupants who had no muskets. Back at Ouokaha the captives had managed to take their guards by surprise and kill them, but to their horror, while they were planning their escape they saw the waka of the taua sweeping back into Crail Bay. The island was retaken ruthlessly, and this time the surviving captives were taken back to Kāpiti.

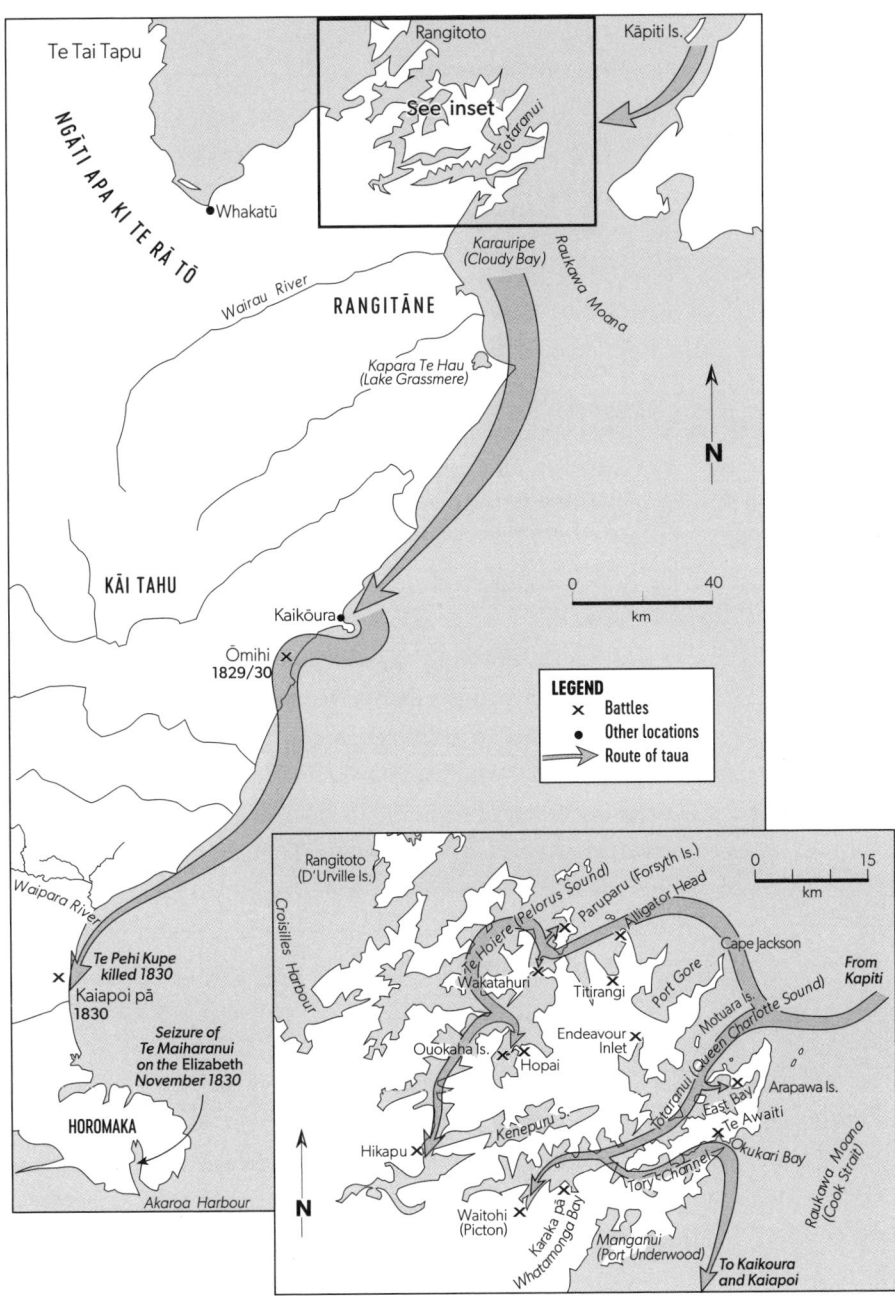

Te Rauparaha's taua to the Marlborough Sounds, Kaikoura and Kaiapoi areas, 1829-30.
INSET: *Te Rauparaha's raid on the Marlborough Sounds, 1829-30.*

> **Worser Heberley**
>
> Worser Heberley was a Pākehā whaler who in 1829 had set up a base at Te Awaiti in Okukari Bay, at the entry to Te Kura Te Au. He recorded the scenes he saw as the taua rested there on 14 April 1830 as it made its way south. Heberley noted that the taua left the remains of 60 or 70 bodies, most of which they had consumed, as well as a number of heads and arms, and many partially cooked body parts that were left lying in the bush.
>
> When the taua returned on 10 May, he recorded that the prows of the waka were decorated with the heads and hands of men. The taua stayed about ten days waiting for good weather for the strait crossing, during which time Heberley saw them force slaves to dig umu, after which they would be killed and their bodies committed to the umu they had dug.

Probably the only aspect of the utu ledger against Kurahaupō iwi that was not satisfied on this taua was the failure to take Pouwhakarewarewa, who was away from Te Hoiere when the taua attacked. With other survivors, he now drew back well up into the bush-clad Te Hoiere River at the head of the sound. Meanwhile Te Rauparaha, filled quite literally with the flesh of his enemies, led the taua on the long journey back to Te Kura Te Au (Tory Channel), from where they headed south to Ōmihi to obtain utu against Rerewaka for his niho mangā curse.

OUTCOMES FOR KĀI TAHU

Rerewaka's pā was located at Ōmihi, a considerable distance south of Kaikōura; the Ōmihi Stream met the sea between Goose Bay and Oaro. Unfortunately for Rerewaka and his people, the advent of the taua coincided with the anticipated arrival of waka of Kāi Tahu relatives at Ōmihi. As the taua arrived off the pā at dawn Rerewaka's people moved down onto the beach in the mistaken belief that they were welcoming their relatives. At the last moment they realised their error, but it was already too late as the muskets of the invaders began to cut them down. The remainder were quickly overwhelmed by the onrush of their attackers.

Huge numbers of Kāi Tahu were said to have been killed or captured at Ōmihi, some accounts suggesting a total of over a thousand. Rerewaka himself was captured and taken back to Kāpiti, where he was ritually killed by having his belly sliced open with a niho mangā.

From Ōmihi the taua moved on to the huge Kāi Tahu pā at Kaiapoi, taking with it about five hundred captives. They left their waka some distance north of the pā, travelling the final stretch overland and camping far enough away that its inhabitants would not be able to see their Ōmihi relatives among the slaves of the taua. The pā at Kaiapoi must have been imposing. It was situated on a peninsula of land surrounded by swamp, accessible by waka on one side but protected on the inland side by a very high set of double palisading, providing good protection against musket fire. It was large enough to hold thousands of people and to have large garden areas, with a constant supply of fresh water.

It is not clear what the true intentions of the taua were at this point. Ngāti Toa accounts suggest that the intention was simply to visit Te Maiharanui, the pre-eminent Kāi Tahu rangatira, and trade for pounamu and other taonga. Te Pehi Kupe, who was with the taua, had met Te Maiharanui the previous year when he was being taken back to Kāpiti on a sailing ship on which Te Maiharanui happened to embark as a passenger at Akaroa; Te Pehi Kupe had actually invited Te Maiharanui to come and visit Kāpiti, but Te Maiharanui had disembarked somewhere along the northeast coast of the Te Waipounamu. Now, Te Pehi Kupe and about twenty other rangatira and toa approached the pā, where they were formally welcomed and invited to enter. Initially all was peaceful, but after some time Te Pehi, or someone in his group, became engaged in a conflict over trade and shooting broke out. Te Pehi bolted for the palisading but was killed by Tangatahara, who was from Ōnawe pā in Akaroa. The remaining members of his party were also killed, and all the bodies were cooked and eaten.

For Te Rauparaha the killing and defiling of the bodies of his own uncle and other close relatives was a severe blow. Outraged at the apparently treacherous killing, he poured musket fire at the pā, but it was protected by its heavy palisading. Te Rauparaha then reacted with the utmost savagery — all of the captives who had been taken at Ōmihi were dragged in front of the pā and ruthlessly killed in sight of their relatives. Te Rauparaha then thundered out that he would be returning, before the taua packed up and began the long journey back to Kāpiti.

TE RAUPARAHA SEEKS UTU FOR THE KILLING OF TE PEHI KUPE

Following the killing of Te Pehi Kupe, Te Rauparaha's desire for utu was increased even further when tales reached him that some of Te Pehi's bones had been taken by the Kāi Tahu rangatira Tuhawaiki to Whakatū (modern-day Nelson) and nearby Whakapuaka for Ngāti Kuia to carve them into fishhooks, a classic way of desecrating the bones of an enemy. Te Rauparaha's desire to obtain utu from Kāi Tahu now knew no bounds.

Despite his fury, Te Rauparaha faced serious problems in his plan to gain utu. Crossing Raukawa Moana again would be no mean feat, and the journey back to Kaiapoi was long and arduous, on a very exposed coast that was dangerous for waka. Added to these problems was the fact that he now knew that, unlike the Kurahaupō iwi in the north of Te Waipounamu, Kāi Tahu had access to some muskets; while he did not know the numbers, the mere presence of muskets added significantly to the risk. And he also knew from having seen Kaiapoi that it was well defended against musket fire.

Perhaps it was all of these considerations that made Te Rauparaha turn his mind to other options. What he was primarily seeking was utu against Te Maiharanui for his perceived treachery to Te Pehi Kupe. He knew enough of Te Maiharanui to be aware that he spent much of his time at Takapuneke pā, in Akaroa. The idea of attacking Te Maiharanui there must have arisen when, a few months later, Kāpiti was visited by the trading brig *Elizabeth*, skippered by one Captain Stewart. Whether the idea emanated from Stewart or Te Rauparaha will never be known, but since Te Rauparaha had never visited Takapuneke it seems highly likely that it may have been Stewart who sowed the seed.

An agreement was reached in which, in exchange for the huge volume of 25 tonnes of dressed flax, Stewart would take Te Rauparaha on a trip south, the results of which would become infamous. Te Rauparaha, Te Pehi Kupe's son Te Hiko o te Rangi and about seventy musket-armed men were taken aboard the *Elizabeth*, which then made its way toward Akaroa. Before the brig entered the harbour the toa were secreted below decks in the hold, while Te Rauparaha and Te Hiko were hidden in cupboards in the captain's main cabin. The vessel then sailed into the harbour and dropped anchor off Takapuneke pā, where it had called previously to trade.

There was nothing to put Kāi Tahu on guard when they came out to the ship by waka. They were asked to send Te Maiharanui out to trade for muskets and powder, but that had happened before and did not raise suspicions. On this occasion, however, Te Maiharanui was absent and word had to be sent to fetch him back to Takapuneke. Some days went by, and anxiety levels on the ship must have become very keen. Finally, however, Te Maiharanui and a small group, which included his wife Te Whe and their daughter Roimata, arrived at the ship by waka and climbed on board.

Te Maiharanui, Te Whe and Roimata were taken below to the captain's cabin, where they were seized by the mate, Clementson, and some of the crew, and Te Maiharanui was shackled by irons to a chair. Te Hiko is said to have stood directly in front of Te Maiharanui and stared at him for over half an hour without speaking. Then he reached forward and spread Te Maiharanui's lips, saying, 'Ko ēnei ngā niho i kai ai i tāku pāpā.' ('These are the teeth that ate my father.')

The other Kāi Tahu up on deck were suddenly confronted by the muskets of the Ngāti Toa, and before any could escape they were herded below. In the early hours of the following morning the ship's boats and the captured waka of the Kāi Tahu were used to ferry the ope ashore, where it launched a sudden assault on the unsuspecting Kāi Tahu kāinga. Once more, many hundreds were reportedly killed and many more captured as Takapuneke fell.

Grisly accounts came back to Sydney of the grim scenes on the *Elizabeth* as the vessel returned to Kāpiti loaded with about a hundred large flax baskets of human flesh, some of which was consumed in cannibal feasts during the voyage. The *Elizabeth* entered Whakaraupō (Lyttelton Harbour) on its return journey,

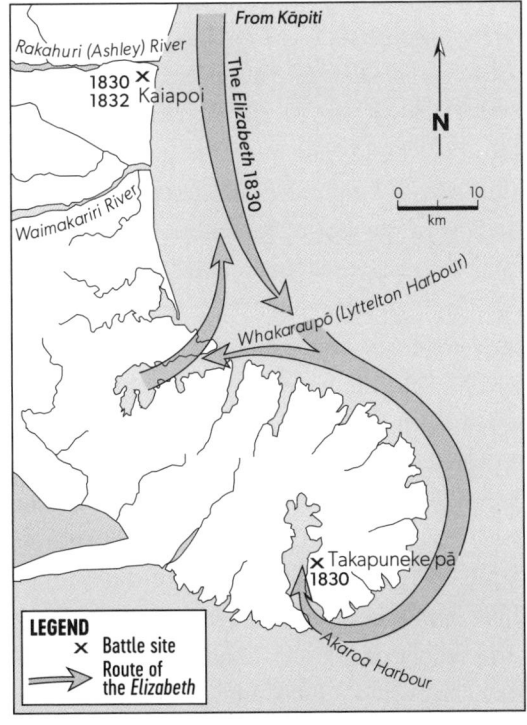

The capture of Te Maiharanui at Takapuneke, 1830.

intending to carry out a similar attack there, but that was frustrated when one of the captives managed to escape from the brig and warn the locals. Several other sailing vessels were present at Kāpiti on the return of the *Elizabeth* and their crews reported their observations when they arrived back in Sydney. Attempts were made by the Governor of New South Wales to prosecute Stewart and Clementson, but these failed for technical legal reasons relating to lack of jurisdiction.

During the *Elizabeth*'s voyage back to Kāpiti, Te Whe and Te Maiharanui made the heart-rending decision to strangle their daughter Roimata to save her from torture at the hands of Ngāti Toa — the fate that they knew awaited them. This did indeed occur, at the hands of Te Pehi Kupe's widow Tiaia and their whānau, following the vessel's arrival back at Kāpiti on 11 November 1830.

The few survivors of the Takapuneke attack, and other Kāi Tahu in north Canterbury, now knew what awaited them when Te Rauparaha returned, as surely he would to gain utu against those at Kaiapoi. In preparation for the inevitable, they began to gather there and improve the pā's defences.

TE RAUPARAHA'S STRATEGIES TO ACHIEVE UTU AT KAIAPOI

Te Rauparaha spent most of the year 1831 planning and gathering a huge taua to invade Te Waipounamu in an extremely complicated series of interwoven thrusts. The taua is believed to have exceeded a thousand toa, all armed with muskets and travelling in more than thirty waka. Late in the year the massive taua crossed Raukawa Moana and headed west to attack Ngāti Kuia in the Rangitoto area. The outcome was initially surprisingly unsuccessful, for an unexpected reason.

As the taua reached Admiralty Bay, to the east of Rangitoto, it was met at sea by some Ngāti Kōata waka led by the rangatira Whakatari. He called on Te Rauparaha to turn around, emphasising that Ngāti Kuia were living under the protection of Ngāti Kōata. An argument ensued, which Ngāti Kōata say ended with Whakatari tipping Te Rauparaha into the water. Whether that actually occurred or not, the taua certainly grasped the message that a direct route to Rangitoto was not available and it turned back to head east — or so Ngāti Kōata believed. In reality the taua turned into Te Hoiere and headed west up Tawhitinui Reach and on to the head of Elaine Bay. There, in a striking demonstration of the initiative, fierce determination and strength of the taua of those times, they undertook the almost incredible task of hauling numbers of their waka up 125 metres through the bush to the saddle on the ridgeline. From there they lowered the waka down the precipitous slope into Whakakitenga Bay in Croisilles

TE RAUPARAHA'S COALITIONS — HEKE, RAUPATU, DISINTEGRATION

Harbour, well south of Rangitoto. This back-door method of entry into Tasman Bay enabled the taua to launch a surprise attack on Ngāti Kuia at Whakapuaka, in which Tutepourangi was killed and large numbers of his people were either killed or captured.

After this devastating attack on Ngāti Kuia, Te Rauparaha and his coalition divided the taua in two in a grand strategy. Te Rauparaha returned to Te Hoiere with Ngāti Toa and some

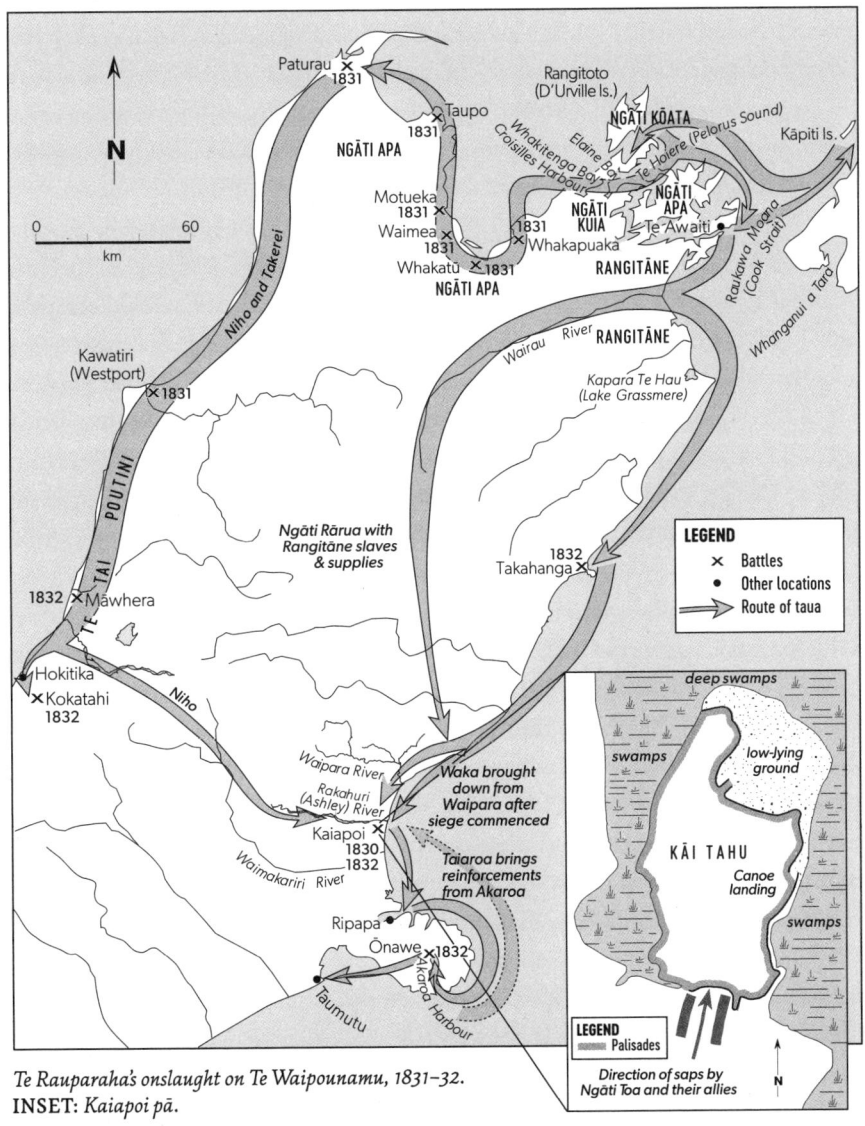

Te Rauparaha's onslaught on Te Waipounamu, 1831–32.
INSET: *Kaiapoi pā.*

of their allies, and then headed south to attack Kāi Tahu at Kaiapoi. The other part of the taua, which included Te Ātiawa under Te Manutoheroa, Ngāti Tama under Takerei and Ngāti Rārua under Niho, headed south to Whakatū then west into Mohua (Golden Bay). From there the plan was to head down Te Tai Poutini (the West Coast) and attempt to cross back over the mountain ranges to join Te Rauparaha in attacking Kāi Tahu at Kaiapoi.

The taua that headed into Tasman Bay and Mohua was involved in a number of successful clashes with Ngāti Kuia and Ngāti Apa; few of their opponents survived, and for refuge they pulled back into the vast hinterland of Te Tau Ihu. Among those killed at Mohua was the Ngāti Apa rangatira Te Ratu, or Te Rato, who had planned the Waiorua attack seven years earlier.

The taua then travelled overland down the very rugged northern coast of Te Tai Poutini, engaging any scattered whānau groupings of Ngāti Apa down to Kawatiri (Westport); further south they started to encounter small groups of Kāi Tahu on food-gathering trips. Continuing south, they took the pā at Māwhera (Greymouth) and Hokitika, capturing the leading Kāti Waewae rangatira Tuhuru and leaving him in the hands of a force that was left in control of the pā. Niho and Takerei then headed east, guided by Kāi Tahu captives up and over Te Tiritiri-o-te-moana (the Southern Alps) to link up with Te Rauparaha, trusting that he was still at Kaiapoi.

The determination and courage of the Ngāti Rārua and Ngāti Tama toa finally paid off in early 1832 as the hardened but weary men at last reached the Rakahuri (Ashley) River and followed it down to the east coast at Kaiapoi. They brought with them the news that with the capture of the Ahaura River area inland from Māwhera, Te Rauparaha's coalition now controlled the most accessible of the Tai Poutini sources of pounamu.

Te Rauparaha, meanwhile, had travelled south, bypassing Rangitoto and moving on to the Wairau, where the taua stopped to resupply and plan the advance on Kaiapoi. The Rangitāne vassals who had been left in the Wairau after the fall of Kōwhai pā now provided the food and guides for an overland ope of Ngāti Rārua. The ope was sent to approach Kaiapoi by a long, arduous journey up the Wairau and through the interior of what is now Molesworth Station, before heading out to the coast down the Waipara River. Meanwhile Te Rauparaha and the main bulk of the taua headed south by waka down the east coast.

THE RAUPATU AGAINST KĀI TAHU BEGINS

The first major blow struck against Kāi Tahu came at the Takahanga pā at Kaikōura. A large ope was landed at night near the pā, and in the darkness the

Alarm in a Maori Pa. A graphic portrayal of the moment of alarm as an approaching taua is observed by the inhabitants of a pā. The artist James McDonald did not accurately portray the hairstyle of the Māori toa of old, but that does not detract from the impact of this hand-coloured lithograph. APG-1443-1/4G, photograph of the reproduction of a painting by James I. McDonald, 'He taua! He taua', painted in 1906. Alexander Turnbull Library, Wellington, NZ

toa secreted themselves in scrub near its main entrance. As dawn broke the waka approached land, and the inhabitants of the pā streamed out to see who was arriving. The members of the ope burst out of hiding as the waka taua rushed ashore, and the pā was captured without the occupants having any chance of securing its defences.

From Kaikōura Te Rauparaha continued south to the mouth of the Waipara River, where he linked up with the inland ope of Ngāti Rārua and Rangitāne. The combined taua now moved overland to approach Kaiapoi, in the hope of also taking that pā by surprise. By now, however, scouts had brought back news of the progress of the taua and the taking of Takahanga as the taua came down the coast, and the pā was strongly defended by many thousands of Kāi Tahu behind its massive palisading. Moreover, messengers had been sent to request urgent assistance from their relatives in Murihiku (Southland), who were more heavily armed with muskets. Taiaroa and about a hundred of his men from Ōtākou (on the Otago peninsula) had been visiting Akaroa when word reached them that the taua was approaching Kaiapoi, and they soon made a night entry into the pā from the Rakahuri River.

As the long siege began, Te Rauparaha moved his fleet of waka to the Rakahuri to dominate and cut off the pā from the sea, and his men also began the laborious process of digging a series of zig-zag sap trenches up to the palisading. At one point Taiaroa and his men attempted to burn Te Rauparaha's waka during the night but they were frustrated by heavy rain. After months of hard work the saps reached almost to the palisading and Ngāti Toa started heaping up huge piles of cut mānuka in preparation for burning the palisading down. At night courageous Kāi Tahu such as Hakopa Te Ata o Tu would enter the saps, attack any Ngāti Toa who were in them, and try to drag away the growing bundles of material. But it was a hopeless task, and after some three months of hard work massive piles had accumulated, reaching well up the sides of the palisading.

While this sapping work was going on, Te Rauparaha received a major reinforcement when Ngāti Rārua and Ngāti Tama arrived from the west coast with their men. Ngāti Toa and their allies were now only awaiting a strong southerly wind to light the piles of mānuka and launch their final attack.

As the outcome was becoming very clear, Te Pehi Kupe's son Te Hiko called out to Taiaroa that he and his Ōtākou men should withdraw as no utu was sought against them. Taiaroa could see the inevitability of what was about to happen, and he tried unsuccessfully to persuade the Kāi Tūāhuriri hapū defenders of the pā to abandon it and flee at night. When they refused, he decided to take the opportunity to depart in the night with his Ōtākou men.

Soon after this, when a very strong northwesterly wind was blowing, the Kāi Tahu rangatira Pureko took the desperate gamble of lighting the huge piles of wood by shoving burning brands through the gaps in the palisading. For a time the tactic seemed to be working, and huge flames and clouds of smoke streamed away from the palisading as the mānuka piles in the saps burned fiercely. But as often occurs at the end of a strong nor'west wind in Te Waipounamu, within about half an hour the wind had suddenly turned southerly and the flames were now driving into the palisading. Heavy smoke and embers poured into the pā for hours, increasing in intensity as the dry palisading caught alight, and choking the defenders.

As the inevitable happened and the palisading crashed to the ground in a huge shower of sparks, it is said that the haka performed by the hundreds of toa outside was thunderous and made the ground tremble. It was followed by a massive volley of musket fire that ripped through the smoke-filled pā as Ngāti Toa and their allies poured into it. Huge numbers of Kāi Tahu were killed or taken prisoner, and for days afterwards a ruthless, wide-ranging pursuit of the survivors was conducted across the plains.

Hakopa Te Ata o Tu

Te Ata o Tu. Described by the artist Lindauer as 'one of Te Rauparaha's slaves', Hakopa Te Ata o Tu was the courageous slayer of Pehi Tahau at Kaiapoi in 1832, just before the fall of the great pā. He and his wife were taken to Horowhenua and lived there as slaves until the end of the Musket Wars.

Gottfried Lindauer, Hakopa Te Ata o Tu, oil on canvas, Auckland Art Gallery Toi o Tāmaki, gift of Mr H.E. Partridge, 1915

Those who managed to survive the carnage at Kaiapoi streamed away towards the refuge of Ōnawe pā in Akaroa Harbour. Unfortunately for them, Te Rauparaha followed up the attack on Kaiapoi by moving south himself to attack Ōnawe, as its leading rangatira, Tangatahara, was the man who had killed Te Pehi Kupe at Kaiapoi in 1830. Ōnawe pā should have been easy to defend, as it stood on a peninsula and had a very narrow ridge entry point that was protected by a short, palisaded gateway. Once again, however, Te Rauparaha employed a cunning kōhuru. On the pretext of seeking to negotiate a peace agreement, several armed Ngāti Toa guards were allowed into the narrow entry to the pā, and mingled with a group of Kāi Tahu survivors from Kaiapoi. It was a fatal slip on the part of Kāi Tahu, as the Ngāti Toa suddenly started firing and the entry gate could not be closed in time to stop others entering. The pā was then rushed, its defenders overwhelmed, and Tangatahara was captured.

Determined pursuits of Kāi Tahu refugees from these two pā and other locations further south continued for some time, with some accounts recording that northern ope possibly reached as far south as Temuka. But then Te Rauparaha started to hear rumours that Tuhawaiki and Te Whakataupuka of Murihiku, together with Taiaroa from Ōtākou, were planning a retaliatory taua to take his men by

> **Te Hiko o te Rangi**
>
> When Tangatahara was brought before Te Hiko, expecting to be killed, others among Te Pehi's relatives demanded that he be handed to them to be slain. Instead, to demonstrate his mana Te Hiko directed that Tangatahara be released — an action that was in dramatic contrast to his cruelty to Te Maiharanui and his wife the previous year.

surprise. He decided he had gained his utu, and it was time to head home.

At this point, Kāi Tahu's fortunes in the Musket Wars were at their nadir. It was not long, however, before they launched two long-distance taua from Ruapuke Island right up to Te Tau Ihu. These taua, which took place in 1833 and 1834, are now known as Taua-iti and Taua-nui and they re-established Kāi Tahu mana. These are discussed in detail in the following chapter: suffice to say here that during Taua-iti in particular Te Rauparaha was fortunate to survive, and he lost many men.

TE RAUPARAHA'S COALITION SEEKS UTU IN THE NORTH ISLAND

On his return to Kāpiti from Te Waipounamu, Te Rauparaha became aware of the arrival in Horowhenua of the very large Ngāti Tama, Ngāti Mutunga and Te Ātiawa heke that was known as Te Heke Tama te Uaua. It comprised more than three thousand people (of whom over a thousand were toa), and had been triggered by Te Wherowhero's onslaught at Pukerangiora and Ngāmotu, in north Taranaki. Te Rauparaha was also told of attacks launched on this heke by Te Atihaunui at Whanganui as it headed south.

He immediately gathered a huge taua, which was supported by both Te Ātiawa and Ngāti Raukawa, and headed north to attack the Te Atihaunui pā Putikiwharanui at the Whanganui River mouth. The leading Te Atihaunui rangatira was Te Pehi Turoa, and a Ngā Rauru contingent also

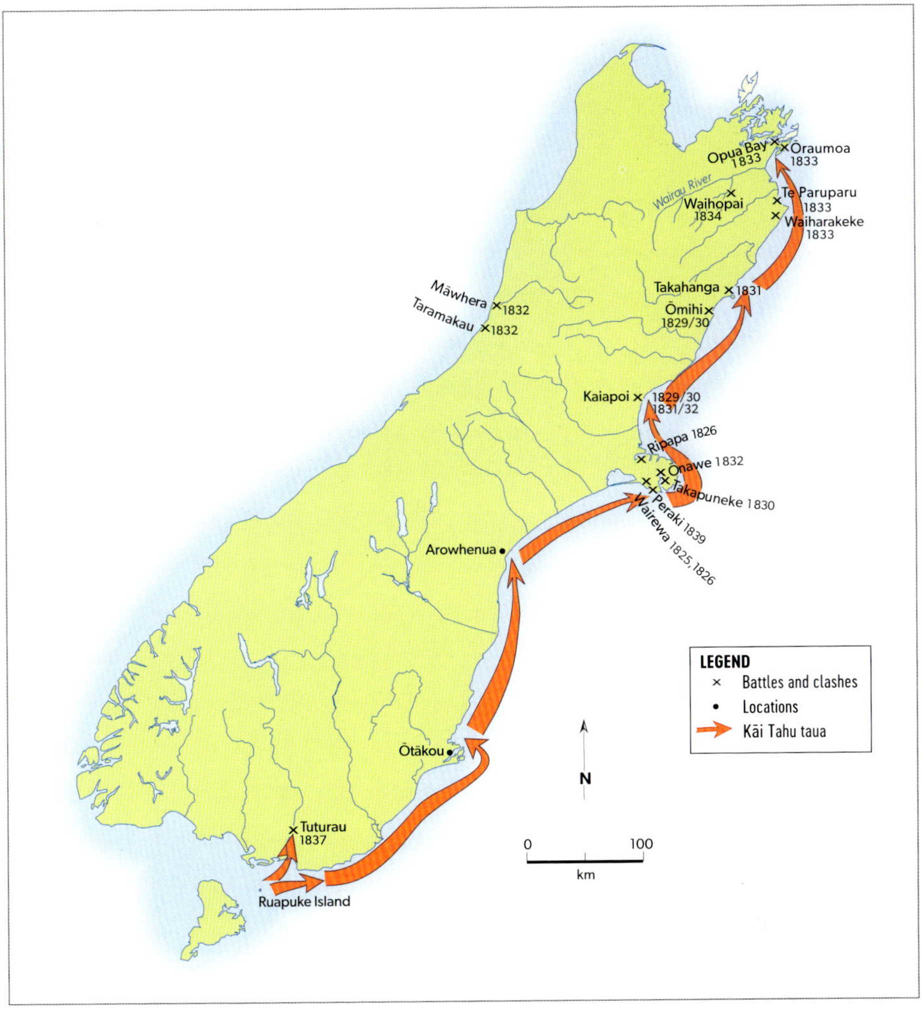

Kāi Tahu: battles sites and taua movements.

RIGHT *Te Hiko o te Rangi. The son of Te Pehi Kupe. He travelled with Te Rauraha on board the* Elizabeth *in 1830, and was also present at the sacking of Kaiapoi and Ōnawe pā in 1832.*

PUBL-0011-04-2, Heaphy, Charles, 1820–1881: Hiko, the son of Te Pehi Kupe (Tupai Cupa). Drawn by Charles Heaphy Esq.re. Day & Haghe. London, Smith, Elder [1845]. Alexander Turnbull Library, Wellington, NZ

Ngāti Apa in Astrolabe Roadstead. The French artist Louis Auguste de Sainson painted this scene at Astrolabe Roadstead (in Abel Tasman National Park) in 1827, while on the Astrolabe. Within five years, the Ngāti Apa featured in this painting would have been killed or enslaved by iwi allied to Te Rauparaha.

B-052-001-a, Sainson, Louis Auguste de, 1800–: Village à l'Anse de l'Astrolabe (Nouvelle Zélande). Villeneuve lith; figures par V. Adam; de Sainson pinx. [Paris, 1833. Alexander Turnbull Library, Wellington, NZ

Akaroa Harbour as portrayed around 1880. The central peninsula in the harbour was the location of Kāi Tahu's Ōnawe pā, which Te Rauparaha sacked in 1832. The cannibal feast after the pā's fall took place in Barry's Bay, in the foreground. Takapuneke pā, which lay on the far side of the harbour, was sacked in 1830 during the Elizabeth incident.

William Watkins, c.1880, Rex Nan Kivell Collection, National Library of Australia, nla.obj-134116080

Te Rangihaeata. The nephew of Te Rauparaha, involved in most of that rangatira's heke and taua throughout the Musket Wars. After the end of the wars he took part in fighting with Europeans at Wairau and the Hutt Valley.

C-025-022, Heaphy, Charles, 1820–1881: Rangiaeata. 1840. Alexander Turnbull Library, Wellington, NZ

Tāmihana Te Rauparaha. Te Rauparaha's son, present as a boy at many clashes with Kāi Tahu. After embracing Christianity, he and his cousin Matene Te Whiwhi courageously travelled to Te Waipounamu in the early 1840s to preach to Kāi Tahu.

C-114-002, Angas, George French, 1822–1886: Tamihana Te Rauparaha [1852]. Alexander Turnbull Library, Wellington, NZ

ABOVE *Kāpiti Island. This watercolour by William McCleverty gives an end-on view of Kapiti Island, which Te Rauparaha made his home base after Te Pehi Kupe wrested the island from Ngāti Apa control in 1823.*

William McCleverty, c. 1851, Rex Nan Kivell Collection, National Library of Australia, nla.obj-134576771-m

Parinui o Whiti, the northern boundary of Kāi Tahu's takiwā claim at the southern edge of the Wairau Valley. In the far distance the mouth of the Wairau River is located beyond the Vernon Lagoons. On its northern side was the Kōwhai pā of Rangitāne, taken by Te Rauparaha in about 1827.

joined those defending the pā. A series of desperate charges by the defenders were cut down by the power of the taua's massed muskets, and when the taua assaulted the pā its defences were broken down in places and it soon fell. Up to a thousand people were said to have been killed or captured in what was a massive loss for Te Atihaunui, although Te Pehi Turoa himself managed to escape and take refuge upriver. The taua then returned to the Horowhenua and Ōtaki areas.

This was the last time Ngāti Raukawa and Te Ātiawa were to be part of a coalition led by Te Rauparaha. However, Te Ātiawa won another victory either near the end of 1832 or in early 1833 at Te Puniunuku on the Heretaunga (Hutt) river, when Te Wharepouri (who led the Ngāmotu people in the huge 1832 heke) attacked Ngāti Kahungunu there. This defeat opened the Heretaunga valley for occupation by Te Ātiawa, in conjunction with their close relatives Ngāti Mutunga, who had pulled back there to avoid Ngāti Raukawa.

Another exhibition of the ruthlessness of the expanding coalition also occurred at about this time, in 1832, when Te Ātiawa under Tuainene invited many of the remaining southern Wairarapa Ngāti Kahungunu to a hākari at Waikanae. As was not uncommon in Māori customary warfare, the guests were set upon and dozens were killed. The cumulative effects of this massacre and the Ngāti Kahungunu defeats at Pehikatea and Te Puniunuku led Tutepakihirangi, in about 1833, to persuade the Wairarapa Ngāti Kahungunu to seek refuge at Mahia Peninsula with Te Pareihe and Te Wera. As a consequence, within a short time the southern Wairarapa lay deserted and open for occupation.

In retrospect, 1832 was the pinnacle of success for Te Rauparaha's coalition. They had a secure base at Kāpiti with access to Pākehā trade and thus muskets, and all opposing iwi to north, south and east had been defeated. Moreover, Te Rauparaha's coalition now controlled Te Tau Ihu, with its major food resources, and northern Te Tai Poutini, with its valued pounamu resources. Within a few years, however, pressures within the coalition in Horowhenua led to its disintegration into open warfare.

THE BREAK-UP OF TE RAUPARAHA'S COALITION

The arrival in Horowhenua of the three major Ngāti Raukawa heke by 1828, followed in 1832 by the Te Ātiawa- and Ngāti Tama-led Te Heke Tama te Uaua, marked the start of pressures for land and resources between the coalition iwi. These pressures grew until in 1834 they erupted in open warfare at Haowhenua, where fighting between Ngāti Raukawa and the combined north Taranaki iwi raged for about three months.

An uneasy truce followed, which saw Te Ātiawa predominantly withdraw into the Whanganui a Tara area, and again seek to expand into the now largely abandoned southern Wairarapa. From 1833 to 1835 the Ngāmotu Te Ātiawa under Te Wharepouri even occupied a pā further north called Tauwharerata, near modern-day Featherston. In 1835, however, Nukupewapewa of Ngāti Kahungunu led a taua back from Mahia Peninsula and surprised Te Ātiawa in a sudden dawn attack, taking Tauwharerata. Te Wharepouri escaped, and with other survivors of the attack first sought safety at Porirua, then moved south to Whanganui a Tara. Among the many who were captured, however, were some important women from Te Wharepouri's close whānau.

In 1835, other opponents of Ngāti Raukawa such as Ngāti

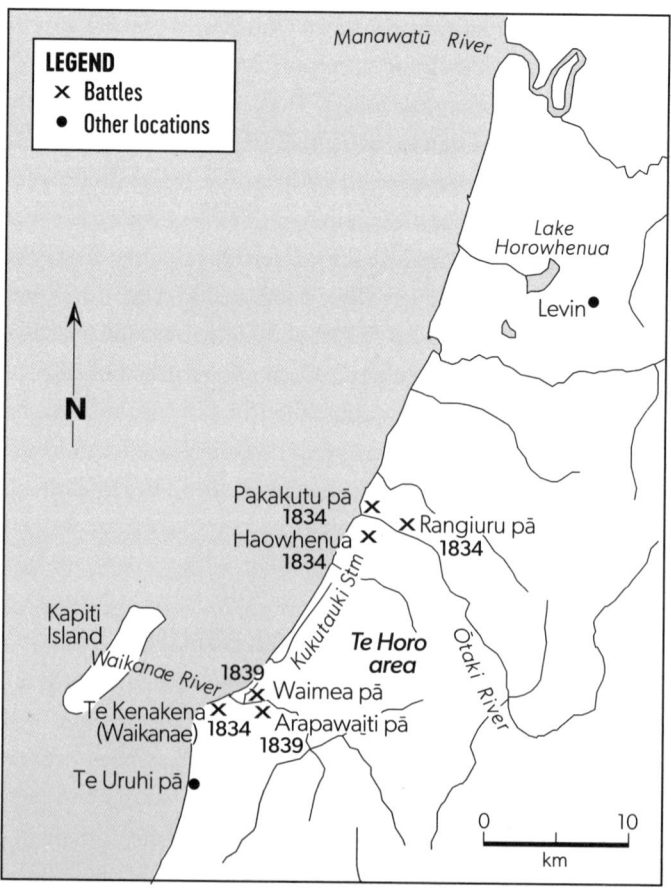

Haowhenua battles 1834, and Te Kuititanga 1839.

> **The women from Te Wharepouri's whānau**
>
> The women from Te Wharepouri's whānau who had been captured at Tauwharerata were released several years later, in about 1840. They formed a major bargaining point for Ngāti Kahungunu, who handed them over in return for solemn customary promises by Te Ātiawa to forgo any claims on the Wairarapa.

Mutunga and Ngāti Tama took the major decision to avoid the threat of further conflict by engaging a Pākehā sailing vessel to take them to Rēkohu/Wharekauri, the Chatham Islands. As they left, Ngāti Mutunga formally handed over their land rights in the Heretaunga valley to Te Wharepouri.

For similar reasons, at around the same time Te Puoho took his people south to Mohua in Te Tau Ihu. Even there, however, he was to find that the best locations had been taken by coalition allies who had settled there earlier. He then decided to embark on the longest overland taua since Te Amiowhenua in 1821. In an absolutely incredible journey that began in 1836 and continued into the following year, Te Puoho led about seventy of his people all the way down Te Tai Poutini, crossing countless major rivers to do so, then traversed Haast Pass and continued through the Otago lakes area and on deep into Murihiku. He was finally killed at Tuturau, just south of Gore, with a few others of his people, while the survivors from the taua were surrounded and captured, with only one escaping.

This taua and its immediate aftermath are also discussed in detail in the following chapter. One consequence of these events, however, was Te Rauparaha's decision early in 1838 to lead a taua south to obtain utu against Kāi Tahu for the loss of Te Puoho the previous year. He arrived at Kapara Te Hau (Lake Grassmere) with his Ngāti Toa taua, the intention being to link up there with a taua of local Te Ātiawa led by Taraua from Tōtaranui, despite the tensions in Horowhenua between Te Rauparaha's people and Te Ātiawa. However, when Te Rauparaha arrived at Kapara Te Hau he found Te Ātiawa had been eating pūhā taken from the area where Ngāti Toa had been killed and eaten by Kāi Tahu on Taua-iti in 1833. To Te Rauparaha, the eating of food taken from such a tapu site was anathema in customary terms, and it demanded some form of utu. The fact that this action had been taken by Te Ātiawa, with whom relations had been strained since the Haowhenua conflicts in 1834, added to his conviction that some degree of utu must be taken, regardless of his previous intention to join with Te Ātiawa on a taua. That night he and his men approached the Te Ātiawa camp and stripped the Te Ātiawa of their muskets and clothing, leaving them naked on the beach. Clearly, combining with Te Ātiawa on the intended raid had now become impossible, and Te Rauparaha returned north.

This was not the end of the matter, however. It was recorded by whalers that when Te Rauparaha's taua arrived at Te Awaiti, Taraua led an assault that lasted for four hours on the afternoon of 7 February 1838. Peace was finally made, but only after some deaths had occurred.

By 1838, then, Te Rauparaha's coalition was in tatters, and incapable of raising the large numbers on a taua that he had been able to assemble six years before. Furthermore, the removal of large elements of Te Ātiawa, Ngāti Mutunga and Ngāti Tama to Te Tau Ihu and Rēkohu/Wharekauri did not bring tensions to an end in the Ōtaki area. In 1839 open warfare once more broke out in the series of battles between Ngāti Raukawa and Te Ātiawa that became known as Te Kuititanga. These occurred among a number of pā right on the coast, and were observed by the New Zealand Company vessel *Tory* on 16 October. Some of the wounded were actually ferried out to the *Tory* to enable the ship's surgeon to attend to their wounds.

Significant numbers were killed on each side in that long day of fighting, during which Te Ātiawa gained the upper hand and captured 55 prisoners, who were taken back to Waikanae pā. There they were made to sit in a long line while they were harangued by Te Manutoheroa, who concluded his tirade with a pūkana (the grimacing that often accompanied waiata, whaikōrero or haka) before ruthlessly walking along the line killing each man with a blow of his patu. These events occurred just four months before the signing of the Treaty of Waitangi, and six months before over a thousand Europeans arrived and settled at Whanganui a Tara, just down the coast.

Meanwhile on Wharekauri, Ngāti Tama and Ngāti Mutunga fell out in 1839 when Ngāti Tama would not share the resources of Waitangi, which was the best harbour and the one that enabled trade with visiting European vessels.

Ngāti Tama had suffered considerable losses the previous year, including the death of their rangatira Ngatuna and the destruction of all their whare and seven waka when the French had bombarded Waitangi with cannon. This bombardment was to seek vengeance for the loss of the French vessel *Jean Bart* and its crew, which the French blamed on Ngāti Tama. Utu was not just a Māori concept! Ngāti Mutunga now took advantage of Ngāti Tama's loss of mana to demand shared rights in respect of European trading vessels, but Ngāti Tama refused.

By the time the New Zealand Company vessel *Cuba* called in at Waitangi in late May 1840, a full-scale conflict over the issue of control at Waitangi was under way. Each side was occupying a palisaded pā by the Waitangi River, and attempting to build pūwhara (towers) higher than their opponent's so that they could fire down into the other's pā. The New Zealand Company took advantage of the situation by negotiating a truce that enabled them to take Ngāti Tama on board the *Cuba* and transport them to the northeast to live with their relatives, after which the company negotiated purchases of land from both iwi. These actions seem to have eased the tension and resulted in an end to the fighting.

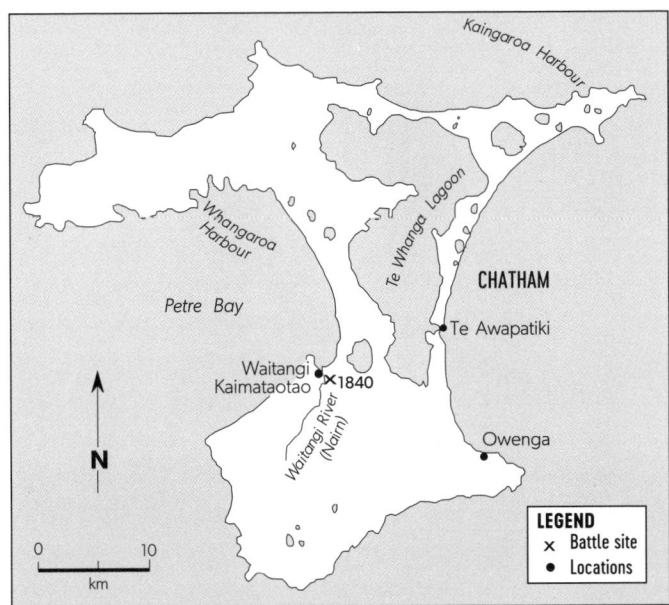

Principal sites on Wharekauri, 1835–40.

THE EFFECT OF THE EVENTS OF 1834–39 ON TE RAUPARAHA AND HIS CONTINUING MANA

Despite the dispersion of the loose coalition of iwi that had comprised his original heke and later taua, Te Rauparaha retained great mana. Among some, such as the north Taranaki iwi who occupied Whanganui a Tara and parts of Te Tau Ihu, this may have been grudgingly accepted, but in other parts of Te Tau Ihu, Ngāti Rārua and Ngāti Kōata were of Tainui descent and remained closely aligned with Ngāti Toa. In Horowhenua, Ngāti Raukawa also acknowledged his mana with warm support.

It is a mark of the significance of his mana in Te Tau Ihu that when it came to the Wairau, no one in Māoridom challenged Te Rauparaha's customary right to assert his mana against European intrusion in 1843. His stand then in defence of his and Ngāti Toa rights in respect of their lands, by destroying surveyors' huts erected without his permission, led to his attempted arrest by Pākehā officials in breach of the Treaty. What is now known as the Wairau Incident developed as shooting broke out and a number of deaths occurred.

But those events belong to the wars sparked by European actions, which would blight Aotearoa over the next 30 years.

Kaimataotao pa. The Ngāti Tama pa of Kaimataotao was located on the Waitangi River at Wharekauri (Chatham Island). The pa facing it was constructed by Ngāti Mutunga in 1839 to enable musket fire to be directed down into Kaimataotao. The elaborate works built to protect people from both pa while gathering water are clearly visible.
Charles Heaphy, 1840; Auckland War Memorial Museum/Te Papa Whakahitu, Auckland

7

IMPACTS OF THE MUSKET ON KĀI TAHU AND MORIORI

Kāi Tahu obtained their first muskets prior to 1825 by trading with vessels that were dropping off and picking up gangs of sealers in the Fiordland and Foveaux Strait areas. Kāi Tahu's main defended areas in this region were on Ruapuke Island, in the eastern approaches of the strait. In those early years very few weapons seem to have been obtained, and none had been seen north of Ōtākou. Few European vessels sought refuge or supplies in those colder, more stormy climes. Even the sealing industry did not last in the way the whaling industry did further north, and it never brought as many vessels.

The first whaling stations in the north of Te Waipounamu opened in Marlborough from 1828, and by that time Te Rauparaha's coalition was in control of those areas. At much the same time a shore whaling station opened at Rakituma (Preservation Inlet) in southern Fiordland, but as there was no local Māori population it had to be self-supporting, and it was a perilous place for waka to visit. Nonetheless, its establishment provided a large supply of muskets for Kāi Tahu in the south. The Rakituma station was established in 1829 by Captain Peter Williams, and enabled by a purchase transaction with Te Whakataupuka of Kāi Tahu, who received 60 muskets, 1000 lb of gunpowder and 1000 musket balls.

The more accessible southerly whaling stations in Kāi Tahu areas of settlement were the Weller brothers' station at Ōtākou and George Hempleman's station at Peraki on Akaroa Peninsula, but they were not established until about 1833 and 1835 respectively. There was a proliferation of whaling stations all around the coast of Aotearoa from about 1838, but by then muskets were more widely distributed and the stations' influence on the Musket Wars was negligible.

FIRST USE OF MUSKETS

The first recorded use of muskets in customary warfare in the southern half of Te Waipounamu was a series of inter-hapū clashes from about 1825 to 1828. These clashes have come to be called the Kai Huanga or Kaihuanga ('Eating of Relatives'). The fighting first broke out because a woman at Waihora (Lake Ellesmere) had worn Te Maiharanui's cloak in his absence. The clothing of a man of Te Maiharanui's exalted status was tapu, so this was regarded as a serious breach of tikanga.

Since at that time only customary Māori weapons were used in this area, when Te Maiharanui attacked the woman's pā at Taumutu, at the southern end of the lake, casualties were restricted and the pā did not fall. However, one of the women at Taumutu was related to the Murihiku (Southland) rangatira Te Whakataupuka, and she had a message sent seeking his assistance. In 1825 a limited taua of her southern relatives arrived and attacked Wairewa pā, at the northern end of Lake Wairewa (Lake Forsyth), to obtain utu for the Taumutu attack. The taua is said to have had two muskets, and these were the first to be fired in warfare in the area.

Travelling with this southern taua was Taiaroa, who had relatives in both the Takapuneke area and Akaroa Harbour, and in Ōtākou where he now lived. He went ahead and forewarned the occupants of Wairewa pā of the impending attack, and most were able to escape by waka onto the lake as the taua came in overland. Some people were killed, but the taua returned home without being satisfied that they had achieved the required utu, and Te Whakataupuka determined to return the following year with more muskets.

One of those who was shot at Wairewa happened to be a relative of Taununu, the rangatira at the Ripapa Island pā in Whakaraupō (Lyttelton Harbour). That provided a direct cause for Taununu to seek utu, which he did by attacking the inland pā of Whakaepa (at modern-day Coalgate), where the inhabitants were of the Kāi Tūāhuriri hapū of Kaiapoi, to whom Te Maiharanui was related. And so the utu wheel moved full circle, with Te Maiharanui now once again having cause to seek utu.

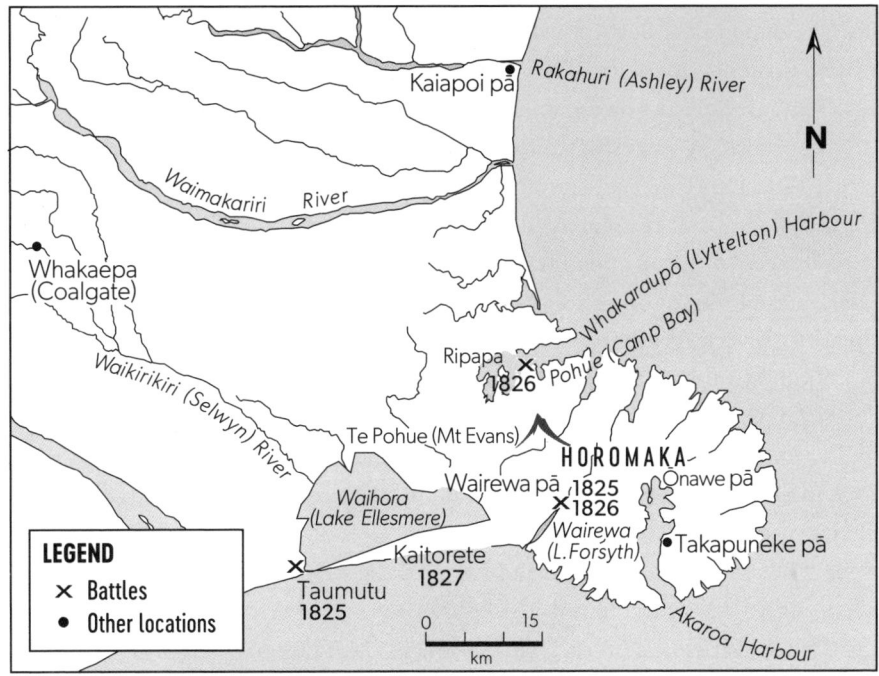

By 1826 Te Whakataupuka had assembled a taua in Murihiku armed with more than twenty muskets. As he headed north he again combined with Taiaroa, but this time he made plans to counter the likelihood that Taiaroa or one of his men might try to forewarn those in Wairewa pā: he would portage the short distance to launch his waka on the lake before the overland assault on the pā began. As he had anticipated, Taiaroa's men did indeed warn those in the pā of the impending attack, but this time when they launched their waka and headed offshore they encountered Te Whakataupuka's waka on the lake. Anyone who was trying to escape came under long-range musket fire from Te Whakataupuka's men, and it was the numbers killed here that gave rise to the name Kaihuanga.

Te Whakataupuka was still not satisfied, however, and the taua now paddled around to attack Taununu at his Ripapa Island pā. Taununu himself had left Ripapa when he heard accounts of the musket power of this taua, but many of his people were still in the pā. Once again Taiaroa and his men tried to forewarn those in the pā, but as they launched their waka in a desperate bid to escape they saw to their horror

Kaihuanga clashes between Kāi Tahu hapū, 1824–27.

Te Whakataupuka's fleet of waka surging out at a furious pace from the small neighbouring Pohue (Camp) Bay.

Te Whakataupuka had aligned his waka so that the 20 muskets were able to fire simultaneous broadsides at those trying to make their escape. The first volley created mayhem and panic, and each following volley added to the slaughter. Those who leapt or fell wounded into the water were killed there, and survivors onshore were pursued and killed. Their only respite came when Taiaroa and his Ōtākou men, seeing the extent of the slaughter, allowed many to escape past them to gain the heights above on Te Pohue (Mt Evans).

When the taua turned back south and the toa met with their relatives at Taumutu pā, such were the tales they told of the ruthlessness and extent of the killing that the people there abandoned their homes and travelled south to relatives in Ōtākou to avoid the almost certain retribution that Te Maiharanui and Taununu would be seeking.

In 1827 Te Maiharanui did indeed arrive at Ōtākou with a taua. However, he announced that he came with the intention of making peace and bringing the Kaihuanga feud to an end, and to return the Taumutu people to their pā to cement the peace-making. He and his taua stayed at Ōtākou for some time to

Taiaroa. The Kāi Tahu rangatira who figured prominently in the Kaihuanga feuds of 1826-27, at the siege of Kaiapoi pā in 1831-32, on the Taua-nui in 1834, and at the killing of Te Puoho at Tuturau in 1836.
PAColl-5800-29, Te Matenga Taiaroa. Alexander Turnbull Library, Wellington, NZ

> **Te Whakataupuka's taua**
>
> This taua of Te Whakataupuka's involved some of the most ruthless features of civil war. The sealer John Boultbee, who spoke with some of the victors soon after their return home, recorded that the musket balls were cut almost in pieces so that they split and caused more damage on impact. He was also told that after the attack at Ripapa groups of women and children were tied together and towed behind waka until they drowned.

ensure all were satisfied that his intentions really were peaceful, and since all there were related, their fears were slowly assuaged. By now the Taumutu people had obtained some muskets, as had their Kaiapoi visitors, so they also seemed to share equality in terms of arms.

So it was that the Taumutu people agreed to return north with Te Maiharanui and his men. All went well as they travelled together for some weeks on the very long, arduous journey to Lake Waihora, which included crossing many major rivers, until they finally reached Kaitorete Spit on the eastern side of the lake. Now, suddenly, Te Maiharanui's men attacked those of Taumutu, who were hindered in their defence by the presence of their women and children. A heavy massacre ensued as Te Maiharanui's men exacted their cruel revenge.

FACING THE STORM FROM THE NORTH

Had Te Rauparaha not launched his first invasions of Te Waipounamu, these events at Lake Waihora would almost certainly have escalated the internecine feud to an even more devastating level. But news soon arrived of the highly armed northern taua that was ravaging areas in Te Tau Ihu (the Top of the South). Thus, from 1828 the iwi of central and southern Te Waipounamu seem to have turned from internal fighting to preparing defences against a likely storm from the north.

Te Maiharanui himself would have been well aware of the

musket power Te Rauparaha's coalition could bring to bear. In 1828 he had happened to board the European vessel that was carrying the Ngāti Toa rangatira Te Pehi Kupe back to Kāpiti, and it is almost certain that Te Pehi Kupe would have told him of the huge supply of muskets he had acquired, and of the iwi that were forming Te Rauparaha's loose coalition. In addition, accounts would have come south of Te Rauparaha's devastating attack on Rangitāne in the Wairau in 1827–28, and Rerewaka's threat to rip open Te Rauparaha's belly with a niho mangā if he ventured south, filling all Kāi Tahu with anxiety.

The early taua led by Te Rauparaha to attack Kāi Tahu at Ōmihi and Kaiapoi in 1830, and the return taua that resulted in the sacking of Takapuneke later that year, and of Kaiapoi and Ōnawe in 1832, are described in chapter 6. However, after the very heavy losses suffered in those events the surviving Ōtākou and Murihiku hapū of Kāi Tahu combined to seek utu, sending north their own retaliatory taua. The first of these, which set out toward the end of 1832, was limited in size as Kāi Tahu sought intelligence on what might lie ahead, while at the same time taking utu in whatever form opened up for them. Because of its limited size, the name given by history to this taua was Taua-iti; it is believed to have comprised about 300 to 350 toa travelling in six or seven waka taua.

ACHIEVEMENTS AND CONSEQUENCES OF TAUA-ITI

By January 1833 Taua-iti, under the leadership of rangatira such as Karetai of Ōtākou and Tutehounuku, the son of Te Maiharanui, had arrived in Kaikōura. Although relatively small the taua was well armed, and on reaching Kaikōura the taua quickly despatched some Ngāti Toa who had been left there. Another clash with a small group of Ngāti Toa occurred further north, at the mouth of the Waiharakeke (Flaxbourne) Stream just south of Te Karaka (Cape Campbell). The taua then stayed there while an exploratory ope was sent ahead overland.

The reason for the exploratory ope was that the taua had learnt from some Ngāti Toa captives that Te Rauparaha had developed the habit of coming to Te Tau Ihu in late summer each year to trap pūtangitangi (paradise ducklings) in nets while they were moulting and unable to fly. It seemed he was expected at Kapara Te Hau (Lake Grassmere) any day.

When the ope crested the last of the low hills between Waiharakeke and Kapara Te Hau they saw in the distance four waka and one whaling rowboat approaching Te Paruparu, the outlet from the lake to the sea. Rushing forward, they hid themselves near the beach, behind the high coastal flaxes and scrub beside Te Paruparu.

Te Rauparaha's son Tamihana was a young boy at the time, but he was in the

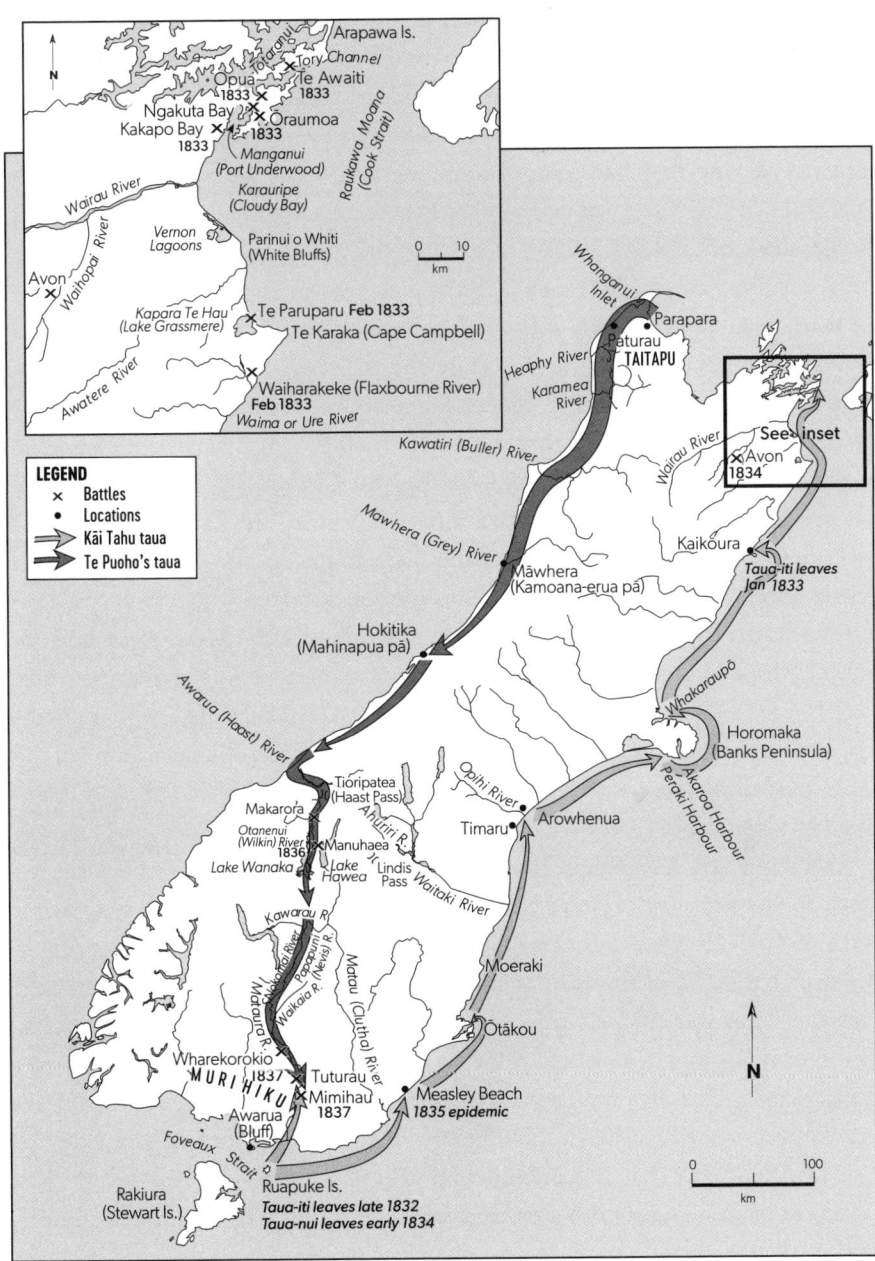

Taua-iti and Taua-nui, east coast of the South Island, 1832–34, and Te Puoho's taua down the West Coast, 1836–37.
INSET: *Taua-iti and Taua-nui engagements.*

rowboat. He has left a graphic account of what occurred as the waka and the rowboat approached the shore. The boat and two of the waka were rowed up onto the beach first, and dragged up beyond the breaking waves. But then, just as the second to last waka was approaching the beach, some Ngāti Toa shouted an alarm, saying they had noticed some excrement on the beach. At the same time some of the Ngāti Toa dogs on the beach started to bark, and just then Te Rauparaha himself saw the heads of some of the Kāi Tahu. He desperately yelled out a warning: 'He taua! He taua!' ('A war party! A war party!')

With that, the Kāi Tahu opened fire from their hiding places and rushed those on the shore. After the first close-range volley the surviving Ngāti Toa, including Te Rauparaha, raced to push the rowboat back into the sea, but as they frantically clambered aboard they realised to their horror that the oars were still on the beach. Jumping out of the boat, they tried to push it from underneath, but by then some Kāi Tahu were swarming out toward them and held the boat back. Te Rauparaha's cloak was seized, but he managed to slip out of it and swim desperately for his life until he reached the waka closest to shore. In all the confusion, Rawiri Puaha, who was in charge of the last offshore waka, was unsure whether those in the waka that was now being furiously paddled out toward him were Ngāti Toa or whether it contained Kāi Tahu. He held his fire, but stayed well clear until he could be certain of who was in the waka. Meanwhile, all of the Ngāti Toa left onshore, and the Rangitāne slaves who had been left there, were killed or taken captive.

Te Rauparaha now found that the strong nor'west wind was blowing his overloaded waka south toward Te Karaka Point, with Rawiri Puaha shadowing it at a distance. It was some time before he managed to persuade Puaha to come close so that some of the load could be transferred to his waka, and all that time the wind was intensifying. They momentarily discussed heading south, doubtless intending to seek help from the group of Ngāti Toa at the mouth of the Waiharakeke. That idea was soon abandoned, however, when they saw that they were being pursued by Kāi Tahu in the two waka that had made it to the beach. It seems likely, also, that Te Rauparaha must have suspected by now that the Kāi Tahu taua would have a waka fleet somewhere around Te Karaka. In fact, before leaving the beach at Kapara Te Hau the Kāi Tahu ope had sent word of their engagement at Te Paruparu back to Taua-iti, urging the fleet to come on.

In an amazing piece of luck for Ngāti Toa, the northwesterly wind at this stage abated before turning to the south, blowing their waka in a northerly direction. Te Rauparaha and Puaha took the opportunity to try to outrun their pursuers, and a long, grim pursuit now took place as the two pairs of waka vied with each other all the way north to Manganui (Port Underwood) through the rest of the afternoon and that night. To lighten his waka Te Rauparaha gave orders for any slaves to be thrown overboard. Finally, at Ngakuta Bay, at the head of Manganui, his men were able to leap ashore and they headed straight up the steep ridge. They traversed through the lowest saddle on the high ridgeline before descending to meet their Te Ātiawa allies in Opua Bay, which opens out onto Te Kura Te Au (Tory Channel). There they were able to borrow waka to take the news of the oncoming Kāi Tahu taua to Te Awaiti, from where waka were sent to seek support from other places in Tōtaranui, Te Hoiere (Pelorus Sound) and Rangitoto (D'Urville Island). A waka was also quickly sent to Kāpiti for help.

Meanwhile, the Kāi Tahu turned back down Manganui to attack the newly established whaling station of Jack Guard and his men at Kakapo Bay. Some of their Ngāti Toa wives were killed, their homes and whale-oil stores destroyed, and their gardens plundered. Kāi Tahu then moved out into Raukawa Moana (Cook Strait) and around to the north to camp at Ōraumoa (Fighting Bay), where they fortified a strongpoint to await developments. They did not have to wait for long. A huge fleet of waka led by Te Rangihaeata appeared one morning, with elements of Ngāti Toa, Ngāti Mutunga, Ngāti Rārua and Ngāti Raukawa from Kāpiti, who were joined by Ngāti Kōata from Rangitoto and Te Ātiawa from Tōtaranui. It must have been a frighteningly imposing sight. One of the Kāi Tahu later recorded that when he saw the northern fleet approaching Ōraumoa the numbers of waka seemed to cover the sea.

But for all its obvious numerical superiority and the apparent co-ordination that had resulted in such a huge taua being assembled so quickly — part of it even having to cross Raukawa Moana — the lack of close practical command and control of tactical planning in such coalition taua now proved its undoing. The unfolding events would demonstrate just how loose was Te Ruaparaha's control of his coalition forces, as each iwi or hapū tended to follow their own leader.

The northerners were soon to find that the Kāi Tahu's fortified position was well protected on the landward side by extremely steep ridges and heavy bush cover, which made it very difficult indeed to attack from the land. As dawn broke on the first morning after the taua's arrival, a Ngāti Mutunga ope decided to show up the rest of the taua and launched an unsupported assault. The result was disastrous, as they were mostly shot down without any noticeable effect on Kāi Tahu.

Skirmishing and a range of attempted assaults followed all that day. There were long, heavy exchanges of fire, during which the Ōtākou rangatira Karetai lost an eye, but despite both sides suffering losses the northerners made no progress. By nightfall, however, Kāi Tahu realised that they had used most of their powder and ammunition, and during the night they surreptitiously launched their waka and headed south. Unfortunately, much further south, as they rounded Te Karaka Point, the waka of Tutehounuku was upset in the very choppy conditions commonly experienced there and he and many of his crew were drowned.

Apart from the serious loss of Tutehounuku and of Karetai's eye, the achievements of Taua-iti had massively rejuvenated Kāi Tahu mana and confidence. They had succeeded in re-establishing Kāi Tahu fires north of Horomaka (Akaroa Peninsula), very nearly capturing Te Rauparaha, and rebuffing the attacks of his huge taua at Ōraumoa over a long day of fighting. The length of Taua-iti, and the courage and hardihood of its kauhoe (paddlers), was staggering. As Tutehounuku had found to his cost, the dangers of waka travel on such a huge, exposed coast demanded extraordinary levels of skill, courage and endurance. Yet, notwithstanding those challenges, and the dangers of a numerically stronger enemy, immediately on the return of Taua-iti plans were afoot for another, larger Kāi Tahu taua the following year to attack the northerners in Te Tau Ihu.

LIMITED SUCCESS FOR TAUA-NUI

Equipped now with knowledge of the geography, hardships and nautical risks that would face any new taua, and knowing the numerical strength and the capabilities of their enemies, Kāi Tahu knew that planning for the larger taua had to be thorough. Te Whakataupuka and Tuhawaiki in Murihiku led the process as the taua was gathered from across their region and headed north, to be joined by Taiaroa and Karetai at Ōtākou. By February 1834 it had left Horomaka after being joined there by more recruits determined to obtain utu for their losses at Takapuneke, Kaiapoi and Ōnawe. By now the taua comprised some seven hundred well-armed toa travelling in thirty large waka and rowboats. This time, most of the waka were lashed together as doubles to provide greater safety during their long and dangerous journey.

As they travelled along the Kaikōura coast they encountered some small parties of Ngāti Toa who were mostly pursued and killed, but they knew some would have escaped, and they could be sure that news of their progress was by now being taken north to Kāpiti. Yet surprisingly, they reached Karauripe (Cloudy Bay) and even Manganui without encountering any opposition. The whaling station at Kakapo Bay was again sacked, with the whalers fleeing to Kāpiti; the taua managed to kill a few Ngāti Toa employees and wives of the whalers, but otherwise encountered no significant numbers of northerners, even when they moved around to Te Kura Te Au. They settled down there for two months to await what they expected to be a massive retaliatory taua as had occurred the year before, but none eventuated.

This must have seemed a total mystery to Kāi Tahu, but they were not to know of the serious fighting that had broken out that year between Te Rauparaha's coalition allies at Haowhenua in Horowhenua. In disappointment, and facing the need to complete the long journey home before winter, most of the taua headed off south. However, a branch of the taua under Tuhawaiki and Taiaroa had heard of a refuge Rangitāne pā well up the Waihopai River, at the beginning of the Avon Valley, and they headed inland to attack it. The take for the raid was the fact that many Rangitāne slaves had been involved in the killing of Kāi Tahu captives after the taking of Kaiapoi pā. The desire for utu was more than satisfied, as somewhere between fifty and a hundred Rangitāne are said to have been killed, and some twenty more taken as captives. Once again, Rangitāne had paid a heavy price for not having access to muskets.

As the members of Taua-nui headed home they had the small satisfaction of having once again asserted their mana

Parinui o Whiti

Over 150 years after these events, on the basis of the assertion of mana involved in these two taua, Kāi Tahu was able to claim that their northern takiwā boundary in Treaty settlement terms should be fixed as being at Parinui o Whiti, the white bluffs at the southern edge of the Wairau Valley. Their claims were challenged during long-running litigation, including in the Waitangi Tribunal, and even the Privy Council, by northern iwi who formed Te Rauparaha's coalition and the original Kurahaupō iwi. Such litigation is a classic illustration of the on-going modern impacts of the Musket Wars era.

north of Kaikōura, but also a deep sense of frustration at not having encountered Te Rauparaha.

This sense of frustration was reflected in a continued desire by southern Kāi Tahu to send taua north. Before doing so, however, Te Whakataupuka sent messages north from Ruapuke to Kāpiti proposing to Te Rauparaha that they meet to settle terms of peace. The offer was high-handedly rejected, with Te Rauparaha responding that when he came south to Ruapuke it would be at the head of a taua, and that Te Whakataupuka would only be spared if he acknowledged Te Rauparaha's authority.

Te Whakataupuka and Kāi Tahu had no intention of acknowledging the authority of anyone else in Te Waipounamu, and so in 1835 they once again put a major effort into co-ordinating a number of taua from their various hapū. As it had been the previous year, the plan was to combine in a huge taua, finally assembling at Horomaka to head north. But now another European influence was to have a devastating effect on Kāi Tahu.

Karetai had been on a visit to Sydney, together with his wife and some other Ōtākou rangatira, and while there, or on the way home, they had contracted measles. A vessel had returned them home to Ruapuke just before the Murihiku taua set off north. By the time the taua reached the mouth of the Tokomairiro River, just over halfway from Ruapuke to Otago Harbour, the whole taua was so badly affected by this new illness, against which they had no immunity, that they had to stop and make camp. Many died at this camp, at what is now called Measley Beach, among them Te Whakataupuka himself. In fact, so many died that the decision was made to abandon the Murihiku contingent of the taua because of a lack of manpower to paddle the waka and boats.

Notwithstanding news of this terrible blow, a taua still assembled at Ōtākou, and at Arowhenua, near Temuka, it combined with other hapū contingents and continued north, heading for Horomaka. However, fate was very cruel to these combined contingents of the taua. As they reached Kaitorete Spit, by Lake Waihora, a severe southerly storm wrecked a number of their craft, and they too, as well as the Horomaka contingent awaiting them, decided to abandon the taua entirely that year.

KĀI TAHU REACTION TO TE PUOHO'S 1836 TAUA

There was to be no opportunity to mount another taua north the following year, however, as news started to filter through of a northern taua coming overland from Te Tai Poutini. This was the small taua of about seventy people led by the extraordinarily determined Te Puoho of Ngāti Tama, who travelled all the way down Te Tai Poutini, over Haast Pass and into the Otago lakes area, where he first started to encounter and capture small groups of Kāi Tahu who were gathering eels there.

One of the first of these contacts did not go well for Te Puoho. At Makarora, north of Lake Wanaka, a group of some ten Kāi Tahu were captured and two of their young children were killed, committed to the umu and eaten before their parents' eyes. One of the other youths who had been captured, Pukuharuru, was visiting this kāika (camp) from his own parents' camp at Lake Hawea, several days' journey away. He was sent with two guards to bring in his father, Te Raki, and the rest of his whānau. It was a fatal error. During the journey, Pukuharuru woke one night and managed to escape from his captors and reach his father. Together Te Raki and his son then killed the two Ngāti Tama guards, hurling rocks onto them in a very narrow gorge where they could not escape and could not respond in time with their muskets. The whole whānau then headed off with another that was camped nearby, making their way down the Ahuriri River and then down the Waitaki valley to the east coast near Ōtākou. In that way the news was conveyed to Ōtākou and Murihiku that a taua was on its way overland, apparently heading for Ruapuke.

Kāi Tahu had only just begun preparations to gather a taua at Ruapuke to meet this threat when news arrived at the mouth of the Mataura River that the northern taua had arrived at Tuturau, about twenty kilometres south of Gore. The manner in which the news arrived was another example of the great courage of some Kāi Tahu prisoners. This time two men and their wives had been captured by a small scouting party of five toa from the taua near the Mimihau Stream, just downstream from the junction of the Mataura and Waikaia rivers. By this stage it was January 1837 and the members of the taua were absolutely on their last legs, exhausted and starving after the long, arduous crossing of the barren central Otago tussocklands. It may have been because of their weakness from hunger that a lax approach was taken to guarding the two captive men, Kukeke and Maruroa.

Each of the Kāi Tahu men surreptitiously armed himself with a mere, and at an opportune time they attacked the four men who were loosely guarding them inside a wharau (temporary shelter), the fifth toa being outside. Three of the men inside were killed, and the two survivors fled. The Kāi Tahu whānau used some mōkihi (flax-stalk rafts) to descend well down the Mataura before heading overland some 10 to 15 kilometres to Tiwai Point, opposite modern-day Bluff. From Tiwai Point the group signalled across to the new whaling station that had just been set up by the Pākehā William Stirling.

Fortuitously, Tuhawaiki and Taiaroa happened to be visiting the whaling station, and thus learnt of the presence of the threatening taua less than 40 kilometres away. Tuhawaiki set off for Ruapuke as messages went out to surrounding kāika for a taua to assemble there urgently. At the time, most Kāi Tahu people were spread out on eeling and fishing trips in inland areas, and after two days Tuhawaiki had only 60 toa available. Nevertheless, he knew he had to act speedily, so with the help of a rowboat manned by another Pākehā named Bill Thomas, he and his men travelled by sea to Toetoe Bay at the mouth of the Mataura.

Meanwhile, despite receiving news of the escape of the Kāi Tahu captives, Te Puoho took no steps to fortify the captured kāika at Tuturau. And so on the third night after the escape, his taua was surprised at dawn by a heavily armed Kāi Tahu ope led by Tuhawaiki and Taiaroa, who were themselves amazed to find the kāika unguarded. Te Puoho was one of the few who were killed in the dawn attack, being shot by 17-year-old Topi Patuki, while the rest of the taua were captured. Only one man, Ngawhakawa, managed the almost incredible feat of getting all the way back to Parapara in Mohua (Golden Bay), carrying news of the fate of the taua to Te Puoho's widow Kauhoe.

On the way, Ngawhakawa stopped in at the pā at Māwhera (Greymouth), which was occupied by Ngāti Rārua under Niho, and informed them of the defeat of Ngāti Tama. This loss, and the sense of being cut off a very long way from support, led Niho and Takarei to make the decision to abandon the two pā at Hokitika and Māwhera. Their withdrawal left the Kāi Tahu rangatira Tuhuru of Te Tai Poutini and his people once more in control of their own takiwā (district) and its valued pounamu.

THE END OF THE MUSKET WARS FOR KĀI TAHU

In December 1837 a small Kāi Tahu taua set out in five whaling boats from Ōtākou, determined to once again seek utu in Te Tau Ihu. They were recorded as reaching the Peraki whaling station at Horomaka on 9 January 1838. While there they heard of the imminent arrival of Te Rauparaha's taua, which had left Kāpiti near the end of 1837 to link with Te Ātiawa of Tōtaranui as described in chapter 6. The Kāi Tahu taua was too small to contemplate a clash with that of Te Rauparaha, and by 12 February it had turned to carry this dreaded news back south.

Later in 1838, Te Rauparaha sent peace envoys to Kāi Tūāhuriri at Kaiapoi accompanied by three captive Kāi Tahu rangatira. This time the proposal was accepted, and by the end of the year peace had been agreed between Te Rauparaha and Kāi Tuahuriri — even though Murihiku and Ōtākou were still seeking utu, as was Te Rauparaha in return for the killing of Te Puoho.

In 1839 Murihiku Kāi Tahu heard of the killing of one of their people who was in captivity on Kāpiti, and that news sparked the gathering of yet another taua. By now Murihiku had more experience on whaleboats, which were recognised as being more seaworthy than waka, and faster through the water on the exposed eastern coast. For these reasons the taua that Tuhawaiki gathered at Ruapuke headed north in whaleboats. One of those on this final taua was Topi Patuki, who had shot Te Puoho some two years earlier.

At Ōtākou they were joined by another taua that had been assembled by Taiaroa and Karetai. The whaling log at Waikouaiti, north of Dunedin, recorded the passage of the combined taua on 17 September 1839. By the end of October the taua had reached Peraki pā and whaling station on the Horomaka peninsula, where Captain Hempleman employed two Ngāti Toa men as whalers. They happened to be on a small waka on Lake Forsyth at Wairewa when the taua arrived and both were seized, with one being killed and eaten. The Peraki whaling log records that the taua was travelling in 20 whaleboats, and as ransom for the surviving Ngāti Toa man it was now given a six-oared boat.

More Kāi Tahu men joined the taua, and on 4 November it left Peraki, heading toward Akaroa. And that was as far as it got. For when the taua reached Akaroa they heard that Ngāti Toa had sold most of the northern portion of Te Tau Ihu to the New Zealand Company. The payment for those lands was rumoured to include 250 muskets, and many kegs of gunpowder and ammunition.

For the Kāi Tahu on the taua this news was devastating. If correct, it meant that Te Rauparaha's military strength would be massively increased. Moreover, much of the land that had purportedly been sold was actually claimed by Kāi Tahu — certainly as far north as Parinui o Whiti at the southern edge of the Wairau. They realised they needed to try to have the sale to the Europeans set aside, but they could not travel through Whanganui a Tara or Kāpiti to do that without being attacked by Ngāti Toa. Their only real option lay in attempting to persuade the Governor of New South Wales in Sydney to intervene.

The taua immediately decided to return home to arrange passage for their rangatira to Sydney. By 2 December it was recorded as being in Ōtākou, and by 10 January 1840 Tuhawaiki, Karetai, Topi Patuki and several others were on a vessel en route to Sydney. Unfortunately the New South Wales Governor had no jurisdiction in New Zealand, and Kāi Tahu had to wait more than a century before they received some sort of justice in a Treaty settlement. While ten years of bitter, bloody warfare between Te Rauparaha's Ngāti Toa-led coalition of

> **Te Waipounamu**
>
> Kāi Tahu were to find to their cost that the signing of the Treaty of Waitangi did not assist them, as only a few years later the Crown embarked on a purposeful process of acquiring Te Waipounamu from Māori. This was almost entirely achieved by about 1859 in a series of transactions using methods that the Waitangi Tribunal found in the Kāi Tahu and Te Tau Ihu reports over 150 years later were in gross breach of the Crown's Treaty obligations to protect Māori interests in land.

iwi and the various hapū of Kāi Tahu had come to a peaceful conclusion, it was as a result of a very doubtful commercial transaction that interfered with and largely ignored customary Māori practices in relation to land.

THE EFFECTS ON MORIORI OF RĒKOHU/WHAREKAURI WHEN THE NORTHERN HEKE ARRIVED

In November 1835, Pomare of Ngāti Mutunga seems to have played the principal role in negotiating with Captain Harwood of the *Lord Rodney* to take Ngāti Mutunga and Ngāti Tama on two voyages to Rēkohu/Wharekauri (the Chatham Islands). The hope of these two iwi was to avoid ongoing exposure to warfare with Ngāti Raukawa and their allies, from whom they felt continuing pressure on the mainland.

Some of their men had crewed on ships that had called at Rēkohu, and what they had heard of the resources available made it sound an ideal location in which to live in security. That was particularly so because the Moriori occupants had been described as peace-loving and non-aggressive — the opposite of how these two iwi regarded Ngāti Raukawa.

Ngāti Tama arrived on the first voyage and settled at Kaingaroa and Waitangi, while Ngāti Mutunga settled at Whangaroa Harbour in the north. The arrival of experienced, warlike toa among a people who had foresworn war, and who did not even have customary Māori weapons, let alone experience in their use, was a recipe for disaster — and so it proved in the events that followed.

The killings of Moriori started in the Waitangi area during the takahi process, in which Ngāti Tama and Ngāti Mutunga walked the new lands they had invaded. The killing and enslavement of Moriori was particularly severe early on, with about three hundred estimated as being killed during the takahi process, but it continued intermittently until all the Moriori survivors of the various takahi had been captured and enslaved. Conditions were extremely harsh for the survivors, who were forbidden to use their own language, forced to work endlessly in labouring roles, and compelled to live on inadequate food in poor accommodation. This state of slavery continued well after the implementation of the Treaty, and long after slavery had completely ceased on the mainland. Slavery of Moriori on Rēkohu/Wharekauri did not finally end until the 1860s.

It has been estimated that the Moriori population numbered about 1660 at the time of the invasion in 1835, based on whakapapa analysis. It is a very grim statistic of the Musket Wars and their effects that by 1862, over the period of one generation, the Moriori population was recorded as being reduced to 101 survivors.

This was one of the most devastating impacts on population of the Musket Wars era, and occurred right at its conclusion.

8

EASTERN IWI RESPONSES TO MUSKET POWER

After the initial Ngāpuhi taua against Ngāti Porou and northern Ngāti Kahungunu (described in chapter 3), which ended when a major peace agreement was made with Pomare in 1823–24, Ngāti Porou enjoyed a welcome period of relief from attack. This came to an end when the killing of the Ngāti Awa rangatira Ngarara at Whakatane by the Ngāpuhi Te Hana was linked to Ngāti Porou as perceived allies of Ngāpuhi, leading to a taua being mounted against Ngāti Porou in 1829 by Ngāti Awa and its Whānau a Apanui and Whakatōhea allies. A series of reciprocal taua then continued until 1834, as each side sought in turn to attain utu. A major factor in the outcomes of these taua was the number of muskets possessed by Te Wera's Ngāpuhi.

The most significant event at the conclusion of the great Ngāpuhi raids had been the return of Te Wera Hauraki and a group of between fifty and seventy of his Ngāpuhi men to Mahia in 1823. They decided to remain on Mahia Peninsula, where they lived alongside Te Wera's brother-in-law Te Whareumu. For Ngāti Kahungunu, the protection provided by the Ngāpuhi muskets was desperately needed as they, and in some cases their northern neighbours of Rongowhakaata, Te Aitanga a Mahaki and Te Aitanga a Hauiti, came under recurrent pressure between 1824 and 1828 by various taua of northern inland iwi.

NGĀTI TŪWHARETOA TAUA AGAINST NGĀTI KAHUNGUNU

The background to the repeated taua to the area around Hawke Bay from 1824 to 1828 lay in conflicts at Lake Roto-a-Tara in 1820, before muskets had reached the central North Island and southern East Coast areas.

A large taua led by the physically imposing Ngāti Tūwharetoa rangatira Te Heuheu Mananui, and his brothers Iwikau and Manuhiri, had entered the Heretaunga Plains from the Ruahine Range to attack Ngāti Kahungunu at the island pā of Roto-a-Tara. There the taua divided, with Manuhiri taking a small ope to attack the coastal kāinga near Maungawharau pā at Waimarama. During that attack Manuhiri was killed.

When Te Heuheu Mananui heard news of Manuhiri's death he was distraught. The response of those in the pā was to mock Te Heuheu, who is said to have responded, 'Ko tēnei rangi anō tēnei!' ('This is but one day!') — words that contained an ominous promise. It was a promise that was to hang over Ngāti Kahungunu for the next four years, as Te Heuheu returned again and again to seek utu for the loss of his young brother.

The first of these taua, which arrived in 1822, not only created further causes for utu, but also had significant consequences in terms of leadership and future strategy for Ngāti Kahungunu. The rangatira who had occupied and fortified Roto-a-Tara against the promised return of Ngāti Tūwharetoa was Te Pareihe, from Ngāti Whatuiāpiti hapū. He led the defence of the pā so courageously and skilfully that it nearly succeeded in rebuffing Te Heuheu's very powerful taua, and his actions during the extended siege secured his reputation among Ngāti Kahungunu.

The siege became known as Te Kahupapa, the name coming from the causeway that Te Heuheu's men laboriously built over months of effort, driving felled trees into the lake bed in an X formation, with brushwood and dirt laid on top. To combat this, Te Pareihe built a tall pūwhara (a tower structure in the palisading) from which boulders were hurled down onto the causeway. One of these boulders killed Te Arawai, a son of the prominent Waikato rangatira Tukorehu. His killing meant that from then on Ngāti Tūwharetoa could expect Waikato support in all future taua against Ngāti Kahungunu.

Despite the efforts of the pā's defenders its fall was inevitable, and the siege ended when Te Pareihe led his people out one night by waka and headed south to the Porangahau area, east of modern-day Dannevirke. The Ngāti Tūwharetoa taua stayed, eating the bodies of their enemies that had been left behind, but the escape of Te Pareihe and most of his people left Te Heuheu unsatisfied.

The major consequence of this siege, however, was the conclusion Te Pareihe reached that Roto-a-Tara could not be held without muskets. He had had to

Te Aute Lake and Roto-a-Tara. A wood engraving made by Charles Barraud of the Hawke's Bay lake, before it was drained by Samuel Williams. The Roto-a-Tara island pā, subject of repeated sieges, was in the closest of these lakes.
PUBL-0016-23-1, Barraud, Charles Decimus, 1822–1897: Te Aute Lake, Hawke Bay. [Engraving, 1877]. Alexander Turnbull Library, Wellington, NZ

abandon the pā the previous year when besieged by Te Amiowhenua, who had some muskets, and now again when attacked by Te Heuheu. He knew that his people would be facing conflict not only from further Ngāti Tūwharetoa taua, but also likely from Ngāti Raukawa, under Te Whatanui, who were contemplating a move to Heretaunga to avoid pressures in Waikato. Te Paraihe believed that all Ngāti Kahungunu needed to combine at one defensible strongpoint like Mahia Peninsula, until they could themselves gain access to muskets.

For some time Te Pareihe faced considerable opposition to these ideas from the various Ngāti Kahungunu hapū in southern Hawke's Bay, which sometimes resulted in significant internal fighting. Te Pareihe could see what they could not — that the arrival of taua from numerous northern iwi armed with muskets would inevitably devastate Ngāti Kahungunu, unless they temporarily left their homelands in order to obtain a safe refuge.

NGĀTI KAHUNGUNU BEGIN TO CONGREGATE ON MAHIA PENINSULA

It was at this time that an extremely fortuitous event occurred that must have been beyond Te Pareihe's wildest dreams. For it was now that, completely out of the blue, Te Wera Hauraki of Ngāpuhi arrived at Mahia Peninsula with Te Whareumu and agreed to stay on with his men at Nukutaurua pā. It is believed that Te Wera's hapū had had a falling out with Hongi Hika's father Te Hotete, and the resultant tension made this alternative home a welcome temporary expedient. For Ngāti Kahungunu, the Ngāpuhi muskets, numbering between fifty and seventy, were literally life-savers.

Te Pareihe's belief in the need to be armed with muskets was reinforced during a confrontation that took place when he was moving north in 1824. Near Tikokino, northwest of Waipukurau, he saw in the distance a major taua emerging from the ranges and moving on towards Te Roto-a-Tara. His scouts ascertained that the taua was made up of Ngāti Tūwharetoa, Ngāti Te Upokoiri from inland Patea, and Ngāti Raukawa. Taking the taua by surprise, Te Pareihe attacked and defeated it at Te Whiti o Tu, in the headwaters of the Waipawa River. At this time, neither side yet had muskets, but Te Pareihe knew this defeat would spark another taua that was highly likely to be armed with the weapons — he knew that by now Waikato had muskets, and that the killing of Te Arawai provided an ongoing cause for utu for Tainui.

It was at that point that Te Pareihe received word that Te Wera and Te Whareumu were visiting Tānenuiarangi pā

Tānenuiarangi pā. The famous Ngāti Kahungunu pa on the banks of the Ngaruroro River, near Pakowhai in Hawke's Bay. It was here that Te Pareihe of Ngāti Kahungunu and Te Wera of Ngāpuhi formed their alliance before retiring to Nukutaurua pā, on Mahia Peninsula.
Henry Bates, 1859. Alexander Turnbull Library, Wellington, NZ

at the mouth of the Ngaruroro River, and he hastened there to meet them. Te Whareumu and Te Wera invited Te Pareihe and his people to move to Mahia, as they too could see that Ngāti Kahungunu needed to gather all their strength there to enable them to withstand the massive forces of inland iwi that were likely to return in the near future. Te Pareihe agreed, but said he would first try to persuade the Ngāti Hawea hapū around the Heretaunga area to accompany them to Mahia.

Te Pareihe's approach to the proud rangatira of those hapū fell on deaf ears. Senior rangatira such as Te Hauwaho, Te Hapuku, Te Moananui and Tiakitai felt secure in their strength of numbers and decided to stay at Te Pakeke pā, near modern-day Napier. So Te Pareihe moved off to Mahia, leaving a warning that they would be fuel for the fires he had lit at Te Whiti-o-Tu.

Within six months Te Pareihe's dire prediction proved correct. Later that same year a massive Ngāti Tūwharetoa and Waikato taua of over a thousand toa descended on Te Pakeke and sacked it — this time aided by muskets possessed by men under the Waikato rangatira Paewaka. A terrible revenge was taken for the losses inflicted at Te Whiti-o-Tu. Te Hauwaho was killed, and other prominent rangatira such as Te Hapuku, Tiakitai and Te Moananui were captured.

For some reason that is now obscure, Tiakitai was allowed to remain at Te Pakeke with a small group of survivors, and Te Hapuku managed to escape near the Titi o Kura saddle as the taua returned inland. Some time later, once again for reasons that are no longer known, Te Wherowhero sent a powerfully armed group back to invite Tiakitai to come to the Waikato to make peace, and to uplift the other captives held there. Tiakitai responded positively and peace was made. In another positive development for Ngāti Kahungunu, in addition to releasing the rangatira, Te Wherowhero sealed the peace agreement with the gift of a barrel of gunpowder and some muskets.

But at the same time as the sack of Te Pakeke in the south, another devastating blow was delivered in the north. This occurred when Titirangi pā, inland from Wairoa, was taken by a taua led by Te Mautaranui, of Ngāti Awa and Tūhoe, assisted by Pomare's musket power. This was sparked by Te Mautaranui's desire to obtain utu for the killing by Ngāti Kahungunu of a Tūhoe rangatira, Te Rangiwaitatao, in the upper Wairoa Valley, events described in detail in chapter 3.

The powerful taua operated in three separate pincers that converged on Titirangi. One of these comprised Tūhoe led by Te Mautaranui and Pomare, who emerged from the Urewera on the upper Ruakituri and attacked Te Papuni pā. They then clashed at Te Waireporepo with an ope of Ngāti Kahungunu led by Te Ua and Tuakiaki, where the former suffered a deep wound in the back following

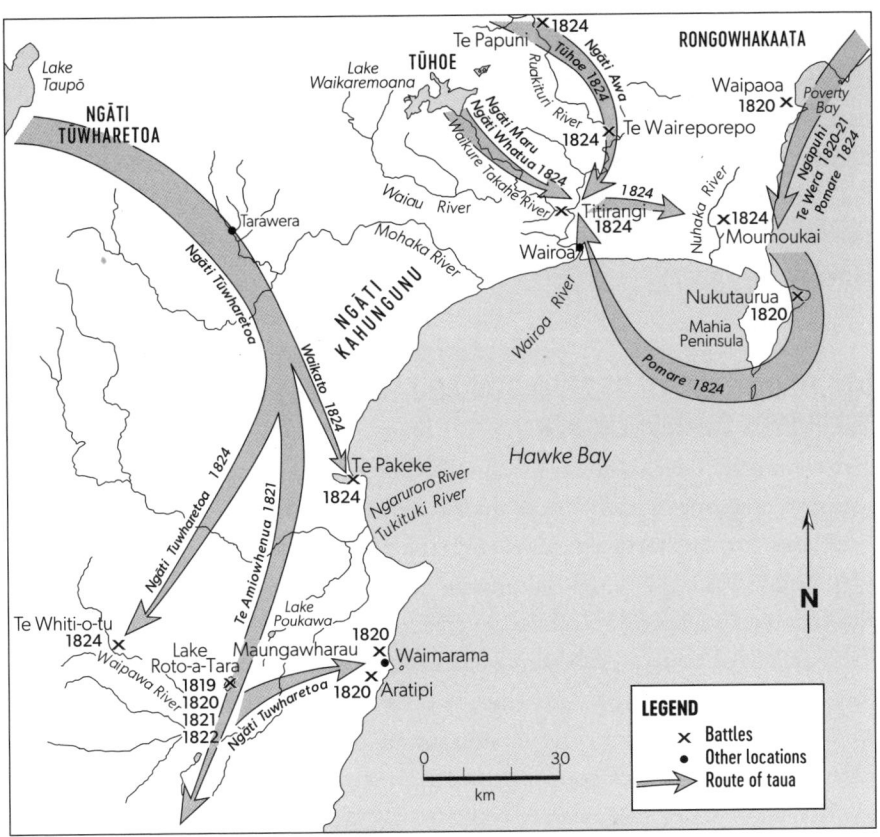

Hawke's Bay battle sites, 1819–24.

a blow from Te Mautaranui's pātītī (tomahawk). Another part of the taua comprised contingents of Ngāti Tamaterā, Ngāti Whātua, Te Arawa and Whakatōhea. The third pincer came from the balance of Pomare's Ngāpuhi, who travelled by waka and moved up the Wairoa to attack Titirangi. After the fall of Titirangi pā, they attacked a number of pā in the Wairoa and Nuhaka areas over several months, before Pomare returned to the north. By that stage the survivors of Titirangi and other pā had fled to Mahia, where they met up with Te Pareihe. Before long they had to endure another siege at Pukekaroro or Okurarenga pā on Mahia Peninsula where, significantly, they were saved by Te Wera's muskets.

The main consequence, then, of the devastating losses at Te Pakeke and Titirangi in 1824 was that Ngāti Kahungunu from all over their extensive rohe, north and south, decided to leave their homelands. The great majority headed for the refuge of Mahia Peninsula, with the aim of remaining there until sufficient stocks of muskets could be acquired to enable them to return with some confidence to their own homes. With the exception of only a few rangatira, such as Tuakiaki at Pohaturoa, on the Ruakituri, and Tiakitai at Heretaunga, most could now see that Mahia was their only safe refuge. And that refuge would be desperately needed when Te Whatanui of Ngāti Raukawa made his long-feared move into Hawke's Bay in 1826.

UTU FOR THE DEATH OF TE MAUTARANUI, AND INLAND IWI TURN THEIR EYES ON HERETAUNGA

Two significant developments for Ngāti Kahungunu were to occur in 1826, one in the north and one in the south of their rohe.

The one in the north was unusual in that it involved Te Wera joining Pomare in an attack on some Ngāti Kahungunu hapū in the Wairoa area. In this case, the taua was seeking to avenge the treacherous killing of Te Mautaranui by Tuakiaki of Pohaturoa. That killing had been intended to obtain utu for the conflict at Te Waireporepo in 1824, when Te Ua had been wounded in the back by Te Mautaranui, but it was the treacherous nature of the killing, and the fact that Te Mautaranui was on such good terms with Pomare, that caused problems.

Tuakiaki's sister had been married to Te Mautaranui a few years earlier, and when they had a child Te Mautaranui naively accepted an invitation from Tuakiaki to attend a celebratory hākari for the baby at Pohaturoa. When they were seated at the hākari, Te Mautaranui and his small group of men were suddenly set upon and killed; not only that, but parts of Te Mautaranui's body were subjected to degrading treatment and sent to other Ngāti Kahungunu hapū further south.

The reaction from both Tūhoe and Ngāti Awa was immediate. Messengers were sent out seeking assistance from the Ngāpuhi rangatira Pomare and from Tainui. Pomare quickly headed south with a taua, linking with Te Whatanui of Ngāti Raukawa on the way, and on arrival at Mahia joining up with his old comrade Te Wera.

Pohaturoa was an immensely strong pā, located at Te Reinga Falls by the junction of the Hangaroa and Ruakituri rivers inland of Wairoa, and it was secured on almost all sides by precipitous cliffs formed in ancient times by the river cutting into the papa rock. Despite this, however, the large numbers and massive firepower of the taua were always going to overwhelm Tuakiaki, who was without muskets. And so it proved, with Tuakiaki himself being killed by

Te Whatanui. Great slaughter is said to have accompanied the fall of this pā and later of Waihau pā on the Tiniroto lakes, where again a causeway was constructed to provide access to the island pā.

The event that took place in the south in 1826 set the scene for a major Ngāti Kahungunu taua the following year. The background to this lay in Te Whatanui's long-held intention of moving to Heretaunga, which Te Heuheu had continually urged him to do. That intention was somewhat undermined for a period after Te Whatanui accompanied Te Ahukaramu in 1825 on the long journey from Maungatautari to Horowhenua. Once there Te Whatanui could see that Te Rauparaha's coalition was in a strong position after the great battle at Waiorua the previous year, and he and Te Ahukaramu were persuaded by Te Rauparaha to return with their people.

On his way back to his people in the Maungatautari area, however, Te Whatanui encountered many Ngāti Raukawa who had been living in west Taupō with their relative Te Momo, a rangatira of the Ngāti Te Kohera hapū of Ngāti Tūwharetoa. Te Momo was determined to lead a heke to take possession of the Heretaunga area, and invited Te Whatanui — with his muskets — to accompany him there instead of returning to Horowhenua. Before Te Whatanui had made a final decision, Te Momo proceeded with his long-planned heke to occupy the abandoned island pā of Roto-a-Tara, accompanied by those Ngāti Raukawa who were living with his Ngāti Te Kohera people. Te Momo himself occupied Kahotea pā at the lake's edge.

Te Pareihe soon heard of the occupation of these pā through Tiakitai's scouts still based at Te Pakeke. He and Te Wera led a taua from Mahia to link with Tiakitai at Te Pakeke, from where the assault was launched. The pā at Kahotea soon fell and Te Momo was killed as he returned from a fishing trip. Initially, however, the taua was unable to attack the island pā of Roto-a-Tara, as it lacked waka, so it returned to Te Pakeke and Mahia with only half its aims achieved. But it did not take long for the new occupants of Roto-a-Tara to start raiding gardens around Te Pakeke pā, and then the inevitable happened after they killed some of the pā's women as they worked in the gardens. Te Pareihe reassembled his taua with Te Wera and Tiakitai, and devised an ambitious plan to take waka up the Tukituki River for 30 or 40 kilometres to the Papanui Stream near Patangata. Then, using the waters of the stream for part of the way, they proposed to portage two waka about eight kilometres to the lake. It was a boldly conceived plan, and it required massive determination to get their huge waka up the braided river, and then to drag them over the long portage to the lake. But their totally unexpected arrival there effectively sealed the fate of the pā.

Even so, it was two months before the siege came to an end. Finally, the starving occupants were overwhelmed in a dawn assault after a group of their attackers had been landed very quietly among the raupō by the palisading during the night. Some Ngāti Raukawa escaped when the pā fell, but the remainder were killed or taken captive, a number of the latter being taken all the way back to Northland by Ngāpuhi with Te Wera.

Some of Te Momo's bones were gifted by Ngāti Kahungunu to one of their hapū rangatira called Wakauna, whose pā was situated well inland at Tarawera, on the route to Taupō. He fashioned them into spear points as a way of denigrating Te Momo's mana. This story got back to Te Kohika of Ngāti Tūwharetoa, who was based at Titiraupenga, a pā northwest of Taupō, and with Waikato assistance he led a powerful taua

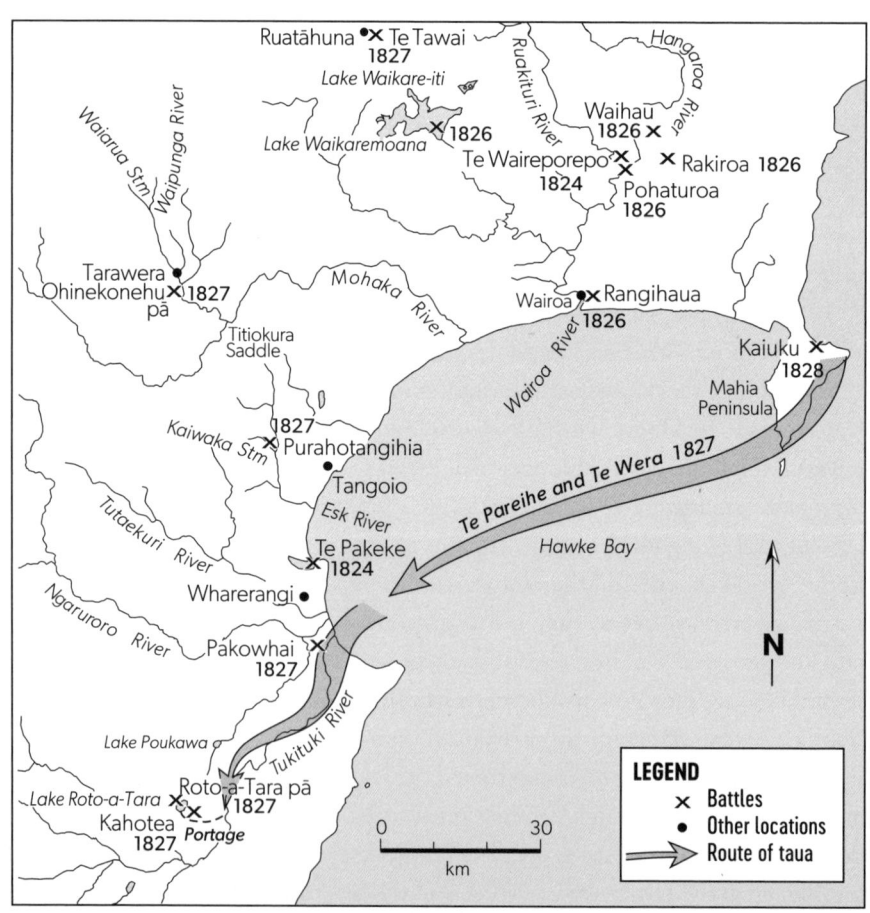

Battle sites involving Ngāti Kahungunu, 1826–28.

> **Renata Kawepō**
>
> Among those captured at Roto-a-Tara in 1827 and taken up to Northland was a young, high-ranking Ngāti Te Upokoiri man called Renata Kawepō. In later years he was released and became a prominent Ngāti Kahungunu rangatira, leading his people against Te Kooti. He lost an eye at the battle of Te Porere in 1869, but later married the woman who had torn it out. She was the wife of a man he had killed during the attack.

to raid Tarawera. Wakauna and his son Nikora were captured when their pā, Ohinekonehu, fell, and Wakauna was killed on the way back to Taupō. Again somewhat inexplicably, given the killing of Wakauna, other captive rangatira and their families were released by Te Kohika some time after their arrival back at Titiraupenga.

Ngāti Kahungunu now lost no time in gathering their own taua to seek utu for Wakauna's killing. After travelling all the way to Taupō the taua attacked the imposing Pohaturoa pā atop a broad volcanic pipe near Atiamuri, but failed to take it. The taua then moved west to attack Titiraupenga, which did fall, with Te Kohika being killed. Ngāti Kahungunu had gained utu for the death of Wakauna in 1827, but all that did was create a further take, or cause for utu, which would be acted on by Te Heuheu the following year.

However, 1827 did at least see the end of a series of reciprocal taua between Ngāti Kahungunu and Tūhoe, which had begun earlier in the year after the Ngāti Kahungunu rangatira Tukitua had travelled into the Urewera with a small ope to seek to make peace. The reward for this courageous act was that he was killed by Ahoaho at Te Tawai pā at Ruatāhuna. In another act of aggression a small Tūhoe taua attempted to attack Purahotangihia pā, at the junction of the Kaiwaka Stream and the Waiohinanga (Esk) River, but it was cut off in a tight gully by Ngāti Kahungunu and two Tūhoe rangatira were killed. After this peace negotiations did begin, with agreement being reached and cemented by several arranged marriages.

NGĀTI KAHUNGUNU COME CLOSE TO DEFEAT IN THE KAIUKU SIEGE OF 1828

In 1828 Te Heuheu started gathering a Ngāti Tūwharetoa-led taua to avenge the killing of Te Momo at Roto-a-Tara and Te Kohika at Titiraupenga. The taua he assembled was massive, both in numbers and in firepower, because he knew it would have to face the muskets of Te Wera Hauraki's Ngāpuhi.

In fact, for Ngāti Kahungunu, Te Wera's presence was now probably as much a liability as an advantage, because it led their attackers to gather massive forces. In forming this taua, Te Heuheu not only approached all iwi who he knew had recent cause to seek utu against Ngāti Kahungunu, such as Ngāti Raukawa, but he also approached those who sought utu against any Ngāpuhi. Because of the presence of Te Wera, that list was not short. The loss of Te Arawai still rankled with Tainui, who also relished any chance to seek utu against Ngāpuhi because of their invasions of the Waikato, as did the Marutūahu iwi and the Bay of Plenty and Rotorua iwi. They all sent ope to join the taua, supplementing the major forces of Ngāti Tūwharetoa under Te Heuheu and Ngāti Raukawa under Te Whatanui.

The taua headed south to attack Okurarenga pā on the Mahia Peninsula, in what became one of the longest sieges of the Musket Wars. The lack of food was so severe after months of being under attack that some of the pā's occupants were forced to try to gain some sustenance by eating dissolved uku (clay) mixed with whatever seaweed, plant, animal or bird they could scavenge. As a consequence the siege earned the name Kaiuku — this being the taunt the besiegers flung at those inside. An attempt by Te Kani a Takirau of Rongowhakaata to break in with supplies for his distant relations was repelled by the taua, and Te Kani barely managed to escape with his life.

Then, just when it seemed the pā must fall, Te Heuheu decided that the Ngāti Tūwharetoa contingent would return home. Some Ngāti Tūwharetoa accounts say the decision was taken to ensure Te Heuheu's home rohe was not exposed to invasion for too long, with most of its toa being absent. It is likely, too, that the aggressors themselves were beginning to feel the consequences of such a lengthy siege, with diminishing food resources in the area outside the pā.

Just after the Ngāti Tūwharetoa withdrawal a Te Arawa rangatira, Te Amōhau, was killed in a skirmish with some of the defenders outside the pā, with his body being dragged inside. His father Te Mokonuiarangi called out seeking the return of his son's body, promising to leave the siege if that occurred. Te Pareihe lost no time in opening the gates so that the body of Te Amōhau could be uplifted, and with that, Te Arawa also withdrew. Waikato and the other iwi now decided they did not have sufficient forces to take the pā, and the siege was abandoned.

Once again, however, after some time the mindset of Ngāti Kahungunu

> **Thunder of Te Heuheu**
>
> On leaving Okurarenga, Te Heuheu is famously said to have called out to Te Pareihe not to follow him into Ngāti Tūwharetoa's rohe, warning him that he would 'leave the thunder of [his] footsteps in case he was to follow'. Te Pareihe's derisive response was that he would use that thunder to guide him as he avenged the siege.

changed from one of relief at their survival, to a burning desire for utu for the losses and the denigration of their mana. The thunder of Te Heuheu's footsteps would have to be followed as soon as enough muskets were acquired.

THE CONCLUSION OF THE LONG-RUNNING WARFARE BETWEEN NGĀTI KAHUNGUNU AND NGĀTI TŪWHARETOA

By 1830 Ngāti Kahungunu were trading vigorously with the American whalers who were starting to frequent their offshore waters, and they soon had enough muskets to largely arm a major taua in conjunction with Te Wera. The taua that set off inland to seek utu against Ngāti Tūwharetoa in their own rohe is said to have numbered over fifteen hundred toa.

Attaining such numbers was now possible as Ngāti Kahungunu at Mahia had also been augmented by Wairarapa hapū under Nukupewapewa and Tutepakihirangi. They had recently arrived after heading north to avoid attacks from Ngāti Tama and Ngāti Mutunga after the defeats they had inflicted at Te Tarata and Wharepapa at Lake Onoke in 1829. Moreover, most of the toa from these Wairarapa hapū now had muskets, having supplemented their previous supply with weapons taken during the capture of these two pā.

The taua made the long, hard journey to Taupō, after which it crossed the Waikato and then advanced on the pā at Omakukara; this was located on a high point immediately west of modern-day Ōruanui, which is about five kilometres northwest of Wairakei. The pā was principally occupied by Ngāti Raukawa who had escaped from Roto-a-Tara when it was taken by Te Pareihe and Te Wera in 1827, and Te Pareihe was keen to inflict utu upon them. More than three hundred people were said to have been killed when Omakukara fell.

From Omakukara the taua headed west for Tutakamoana pā, beside Tihoi. This was another naturally very strong pā, situated on a volcanic peak and protected by steep cliffs. Unable to overcome these natural defences, the taua travelled down the full length of the west coast of Lake Taupō, heading for Te Heuheu's own pā at Waihi at the southern end of the lake. Hearing of the approach of this huge taua, Te Heuheu told his people to take to their waka and head offshore to the refuge of his strongly fortified pā on Motutaiko Island. At this stage Te Rohu, one of Te Heuheu's daughters, asked to be given the opportunity to try to make a peace accord with Te Paraihe, and Te Heuheu consented.

With extraordinary courage, Te Rohu succeeded in persuading Te Pareihe to enter negotiations directly with Te Heuheu, and the two great leaders managed to reach a binding agreement. During the negotiations Te Heuheu stressed the fact that he was able to call on Waikato once more if a peace agreement was not concluded, emphasising the huge arsenal of muskets they would be able to bring south. Te Pareihe's recent memory of the Kaiuku siege helped persuade him of the sense of that argument and so, with a peace accord agreed, the taua turned for home.

One relatively small clash occurred later when Ngāti Te Kohera sent a limited taua to seek utu for the losses at Omakukara, raiding the pā at Maungaharuru in the Tarawera area, but that did not upset the peace that the principal rangatira had forged. And that overall peace was further cemented the following year when Te Rohu married Te Hapuku, thus finally bringing to a peaceful conclusion some ten years of fairly constant war between these two major iwi.

CONFLICT IS SPARKED BY AN UNPROVOKED ATTACK IN THE EASTERN BAY OF PLENTY

In 1829 the trading vessel *Haweis* anchored at Motuhora Island, which lies 7 or 8 kilometres offshore from Whakatane, from where the crew proposed to trade with the Ngāti Awa rangatira Ngarara and his people. A number of pigs were purchased, then taken by the captain and eight of his crew on the ship's boat to be prepared using the hot spring on the island. Four men, including the mate, Atkins, were left on board.

With the captain and most of the crew of the *Haweis* on the island, Ngarara

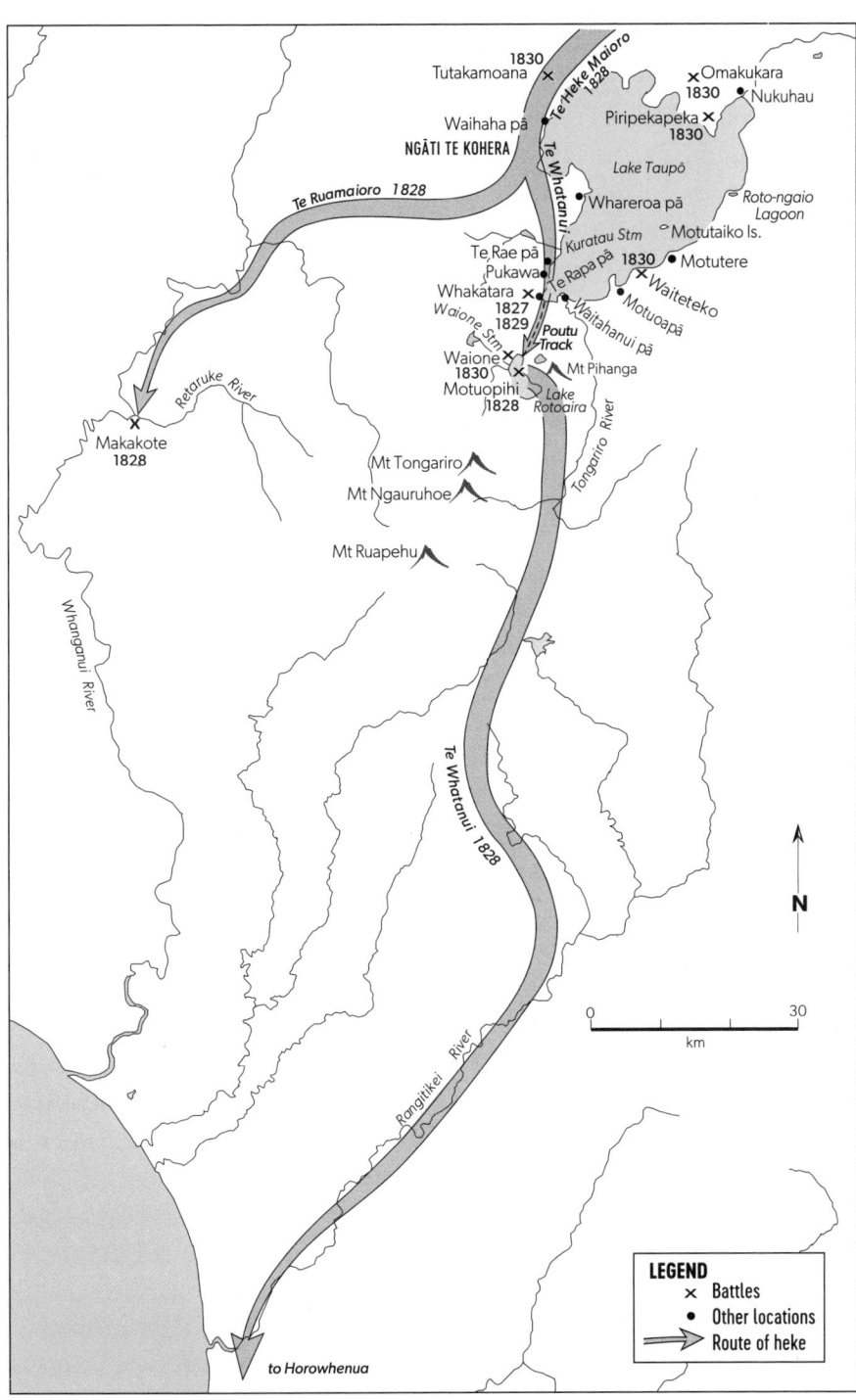

Location of Ngāti Tūwharetoa, Ngāti Maru and Ngāti Kahungunu clashes in the Taupō and Whanganui areas, 1827–30.

returned to the vessel and took the opportunity to take it over. During a short fight on board three of the crew members were killed and Atkins was badly wounded when Ngarara shot him in the arm, breaking it. Atkins was taken captive and after the ship had been stripped of anything of value, including a small cannon, Ngarara's waka headed ashore.

Hearing the shooting, the men on Motuhora headed out to sea in the ship's boat and were fortuitously picked up by a passing schooner, the *New Zealander*, the following day. When the schooner approached the *Haweis* they found the grisly aftermath of the attack, with portions of human flesh and remains of fires visible on board. Unaware of Atkins' survival, the schooner then headed for Tauranga to seek help. Meanwhile, Atkins had managed to persuade Ngarara that he could provide a valuable ransom if word of his capture was sent to Tauranga.

In response to the captain's appeal for assistance, a limited Ngāiterangi taua attacked Puketapu pā, above what is today the town of Whakatane. Thanks in part to the cannon that had been taken from the *Haweis*, the assault was rebuffed and a number of the attackers were captured. In addition to the physical trauma he had undergone, Atkins now had to watch as these men were killed and their bodies eviscerated, cooked and eaten. After some days, to his relief, a ransom of muskets arrived and Atkins was taken back overland to Tauranga. His experience has survived in a written account, and it reflects the common fate of those unfortunate enough to be taken captive during this era.

To many Māori the news of these events was unsettling, as they were heavily reliant on trade with European ships for muskets, powder and ball. Ngāpuhi rangatira, in particular, reacted strongly against Ngarara's actions. One graphic illustration of this occurred when Tamati Waka Nene happened to be peacefully visiting Tauranga. A Ngāpuhi man who was married to a Ngāiterangi woman had just returned to Tauranga from Whakatane, and he was known to have been with Ngarara during the attack on the *Haweis*. Waka Nene approached the man on the beach and berated him, saying that Ngāpuhi did not attack European vessels, then without warning shot him dead in front of his relatives.

Had matters rested there perhaps nothing more would have developed. However, the *New Zealander* carried news of the fate of the *Haweis* to Pēwhairangi, and Ngāpuhi there persuaded the captain to take a rangatira called Te Hana with him when he returned to Whakatane. When the *New Zealander* arrived at Whakatane, Ngarara called out to the schooner from his waka to trade. His trading was apparently successful, and Te Hana sat quietly on the side of the vessel, cradling his musket and smoking, while the trading was undertaken. When it was complete Ngarara was the last to descend the ladder back to his waka; as he did so, Te Hana suddenly took up his musket and shot him dead.

Ngarara had exalted status with Ngāti Awa and their close relatives in Whakatōhea and Whānau a Apanui. All three of these iwi had suffered severely from Ngāpuhi musket power in the past, for which they still desired utu, and these feelings were powerfully rekindled by the purposeful execution of Ngarara by the Ngāpuhi Te Hana.

Unfortunately for Ngāti Porou, also present on the *New Zealander* were a number of innocent members of their iwi who had been captured during previous Ngāpuhi raids but had been released to return to the East Coast. Their presence on the vessel when Ngarara was shot was sufficient in the eyes of the eastern Bay of Plenty iwi to mean Ngāti Porou became the closest objective against whom utu could be sought.

NGĀTI POROU COME UNDER ATTACK, WITH LONG-TERM CONSEQUENCES

Some time later in 1829, a taua of Ngāti Awa, Whakatōhea and Whānau a Apanui was assembled to attack Ngāti Porou. The target chosen was two European traders who were living with Ngāti Porou at Omuru-iti in Wharekahika (Hicks Bay) — utu in this manner against both Europeans and Ngāti Porou being regarded as particularly fitting.

The taua's attack at Omuru-iti was partially successful, with one of the Pākehā being killed and the other managing to escape. But the consequence, of course, was to provoke Ngāti Porou and provide them with a reason to seek utu themselves. However, in 1829 Ngāti Porou were still trying to build up their supply of muskets.

In 1831, their desire to seek utu for Omuru-iti was renewed and strengthened by an event that followed news reaching Whānau a Apanui of the intended passage of a Ngāpuhi waka that was returning from a friendly visit to Ngāti Porou. By now Ngāpuhi were bound in peace with Ngāti Porou through Pomare's actions and those of Te Wera to the south. Whānau a Apanui decided to stage a surprise attack on the Ngāpuhi waka, which happened to have some Ngāti Porou on board, as it passed Whakaari (White Island). The waka kauhoe were outnumbered and overcome, with two prominent Ngāpuhi rangatira, Ngaure and Wharetomokia, being among those killed.

The consequences of this attack were far-reaching, in that it in turn renewed not just the Ngāti Porou desire for utu, but also the long-standing Ngāpuhi desire for utu against people in the Bay of Plenty. Between 1831 and 1833 a series of Ngāpuhi taua were launched from the north, although as it turned out they did not get past Mōtītī Island. On the East Coast, however, reciprocal taua by joint forces of Ngāti Porou and Ngāpuhi from Mahia culminated in attacks on Whakatōhea at Kekeparoa, inland of Turanga (Gisborne), in 1832 and on Whānau a Apanui at Te Kaha in 1834.

WHAKATŌHEA BECOME INVOLVED

In the 1832 attack on Whakatōhea the two iwi of Ngāti Porou and Ngāpuhi were joined by Rongowhakaata and Te Aitanga a Mahaki, whose rohe was being occupied at Kekeparoa pā by Whakatōhea. The occupation had come about after Whakatōhea had suffered repeated raids by Ngāpuhi taua in the early 1820s, followed after 1828 by severe raids by Ngāti Maru under Te Rohu. In addition, they had been involved in long-running clashes with Ngāti Awa in the disputed area around Ōhiwa Harbour.

In response to this continued pressure some hapū of Whakatōhea had withdrawn deep into the hinterland. They had traversed up and over the Raukumara ranges, from which the Motu catchment flows into the Bay of Plenty, to the refuge of the Waipaoa and Tūranganui river systems that drain to the southeast into Poverty Bay. There, with the agreement of the Ngā Potiki hapū of Te Aitanga a Mahaki, they had built and occupied Kekeparoa pā near the junction of the Waihuka and Waikohu rivers. This was just upriver from Te Karaka, about 25 kilometres from Turanga, which meant that in the eyes of the other hapū of Te Aitanga a Mahaki they were transgressing into their rohe. Slowly, tensions began to build.

After failing in their attempts to persuade Ngā Potiki to urge Whakatōhea to leave Kekeparoa, the other Te Aitanga a Mahaki sent for assistance to their relatives in Rongowhakaata; they in turn sought the assistance of northern Ngāti Kahungunu and the Ngāpuhi Te Wera. Ope from Te Aitanga a Hauiti were also involved, and when the whole taua assembled it is believed to have had more than six hundred toa. It also had the added advantage of Te Wera's experienced men armed with muskets. The pā is believed to have had only about four hundred occupants, including men, women and children.

Kekeparoa was not well located, being on a river flat with no particularly strong natural defences, and after being besieged for some time the pā fell as its occupants succumbed to starvation. There are varying accounts of the harshness of the treatment meted out to those captured on the fall of the pā. One rather highly coloured account by the European Barnet Burns, who was present at some stages of the siege, suggested that the usual heavy slaughter occurred. However, most accounts from iwi sources suggest that the majority of the Whakatōhea were spared, but forced to go north back to their own rohe.

EARLY CONFLICTS BETWEEN NGĀTI POROU AND WHĀNAU A APANUI

In 1832 a limited Ngāti Porou taua had set out to attack Whānau a Apanui just south of the Raukokore River, which flows into the Bay of Plenty just south of Waihau Bay and the Whangaparaoa Bay area. As was common, news of the taua's progress reached its intended victims ahead of it, and Whānau a Apanui withdrew into the pā at Wharekura, near Te Kaha. This was a well-defended pā, and when the taua attacked it was repelled and two prominent Ngāti Porou rangatira were killed. One of these was Pakura, whose son Kakatarau became the senior rangatira at Rangitukia pā, in the heart of Ngāti Porou country, after his father's death; Pakura's other son was to become well-known as Mokena Kohere during the period of the New Zealand Wars.

The losses of their rangatira and the failure to take Wharekura pā gave further impetus to the Ngāti Porou desire to obtain utu against Whānau a Apanui for the earlier killings at Omuru-iti and Whakaari. But before that was possible they faced the inevitable riposte to the Wharekura attacks when, in 1834, Whānau a Apanui sent a strong taua to attack Rangitukia pā. The taua travelled by waka to the pā, which was situated on the northern side of the Waiapu River, east of Tikitiki. The pā was strongly palisaded, and defended by the fiercely determined Kakatarau and his people. The taua took a few days to plan their tactics for the forthcoming assault, during which time Kakatarau's scouts managed to find out that a treacherous attempt was to be made to enter under a flag of truce.

Ngāti Porou men armed with muskets hid themselves while Kakatarau is said to have hummed a popular waiata as a large party of Whānau a Apanui slowly approached under a flag of truce. Then, at a signal from Kakatarau, the hidden marksmen opened fire, killing many of the Whānau a Apanui party. The survivors returned later, with Kakatarau's approval, to uplift their dead, but rather than risking the bodies being desecrated by Ngāti Porou, the Whānau a Apanui burnt them before the taua departed.

Despite their own losses, as they returned home Whānau a Apanui must have realised that Ngāti Porou would soon be calling to avenge their losses and the assault on their mana at Rangitukia.

THE FIGHTING FINALLY COMES TO A CONCLUSION

Later in 1834, that is exactly what happened as Ngāti Porou assembled a huge taua. They were joined by Te Wera leading an ope of his musket-armed men, and by an ope from Rongowhakaata led by Te Kani a Takirau.

A major influence on Ngāti Porou plans at this stage stemmed from the return to the East Coast earlier that year of a number of Christian converts. These were some of the captives who had been taken back to Pēwhairangi by Ngāpuhi during the series of taua they had undertaken ten years or more earlier. Among those who had been released was a notably persuasive rangatira called Taumata a Kura (later baptised as Piripi). He was particularly strongly committed to his Christian beliefs and had come back with the intention of training others as missionary teachers.

Now, Taumata a Kura found himself having to balance his beliefs as a peace-loving, God-fearing man against his deeply embedded desire to lead Ngāti Porou in obtaining utu for their recent losses. He coped in part with that inherent conflict by refusing to accompany the taua unless it followed some specific edicts. Among the most important of these was a requirement to forgo the ancient customs of killing captives and cannibalising their bodies. Nor was there to be wanton and unnecessary destruction of enemy waka or gardens. Taumata a Kura's own mana increased during the lengthy siege that followed, as a result of his repeated leadership at the front of engagements while literally holding a Bible in one hand and a musket in the other. He came through all the fighting unscathed, and the power of his personal mana saw his demands respected on the battlefield.

The taua travelled by waka to besiege Whānau a Apanui who had assembled at the strongly palisaded and defended pā site of Toka a Kuku at Te Kaha Point. The siege is said to have lasted about six months, the defenders being aided by the fact that the pā had sea access on two sides of the narrow peninsula on which it was located; this meant some level of food supplies were able to be brought in by waka at night.

The exact numbers of the attacking taua or of the defenders will never be known, but both must have been very large. About sixteen hundred Whakatōhea, Ngāi Tai and Ngāti Awa were said to have responded to a call from Whānau a Apanui to come to their aid. They headed off toward the pā in two groups, two hundred travelling by waka and the balance overland. The sea-borne group managed to make it inside the pā, but those travelling overland were heavily defeated by Te Wera and Kakatarau at Puremutahuri Stream just to the south of Te Kaha.

> **Whata tangata**
>
> Piripi Taumata a Kura's influence did not remove all vestiges of the brutality involved in customary warfare. To weaken the resolve of the besieged, after one heavy engagement during the siege of Toka a Kuku a very high whata (an upright stage-like structure) was erected in front of the pā. The bodies of those killed were tied in pairs by the feet and suspended, with one body hanging down each side of the structure. The besiegers termed this a 'whata tangata' — a distressing wall of men, as indeed it must have been.

During the siege the defenders sallied out on a number of occasions, and while these sorties were ultimately unsuccessful, and some heavy losses were sustained, the pā did not ever fall. In the end, when it became apparent that the pā was unlikely to fall, and the supplies around the Te Kaha area had mostly been consumed, Te Kani a Takirau left with his Rongowhakaata men. After a few more months he was followed by the balance of the taua.

The siege of Toka a Kuku was the last major engagement between these iwi. Taumata a Kura had considerable success afterwards in spreading the message of Christian peace, as he and others converted a number of prominent Ngāti Porou rangatira to that religion. As a consequence a formal peace was entered into between Ngāti Porou and Whānau a Apanui in 1837.

9

THE LAST CONFLICTS

It is a common misconception that the Musket Wars quickly ground down after the major sieges at Kaiapoi and Pukerangiora in 1832, as a result of the balance of musket power that now existed. While the relative equality in musket power did play a significant part in the eventual cessation of the wars, it was not enough on its own to bring all conflicts to an end.

That was particularly apparent in the Bay of Plenty area between 1836 and 1840, when a long-running series of conflicts broke out between Ngāti Hauā and Ngāiterangi on the one hand, and most of the Te Arawa hapū on the other. In the south Taranaki and Whanganui areas between 1840 and 1845 clashes occurred between Ngāti Tūwharetoa and some upper-river Te Atihaunui a Pāpārangi on the one hand, and Ngā Rauru and Ngāti Ruanui on the other. Very heavy casualties occurred in some of these clashes, particularly in 1836 and 1840.

THE DESIRE FOR UTU SPARKS A SERIES OF CONFLICTS IN THE BAY OF PLENTY

The initial trigger for the Bay of Plenty conflicts appears to have been an action steeped in the convoluted train of thought regarding utu that sometimes guided rangatira in customary Māori warfare. A Te Arawa rangatira, Haerehuka, of the central Rotorua hapū of Ngāti Whakaue, became incensed after members of his own hapū received payment for dressed flax by way of trade goods from the

Pākehā trader Hans Tapsell while Haerehuka was away in Maketu. Haerehuka's people had been involved in preparing and selling the flax, but he had not received a share of the payment. His reaction was to seek utu on his own iwi by bringing down on them a desire for utu by another iwi.

To achieve this, Haerehuka killed a Ngāti Hauā rangatira called Te Hunga on 25 December 1835 at the Ngāti Rangiwewehi kāinga of Parahaki, a pā that then existed on the northwestern side of Lake Rotorua. He then took the body to the northeastern side of the lake, where it was cut up and parts sent to all of the Te Arawa hapū for them to share.

At this time the bulk of Ngāti Hauā under Te Waharoa were living in their pā at Matamata, which was in a strong position, surrounded by deep swamps that were dominated by kahikatea forest. Their long-time allies Ngāiterangi, with whom they were interrelated, occupied a number of pā at Tauranga as well as a smaller pā at Te Tumu, about 10 kilometres east of Tauranga. A similar small group of Ngāiterangi under Tamaiwahia held Otamarakau pā, about 20 kilometres east of Maketu. Maketu itself was held by Te Arawa, who traded heavily there for muskets with Hans Tapsell, who was married to a Te Arawa woman, Hine-i-turama.

Te Waharoa's reaction to the killing of his relative Te Hunga and the desecration of his body was exactly as Haerehuka had anticipated. Three months later, in March 1836, Te Waharoa led a huge taua from Tauranga to attack the Te Arawa pā at Maketu. The taua numbered more than sixteen hundred toa, with Te Waharoa's own men augmented with contingents from Ngāti Maniapoto and other Tainui hapū as well as Ngāiterangi from Tauranga. The defenders' numbers, by comparison, were tragically small. Haupapa, the senior Ngāti Whakaue rangatira at Maketu, and Nainai, his Ngāti Pukenga ally, had only about sixty toa between them, together with their whānau.

Tapsell and Haupapa stood outside the pā watching as the first skirmishers approached the river below. Haupapa shot two of the attackers before he himself was hit by a musket ball and badly wounded. Tapsell carried his friend into the pā and into his own house, where Haupapa's wife Kata was with the pregnant Hine-i-turama. Meanwhile the taua split in two, enabling it to attack the pā from the south and west simultaneously. Nainai and the other defenders fought bravely until evening, but in the end they were simply overwhelmed.

The fall of Maketu in 1836 was one of the rare occasions during the Musket Wars where a pā held by musket-armed defenders fell — the imbalance in numbers was simply too great.

> **Maketu survivors**
>
> Although Haupapa died from his wounds, Tapsell managed to save his own life, and Hine-i-turama and Kata as well as five other Te Arawa women, because of the relationship he had forged in earlier trading with the Ngāiterangi rangatira Tupaea. Tupaea sent his own wife to accompany the small group of survivors to the Ngāiterangi pā Te Tumu, about five kilometres to the west, from where they travelled in a rowing boat of Tapsell's to Matata, before travelling overland to Rotorua.

TE ARAWA'S RESPONSE TO THE LOSS OF MAKETU

After the capture of Maketu, Ngāti Hauā and Ngāiterangi withdrew their main forces for the time being to their bases at Matamata and Tauranga respectively. Strangely, as they should have been expecting retaliatory raids from Te Arawa, Ngāiterangi left only a relatively small force at Te Tumu pā, which lay on exposed sand-dune country just 5 kilometres west of Maketu. Its defence was in the hands of small garrison under Tupaea, Kiharoa and the elderly Hikareia.

After Maketu fell, a series of hui (meetings) were held by hapū throughout Te Arawa country, resulting in the assembly of two taua to avenge the loss by attacking Ngāiterangi. The outcome of those hui was a strategy whereby a smaller taua under Tautari would attack Tuhua (Mayor Island), about 40 kilometres northwest of Tauranga, while a larger one would attack Te Tumu pā.

This larger taua comprised over a thousand toa, and its attack on Te Tumu on 6 May achieved the same rare success as had the massive Ngāti Hauā and Ngāiterangi taua against Maketu, and for the same reason. The huge imbalance of numbers was so marked that the attack could not be rebuffed, despite an initial valiant defence by the muskets of the defenders, during which Kiharoa was killed. When it became clear that the pā was doomed to fall, Tupaea and Hikareia led a desperate break-out and dash along the sand dunes toward distant Tauranga. They were closely pursued and while some prisoners were taken, most were run down and killed, among them Hikareia.

Meanwhile, Tautari's taua, comprising about three hundred Ngāti Pikiao toa, had set off by waka, intending to arrive at Tuhua under cover of darkness so that it could make a surprise landing. The journey must have been mistimed, however, as the waka were observed by Ngāiterangi lookouts on the heights. The pā was protected on both sides by unscalable bluffs and the only approach was up a narrow pathway. Forewarned, the Ngāiterangi defenders released huge piles of large boulders that had been stored as part of a defensive plan. They smashed into the attackers with a huge roar, causing death and mayhem, made worse by a follow-up series of musket volleys.

Tautari's men withdrew with their dead and wounded, and although they destroyed gardens and buildings on the rest of the island, this was inadequate for the utu they sought. But the taua now had no option other than to head back to the mainland, where to their chagrin they arrived at Te Tumu to find that it had just fallen.

Te Arawa raiding parties still seeking further utu stayed in the areas around Tauranga and Matamata over the winter months, killing any Ngāti Hauā or Ngāiterangi travellers they came across.

TE WAHAROA MOVES AGAINST NGĀTI WHAKAUE

In response to all these various attacks by Te Arawa, in late July 1836 Te Waharoa assembled a fresh taua to launch a further assault on Ngāti Whakaue, this time at their principal base, the lakeside pā of Ōhinemutu (in modern-day Rotorua city). By 1 August his powerful taua was setting up camp at Te Koutu, a few kilometres away from Ōhinemutu.

The attack began on 6 August when a small ope under Wetini Taiporotu launched an assault that was relatively quickly repulsed. As the ope withdrew in apparent confusion the gates of the pā opened and Te Arawa defenders streamed out to pursue them. As had happened so often before in Māori customary warfare, what turned out to be merely a kōhuru (stratagem) worked perfectly. When the pursuers were strung out an ambush was sprung and the tables turned. Only the courage of Tohi Te Ururangi in making a stand at the Utuhina Stream provided time for many Te Arawa to make it back to the pā, but their losses were heavy. Many now wished to abandon the pā and paddle out to Mokoia Island as a safe refuge, but again the courage of one rangatira, Korokai, stayed their hands. After an extended period of desperate exchanges of fire Ngāti Hauā realised they

> **Samuel Knight**
>
> Among the prisoners taken back to Rotorua after the fall of Te Tumu was a young Ngāiterangi woman who had relationships with various Te Arawa, to whom she appealed for mercy. Despite the missionary Samuel Knight attempting physically to prevent it, this young woman was killed by Kata, the widow of Tapsell's friend Haupapa, who took a dreadful revenge by despatching her with a tomahawk. Shocked as Knight had been by the brutality of this killing, a few months later he was traumatised once more after Mataipuku, as Ngāti Hauā made him witness the horrendous scenes of their cannibal feast on the Arawa dead.

were unlikely to be able to breach the palisading of the pā under heavy musket fire, and the taua withdrew.

Satisfied with the heavy losses they had inflicted, the taua moved back to their camp near Te Koutu to celebrate with a cannibal hākari lasting some days — the conflict afterwards becoming known as the battle of Mataipuku, referring to the locality just west of Ōhinemutu where much of it was fought.

NGĀITERANGI RESPONSE TO THE TE ARAWA ATTACKS

On the same day as Ngāti Hauā launched their attack on Ōhinemutu, 6 August 1836, a small ope of Ngāiterangi attacked the Ngāti Rangiwewehi pā of Puhirua, on the western side of Lake Rotorua, in a diversionary attack. Its purpose was to distract attention from a large taua under Tamaiwahia that was heading east by waka to attack Ngāti Pikiao at Okahu pā at Lake Rotoehu. The Ngāti Pikiao rangatira at Okahu was Tautari, who had been among those who had failed in their attempt to take Tuhua some months earlier. Now Tautari at least had the satisfaction of seeing the Ngāiterangi attack repulsed, with 17 of Tamaiwahia's men killed.

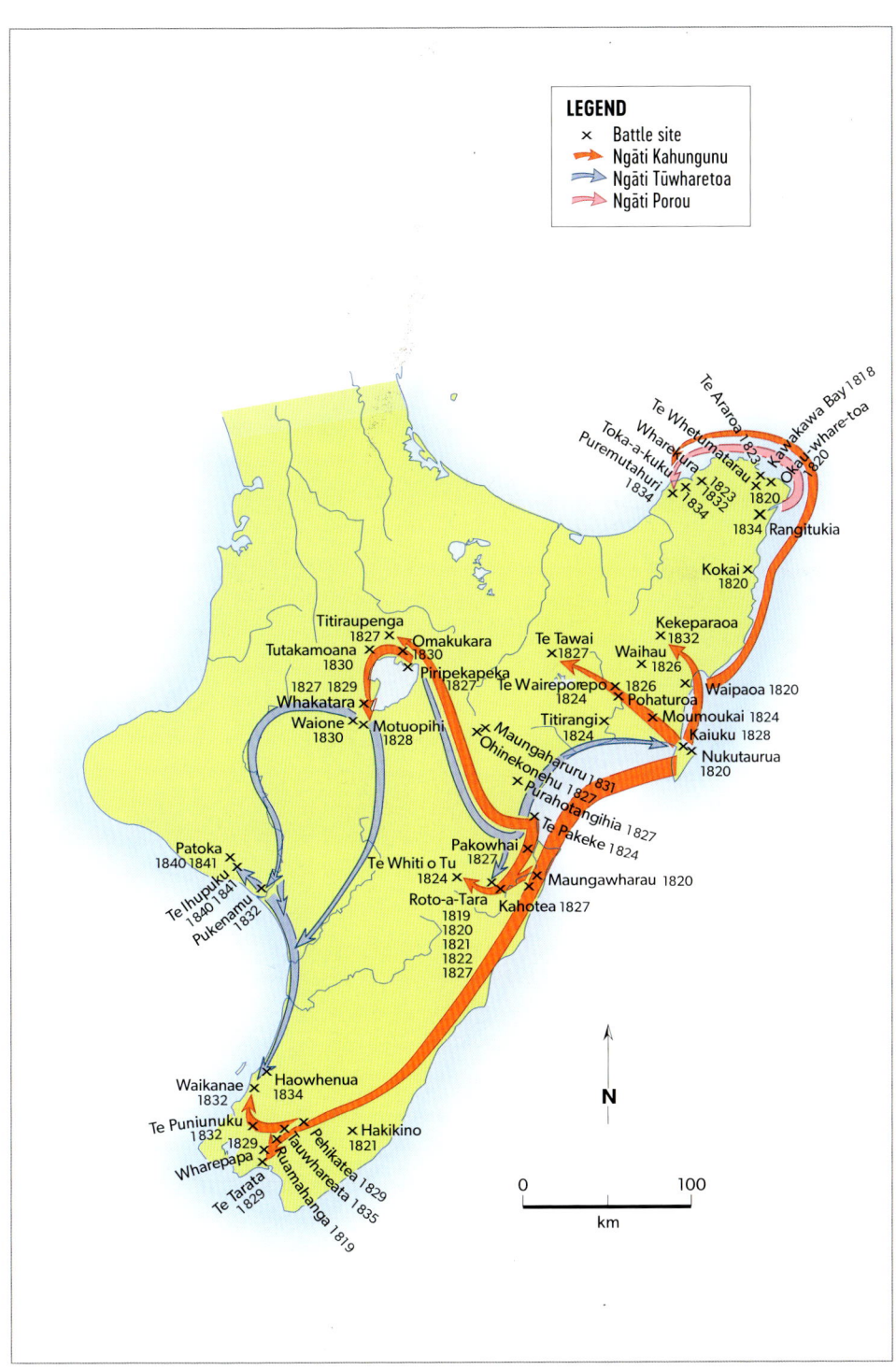

Ngāti Kahunganunu, Ngāti Tūwharetoa and Ngāti Porou: battle sites, and routes of taua and migrations.

Te Hapuku. Captured in 1824 on the fall of Te Pakeke pā at Napier, this famous rangatira of Ngāti Kahungungu escaped from his Waikato captors and survived the Musket Wars.

Gottfried Lindauer, Te Hapuku, oil on canvas, Auckland Art Gallery Toi o Tāmaki, gift of Mr H.E. Partridge, 1915

Renata Kawepō. The Ngāti Te Upokoiri rangatira captured in 1827 at the fall of Rota-a-Tara pā in Hawke's Bay, and taken as a slave by Ngāpuhi back to the Bay of Islands. He was subsequently returned to his people, and decades later fought against Te Kooti.

Gottfried Lindauer, Renata Kawepo, Tama ki Hikurangi, 1885, oil on canvas, Auckland Art Gallery Toi o Tāmaki, gift of Mr H.E. Partridge, 1915

RIGHT *Te Heuheu and Iwikau. Te Heuheu Tukino Mananui (front) was the great Ngāti Tūwharetoa rangatira, a huge man who successfully led his people's defence of their territories. He led the last of the great taua to Te Ihupuku pā on the Waitōtara River in 1844–45. Iwikau, his warrior brother, was involved in the dramatic clash with Te Matakatea in 1840 on the Whanganui River.*

PUBL-0014-56, Giles, John West, 1801–1870. Angas, George French 1822–1886: Te Heuheu & Hiwikau, Tanpo [sic]. George French Angas [delt]; J.W. Giles [lith]. Plate 56, 1847. Alexander Turnbull Library, Wellington, NZ

BELOW *Maketu pā. One of a series of paintings by Major-General H.R. Robley done after the end of the Musket Wars featuring the ornate carved waha (gateways) of Maketu pā, the coastal stronghold of Te Arawa just east of Tauranga.*

A-080-051, Robley, Horatio Gordon, 1840–1930: Maketu. 1865?. Alexander Turnbull Library, Wellington, NZ

ABOVE *A graphic portrayal of a haka being performed in front of Ōhinemutu pā at Lake Rotorua — the pā that withstood the assault by Te Waharoa in 1836.*

PUBL-0014-53, Angas, George French, 1822–1886: War dance before the Pah of Oinemutu, near Rotorua Lake. J.W. Giles lith., 1847. Alexander Turnbull Library, Wellington, NZ

LEFT *The famous fighting rangatira of Ngāti Tamaterā, Taraia Ngakuti Te Tumuhia. He took part in numerous Ngāti Maru taua and was involved in one of the last acts of cannibalism in New Zealand after his capture of Ongare pā, near Katikati, in 1842.*

Gottfried Lindauer, Taraia Ngakuti Te Tumuhuia, 1874, oil on canvas, Auckland Art Gallery Toi o Tāmaki, gift of Mr H.E. Partridge, 1915

TE ARAWA SEEK UTU AGAINST NGĀTI HAUĀ

To some extent, the victory at Te Tumu in May had satisfied Te Arawa desire for utu against Ngāiterangi, but so far they had not achieved similar utu against Ngāti Hauā. Yet it was Ngāti Hauā who had inflicted such heavy losses on them at Maketu in March, and later against Ngāti Whakaue in particular at Ōhinemutu. So, in late 1836, a large taua again principally comprising Ngāti Whakaue was assembled and headed for Matamata to seek the necessary utu against Ngāti Hauā.

At Matamata, however, the pā defences were found to be too strong to overcome. The swamps surrounding the pā were so numerous and deep that lines of attack were channelled onto narrow land routes, rendering the attackers vulnerable to concentrated musket fire.

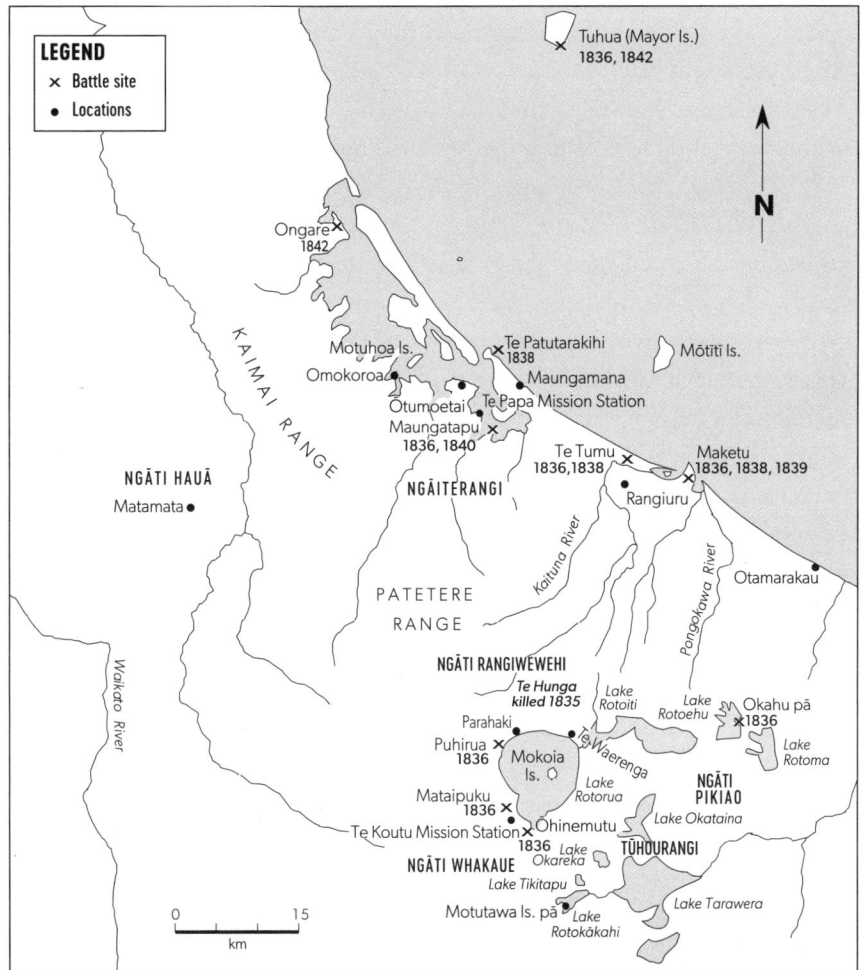

Principal battle sites involving Ngāti Hauā, Ngāiterangi, Te Arawa and Ngāti Tamaterā, 1836-42.

Some Ngāti Hauā converts to Christianity, though, were encountered living outside the palisaded pā in a large house, and they were mostly killed, with a few being taken captive. Among those captured was a high-ranking youth called Teiteinui, whose grandfather was the prominent Waikato rangatira Muriwhenua. Teiteinui's presence as a captive in Rotorua was to prove significant the following year.

For now, frustrated in its principal aim of taking the main pā, the taua headed back to Rotorua as the tumultuous year of 1836 came to an end.

PEACE IS AGREED AT ŌHINEMUTU, BUT CONFLICT CONTINUES IN THE BAY OF PLENTY

Although they had maintained control of the pā at Matamata, Ngāti Hauā still felt the need to seek utu for the loss of the Christian converts. In early 1837 a taua was assembled and headed for Rotokākahi (Green Lake), where they had heard Teiteinui was being held. When they arrived there, they found that the people had left by waka for the island refuge of Motutawa. Having no waka available to them, the Ngāti Hauā turned to head for home, travelling via Rotorua. Taking advantage of the presence of the taua nearby, the prominent Ngāti Whakaue rangatira Te Pukuatua invited Ngāti Hauā to enter peace negotiations, offering Teiteinui's release as part of any agreement.

Tensions must have been high on both sides as the taua arrived at Ōhinemutu, where they had engaged in such bitter fighting just six months earlier. On this occasion, however, wise heads prevailed and Teiteinui was handed back in a huge ceremony at which peace was formally agreed. The following day a similar accord was reached with the redoubtable Hikairo and his Ngāti Rangiwewehi people at Puhirua pā, on the west coast of the lake.

These peace agreements between Te Arawa and Ngāti Hauā would be honoured in the Matamata and Rotorua areas in the years ahead, but relations between Ngāiterangi and Te Arawa remained unresolved. Most significant was the issue of who controlled Maketu.

Te Arawa desire for utu against Ngāiterangi had deep roots, going back as far as the assistance some Ngāiterangi had given Ngāpuhi in its massive raid on the Rotorua lakes in 1823. This desire now came to a head when a Te Arawa taua attacked Maungatapu pā near Tauranga on 27 January. Maungatapu had successfully resisted attacks by Ngāti Maru in 1828, and by Ngāpuhi in 1832 and 1833, and Te Arawa were to have no better fortune in 1837. Within a matter of weeks the missionaries at nearby Te Papa had recorded that the taua had left for

Rotorua after managing to kill only a few Ngāiterangi stragglers who were found outside the pā.

Meanwhile Te Puehu of Ngāti Pikiao remained determined to reoccupy Maketu, which had remained abandoned since its sacking. The major problem was that its palisading had been burnt during the attack on the pā. Te Puehu also found that the hapū closest to Ngāti Hauā in the west, Ngāti Whakaue and Ngāti Rangiwewehi, were resistant to his aim of moving back into the pā. They were concerned that Te Arawa reoccupation of the pā, being so close to Tauranga, would incite Ngāiterangi to again call on Te Waharoa to join them in an attack on Maketu.

Te Puehu had better luck with his own Ngāti Pikiao, and with Tūhourangi and other hapū from more easterly areas, such as Tapuika and Ngāti Tarawhai. They realised, however, that a reoccupation would entail considerable planning and speedy construction of defences, including new palisading. Two huge waka, *Ngareua* and *Hokowhitu*, were dragged over to the upper headwaters of the Pongakawa Stream, following the route that Ngāpuhi had used in the opposite direction to reach Lake Rotoehu in 1823, then the taua descended the stream to the Waihi estuary. A number of large trees were felled on the way and carried to the estuary, where they were prepared for use as support posts and railing for palisading.

Finally, after spending most of the year in preparatory work of constructing the waka, and felling and transporting the logs for palisading, one night in late 1837 the prepared timber was ferried by waka to Maketu and temporary earthen defences were thrown up. The following day, with a huge effort, the entrenchments were dug out afresh, the support posts dug in, and the palisading fixed in place. By the time Ngāiterangi became aware of what was happening, Maketu was a fully defended, palisaded pā. It was now reoccupied by a large force well armed with muskets, and gardening and flax-gathering for trade were already beginning. The gauntlet had been well and truly thrown down by Te Puehu.

Ngāiterangi mana now demanded that they remove this threat to their occupation of the western Bay of Plenty. To ensure their success against what was clearly a much more formidably defended pā than it had been in 1836, they again turned to Te Waharoa and his Ngāti Hauā for assistance.

By mid 1838 the local missionaries had recorded that Te Waharoa had moved to live on Motuhoa Island in Tauranga Harbour as a preparatory step to the assembly of a taua. In response to their entreaties that he desist from further warfare he said that he was only awaiting the arrival of a Waikato taua to join with him before he and Ngāiterangi would launch a fresh assault on Maketu.

Suddenly, however, on 2 August, the missionaries heard that Te Waharoa had fallen ill and had been taken to Omokoroa pā on the southern side of the harbour. Visiting him there, they found that he had a very serious skin infection that appeared to them to be bordering on gangrenous. On 7 August he was carried off on an amo (litter) towards Matamata, and in early September news arrived that he had died there.

On 19 October the missionaries noted that Muriwhenua had passed through Maungatapu pā in Tauranga with the Waikato taua that Te Waharoa had been awaiting. A few days later the taua, comprising Ngāti Hauā, Ngāiterangi, Ngāti Ranginui and now Waikato, linked up east of Tauranga and moved to occupy Te Tumu. But the death of Te Waharoa had badly weakened the resolve of the taua, and now in his place they were being lectured by his son Tāmihana Te Tarapipi Waharoa, who was a Christian convert. He now argued for peace, literally with Bible in hand, supported by the missionaries. Muriwhenua added little if any fire to the taua, being described by the missionaries as by then so old as to be enfeebled.

It is probably not too surprising that apart from a few half-hearted advances, and the killing of several women who were captured outside the pā, no firm attack was pressed. After some desultory exchanges of fire the taua withdrew in late October, doubtless to the great relief of Te Puehu and his Te Arawa.

LAST TAUA IN THE CONFLICTS BETWEEN NGĀITERANGI AND TE ARAWA

One of those killed at Maketu in these desultory exchanges was a Te Arawa woman called Tamiuru, who was related to the great Ngāti Rangiwewehi rangatira Hikairo. An account reached Hikairo that as the taua passed through Tauranga some of the toa had taunted Ngāiterangi converts in the CMS mission station by waving one of Tamiuru's severed hands at them. To a rangatira of Hikairo's mana, the killing of his relative and the desecration of her remains in this way demanded utu.

So it was that more waka were portaged to the Pongakawa and descended the stream in preparation for another attack on Mount Maunganui. On the night of 23 November, 14 waka arrived off the Mount and intercepted a Ngāiterangi waka whose occupants were fishing for tarakihi. All 11 were killed. Their bodies were then taken to be cooked and eaten in front of the pā at Maungatapu, where once again a missionary, this time John Morgan, was forced to observe the grim scene. Utu in this manner, which became known as Te Patutarakihi, was regarded as sufficient for the killing and demeaning of Tamiuru, so no other attacks were launched by the taua.

But of course the killing of 11 Ngāiterangi was always going to cause a renewed desire for utu on the part of their people. On 27 February 1839 the missionaries recorded the departure of yet another taua of Ngāiterangi and Ngāti Hauā, but this time comprising more than six hundred toa. Despite the size of the taua, however, and determined attacks on the palisading at Maketu, the pā's defences held, supported by heavy musket fire. Within three days the taua was back at Tauranga with 14 bodies of its toa and 20 wounded.

Later in the year, on 6 October, an even more determined Tainui taua arrived at Maungatapu pā to link up with Ngāiterangi and head for Maketu. Once again Muriwhenua was one of its rangatira. Twenty waka headed off, as well as hundreds of toa travelling overland. The weather over the next three days was appalling, with continuous heavy rain, and the dispirited taua had to survive in temporary shelters before moving on to set up camp at Maketu just out of musket range.

A high-ranking Te Arawa woman called Titia was killed at the Waihi estuary to the east of Maketu, but other than her death the taua did not achieve anything before the missionaries arrived on 28 October to try to persuade the two parties to make peace. The taua allowed the missionaries through their camps to enter the pā, but no peace was able to be arranged. The missionaries left on 30 October to return to Tauranga, fearing the worst of outcomes.

However, by now the taua, which the missionaries estimated to number more than eight hundred, was seriously short of food. Moreover, as the earlier taua had found in March, the taua rangatira realised that the Maketu pā was now so strongly defended by musket fire, and had such substantial palisading, that it was almost impossible to take. The taua withdrew, but both sides were still left with a deep-seated and unsatisfied desire for utu, which for Te Arawa had only increased with the killing of Titia.

The final event in this see-saw of utu was the taua launched by Te Arawa in February 1840 against Ngāiterangi in Tauranga, at the urging of Tūhourangi. The taua had assembled over some months and numbered between five and eight hundred toa. The main body of the taua left in 36 waka from Maketu, arriving off Maungatapu pā on 13 February, a week after the Treaty had been signed at Waitangi.

Once more the fiercely defended pā at Maungatapu resisted the initial assault. The missionaries recorded that over the first few days of conflict thousands of musket rounds were exchanged, with very low casualties inflicted by either side. A similar result followed when the taua attacked Otūmoetai pā to the west. On 20 February a Ngāti Hauā taua arrived to reinforce Maungatapu pā, but bad weather again prevented any fighting for several days. On 26 February Te Arawa launched a last effort against Maungatapu pā; then, after a heavy exchange of fire in which only three men were wounded on each side, the taua pulled back. It left Tauranga the following day, 27 February 1840.

This was to be the last taua undertaken by these enemy iwi as each in turn sought utu sparked by the series of events that had followed after the killing of Te Hunga four years earlier.

MUSKET WARFARE IN THE BAY OF PLENTY AFTER THE SIGNING OF THE TREATY

One of the last acts of warfare near Tauranga occurred on 9 April 1840 when the Ngāiterangi rangatira Ponui travelled to Maketu in a courageous attempt to negotiate peace. He was invited to enter the pā, but when he did so he was speared in the back and killed by three senior Te Arawa rangatira — Te Pukuatua, Te Amohau and Tohi Te Ururangi. His body was then cooked and eaten in the old style. The Treaty was plainly not yet having any effect on Te Arawa in the Bay of Plenty.

At this time the Treaty had not been signed in the Tauranga area, however, and it seems likely that when it was signed, shortly after Ponui's death, it may well have influenced Ngāiterangi in their decision not to seek utu for his killing.

The missionary Alfred Brown had raised the issue of the signing of the Treaty at Tauranga on 10 April, the very day after Ponui's killing. Over the next few weeks 21 Ngāiterangi rangatira were persuaded to sign, but Tupaea and many of the Otūmoetai rangatira were among those who refused. Those who did sign, however, included Te Haereroa and Nuka of Maungatapu pā, the two rangatira who had led its stout defence against so many attackers between 1828 and 1840.

But if the Treaty was starting to have some effect on retaliatory action in the Bay of Plenty, this was still intermittent for some years. This was graphically demonstrated when Taraia of Ngāti Tamaterā led a final taua of Marutūahu hapū to seek utu from Ngāiterangi in May 1842. The taua travelled overland and attacked a small Ngāiterangi coastal pā called Ongare in the western reaches of Tauranga Harbour, not far from modern-day Katikati. Taraia had become enraged over the claims of Te Whanake, the rangatira at Ongare, that he had the authority to declare rāhui on fishing rights in the western Tauranga Harbour and to occupy Ongare. Both of those areas Taraia viewed as being within his rohe entitlements, but in addition he had always harboured a deep-seated resentment against Ngāiterangi, who years earlier had killed his mother, then cooked and eaten her body.

Taraia's taua, which was limited in size to about seventy heavily-armed toa, surrounded Ongare one night and at dawn fired a heavy volley into the pā. This was followed up immediately by an assault over the palisading. Te Whanake's wife and about fifteen others managed to escape, but Te Whanake himself and 11 of his people were killed, and another 17 taken prisoner. The bodies of those who had been killed were cut up and the prisoners were forced to carry the baskets of meat taken from the bodies of their relatives. On the ridge above Ongare the taua stopped and cooked some of the body parts, with Taraia himself eating portions of Te Whanake's body. Another hākari occurred at the Waihou River in Ngāti Maru country. These two hākari were among the last cannibal hākari in Aotearoa.

Probably the most significant aftermath of all of these events came when the Governor, William Hobson, ordered George Clarke, the newly appointed Chief Protector of Aborigines, to travel to the area to obtain a peaceful resolution and avoid a Ngāiterangi taua seeking utu. Despite Tupaea being one of the rangatira who had refused to sign the Treaty, Clarke was able in the end to arrange a commercial resolution by buying the disputed land for the Crown, and to obtain the agreement of both Tupaea and Taraia to a lasting peace between their iwi. It was one of the first occasions of the Musket Wars in which the outcome was affected by the new government in place under the Treaty.

THE FINAL TE ARAWA AND NGĀITERANGI CONFLICTS

The immediate aftermath of Ongare was that Ngāiterangi declared the pā site tapu and it remained abandoned. However, it was known that a considerable stock of potatoes had been left in the pā. In late November 1842 a European trading vessel, the *Nimble*, anchored off the pā during a trading voyage from Maketu into the northern reaches of Tauranga Harbour. Two Te Arawa men were on board, accompanied by Ngaki, the 11-year-old son of the senior Te Arawa rangatira Tohi Te Ururangi. They persuaded the captain to row them all ashore to retrieve some of the potatoes, but while they were doing this a Ngāiterangi waka shot out from the shore and captured the *Nimble*. The Te Arawa men, observing what had happened, wisely hid until they were able to flag down another passing vessel and return to Maketu. But they brought back to Tohi Te Ururangi the tragic news that they had lost touch with Ngaki, who was never seen again.

Tohi was convinced that his son had been killed by Ngāiterangi. Taking a rowing cutter he had seized from another European vessel, he led a small ope out to Tuhua to exact utu against the Ngāti Tauwhao hapū of Ngāiterangi. When the cutter arrived at the island all but one of the Te Arawa lay in the thwarts. The remaining man, wearing European clothing, awaited the arrival of a small

Ngāiterangi waka that came out from the island carrying three men and two boys. When the waka drew close, the men lying in the thwarts leapt up and shot and killed two of the Ngāiterangi men, captured the two boys, then killed the third man, who had attempted to swim to shore after being wounded. The bodies were brought back to Maketu, where Tohi Te Ururangi presided over the last known cannibal hākari of the Musket Wars era.

Acting Governor Willoughby Shortland, who had recently replaced the very ill Hobson (who actually died on 10 September 1842), again intervened with Tupaea to avoid a repeat round of utu killings, and to regain for the European owners the boats that the two iwi had taken. Initially both Tupaea and Tohi Te Ururangi were unwilling to recognise any other authority, or return the boats. In December Shortland

Tohi Te Ururangi. A leading Te Arawa rangatira who was prominent at the battle of Mataipuku in 1836 and the defence of Maketu pā in 1839. He was involved in one of New Zealand's last acts of cannibalism, at Maketu in 1842.

PA1-o-328-11, Tohi Te Ururangi. Mantell, Walter Baldock Durrant: Family photograph albums. Alexander Turnbull Library, Wellington, NZ

ordered a force of 53 Imperial Army soldiers to be brought from Auckland on HMS *Victoria*, and they set up camp at Mount Maunganui together with 15 sailors from HMS *Tortoise*, supported by two 18-pounder carronades. In the face of this show of government power Tohi agreed to forgo cannibalism, and both he and Tupaea agreed to return the boats they had in their control. The reality of British military might was thus recognised by two rangatira who had refused to sign the Treaty, while at the same time they still professed not to be bound by it. The consequence was a cessation at last of Te Arawa and Ngāiterangi warfare.

THE OUTBREAK OF WAR IN THE WHANGANUI AREA

In early January 1840 a rangatira of Te Atihaunui a Pāpārangi called Te Kotukuraeroa heard that one of his relatives had been killed by Ngā Rauru, the iwi centred around the Waitōtara River sytem west of Whanganui. Te Kotukuraeroa's sister had married Tauteka, a prominent Ngāti Tūwharetoa rangatira (who had been one of those hunting for Te Rauparaha at Motuopihi when he composed Ka Mate). Te Kotukuraeroa journeyed to Taupō to ask Tauteka to raise a taua to help him seek utu against Ngā Rauru.

Tauteka and his son Te Herekiekie were keen to assist, and a limited taua was soon raised. However, when it reached Te Rapa pā, at the head of the lake, Te Heuheu was reluctant to join. This was because he was in the middle of building a major wharenui, and it was seen as a bad omen to interrupt the building of a whare to head off on a taua. His brother, the aggressive Iwikau, had no such qualms, however, and he enthusiastically joined the taua with his men.

In the headwaters of the Whanganui the taua had stopped to gather more supporters when it received an unexpected visitor, the Ngā Rauru and Taranaki rangatira Wiremu Te Matakatea. News of the taua's movements had travelled ahead of it, as was common, and Ngā Rauru and Ngāti Ruanui had become aware of its impending arrival. Wiremu Te Matakatea had stood out for his courage and leadership ever since the outstanding south Taranaki defence against Waikato taua between 1832 and 1834, and all three iwi, Taranaki, Ngāti Ruanui and Ngā Rauru, gravitated to him for leadership. Te Matakatea had made the bold decision to travel up the Whanganui in an effort to dissuade the taua from continuing.

Te Matakatea's plea fell on deaf ears with Iwikau, who famously held up a large carved calabash and said that it would hold Te Matakatea's stinking head the next day. A more direct and aggressive threat to a rangatira could not be imagined. Te Matakatea rose and left with his men, warning Iwikau as he boarded his waka not to pursue them as they left. With that, his small group of waka headed away on the long journey of some 250 kilometres to their home pā to prepare their defences.

After some time as they were paddling through one of the long stretches of high, steep-walled river banks on the upper Whanganui they started to hear behind them the loud, rhythmic chant of kaihoe. Turning, they saw in the distance a group of the taua's waka flying downriver in pursuit. Standing on the prow of the leading waka, stripped for fighting and holding a taiaha (an elongated stabbing spear), was Iwikau.

Te Matakatea had his waka turned to meet the oncoming Iwikau, and he too stripped for combat, taking up a long-handled pātītī (tomahawk) as he stood at the prow of his waka. The taiaha being longer than the pātītī meant he had to accept the reality that Iwikau would swing first, and he must try to parry that blow before he could respond. Iwikau was bracing himself against the movement of his rushing waka by holding on grimly with his toes as he prepared to swing his taiaha. Suddenly, just as he was about to do so, he was gripped with cramp in the leg. As a consequence he did not swing his taiaha at all as he struggled to release the pain of the cramp. The two waka slid rapidly past each other and the taua kaihoe stopped paddling at this kōhera or bad omen.

Te Matakatea's small group of waka continued rapidly on their way as the taua stopped to take stock of what had just happened. Later the taua continued as far as Whanganui, where Iwikau's Ngāti Tūwharetoa contingent decided the two omens — interrupting the building of the wharenui at Te Rapa and now the cramp hitting Iwikau — meant they should retire, and they headed back to Taupō.

Tauteka and Te Herekiekie, however, decided to carry on with Te Kotukuraeroa's men. The taua, now numbering only about three hundred toa, found the Ngā Rauru pā of Patoka, near the mouth of the Waitōtara, had been abandoned, so it headed several kilometres up the river to attack and take Piraunui pā before returning to occupy the abandoned pā at Patoka. But now Tauteka and Te Kotukuraeroa made the fatal error of deciding to stay at Patoka, as the crops in the extensive gardens around it were starting to mature.

Meanwhile Te Matakatea and his people were not being idle. They were at Patea preparing a major taua of their own to seek retribution and to drive Tauteka out. Soon enough, with a taua numbering about five hundred toa they headed south to occupy an ancient pā site just downriver from Patoka, called Te Ihupuku. The imbalance in numbers between the two taua was added to by the fact that Patoka was a modern pā with shallow trenches and light palisading.

A typical head-on view by Charles Heaphy of approaching waka on the Waikato River. This is very much the view that Te Matakatea would have had in 1840 on the Whanganui River when being pursued by Iwikau of Ngāti Tūwharetoa.

PUBL-0075-TP, Heaphy, Charles, 1820–1881: [War canoe, Waikato River]. [Drawn by Charles Heaphy; engraved by J. Whymper. London, John Murray, 1855]. Alexander Turnbull Library, Wellington, NZ

It relied on vigilance and heavy enfilading musket fire for protection.

Te Matakatea had had long experience of sieges during the Musket Wars and now he surrounded Patoka and began a siege of some months, designed to weaken his opponents' resolve and vigilance through starvation. At long last, as dawn broke on 24 August, he launched his assault from all quarters, breaking down the palisading at a number of places and quickly overcoming the weakened defenders. Te Kotukuraeroa was shot and killed during the assault, and Tauteka, trapped in a whare, called out for Te Matakatea to pay him the honour of killing him. As he moved through the door of his whare in a stooped position Te Matakatea gave him his wish, using his pātiti.

A large number of prisoners were taken at Patoka, among them Te Herekiekie. Soon after the pā fell the missionary Richard Matthews arrived from Whanganui, and asked that the prisoners be released. Just as these discussions seemed to be bearing fruit, a contingent of Taranaki arrived to join Te Matakatea. All the new arrivals were greeted, then the captives were lined up to greet the newcomers, who advanced in a dignified manner in a similar line. But as they leant forward to hongi the visitors, to Matthews' horror each of the

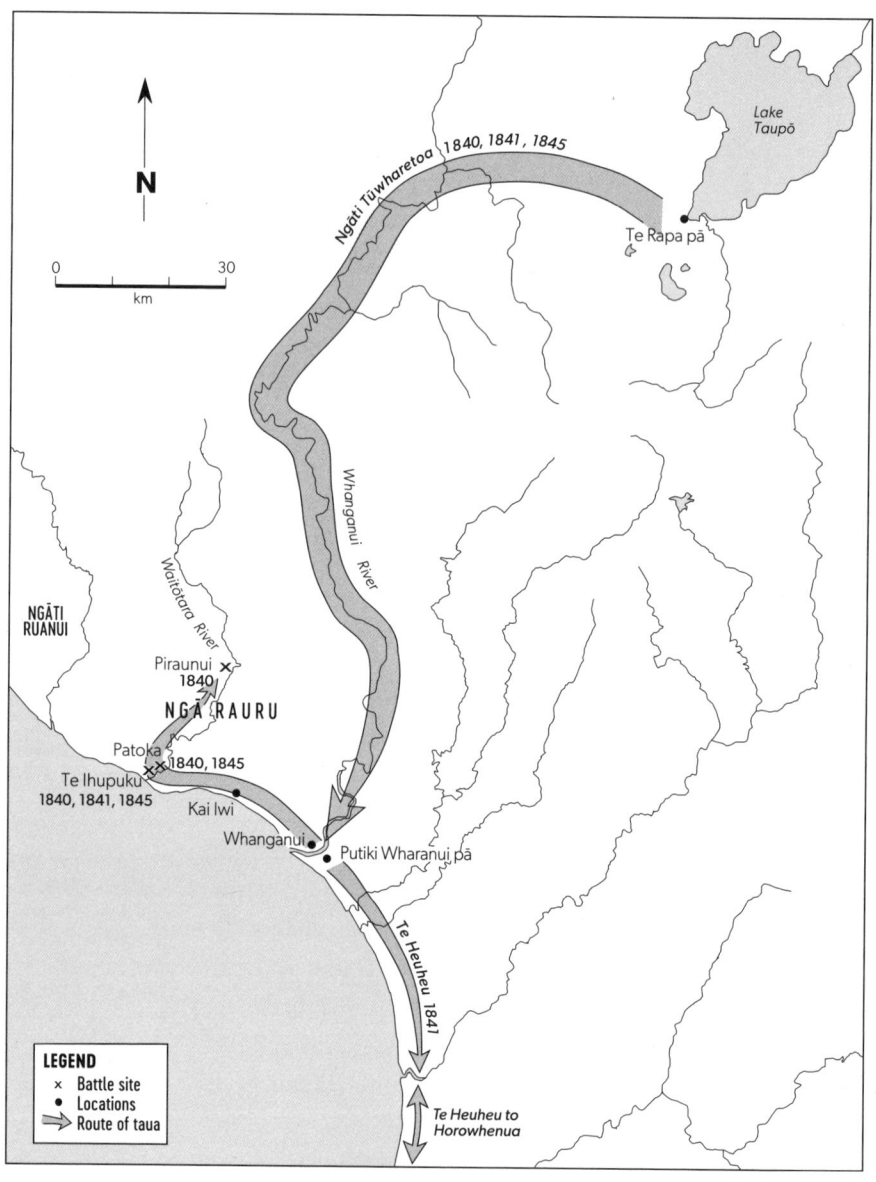

Ngāti Tūwharetoa taua to the Waitotara area, 1840–45.

Taranaki men drew a concealed weapon and swung it. Fighting broke out, with most of the captives being killed by hand-held weapons or shot. Among the few who survived was Te Herekiekie, who was allowed to return with news of the slaughter to Taupō.

Hearing what had occurred, the enraged Te Heuheu and Iwikau immediately set about raising a taua. Te

Heuheu requested assistance from Waikato, and their contingent brought the total to about six hundred toa. In February 1841 the taua headed south. It was a year after the first Treaty signings, but the Musket Wars were still well and truly alive in southern Taranaki.

THE TAUPŌ REACTION TO PATOKA

When the taua arrived in the headwaters of the Whanganui, Te Heuheu and Iwikau experienced for the first time a major change in attitude by experienced and respected Whanganui rangatira, a change that was increasingly gaining momentum throughout Aotearoa. For when they sought the assistance of Te Pehi Turoa, the Ngāti Patutokotoko rangatira who had fought so fiercely in the past, his response was in the negative. He informed them that he was in the process of converting to Christianity, and advised the taua to turn around and go home.

Te Heuheu was incensed at this and made a powerful speech that later became famous, deriding the Whanganui for having signed the Treaty, and asserting that they had lost their mana to a mere woman in Queen Victoria. He appealed to the age-old custom of supporting taua to avenge treacherous killings of their relatives and to recover their bones. But his oratory made no difference, and the most he achieved was an assurance that the taua would not be opposed as it passed down the Whanganui.

Meanwhile, news of the taua had reached Ngā Rauru and Ngāti Ruanui, who abandoned Patoka and Te Ihupuku pā. When the taua arrived there, both pā and some waka were destroyed, but these actions were insufficient to satisfy the desire for bloody retribution. Yet again, the decision was made to seek utu against iwi related to those who had inflicted the losses at Patoka.

Te Heuheu believed he could link up with his long-standing ally Te Whatanui of Ngāti Raukawa, who he knew was in a state of constant tension with Te Ātiawa, who were in turn closely allied with Ngāti Ruanui and Ngā Rauru. What could be better than to attack them in Horowhenua, thus gaining utu both for losses inflicted by these iwi and for his taua's Waikato contingent's losses at Ngamotu, Te Namu and Waimate in the years beween 1832 and 1834? With those aims in mind the taua travelled all the way to Horowhenua. To Te Heuheu's amazement, however, he found that Te Whatanui, just like Te Pehi Turoa, had converted to Christianity and no longer pursued war.

The taua had no option but to reluctantly turn and begin the long journey home without having achieved utu against Te Ātiawa — or Ngā Rauru or Ngāti Ruanui. The awareness of that lack of utu grew and gnawed at Te Heuheu and Iwikau for three more years, until they decided to raise another taua in December 1844. This time the taua was initially of moderate size, with just 170 Ngāti Tūwharetoa men. But once more it was swelled by a Waikato contingent of similar size, and the now powerful force once more descended the Whanganui to attack Ngā Rauru and Ngāti Ruanui.

On arriving at the mouth of the Whanganui, they found that in the intervening three years events had developed apace. There was now a small but permanent European township called Petre (modern-day Whanganui) opposite Putiki pā, and furthermore, most of the Te Atihaunui in Putiki had now converted to Christianity.

The taua made its camp on the northern side of the river, the side on which the European town stood, but being contemptuous of the Christian Māori (particularly as they still regarded the missionary Matthews as having been complicit in the massacre of the Ngāti Tūwharetoa captives at Patoka), they began to steal potatoes from the pā māra (gardens) across the river. Te Atihau reacted angrily and the Europeans, fearing an outbreak of violence, sent to Wellington for the Navy's help. Meanwhile a Te Atihau rangatira called Maewe one day drew a line in the māra and, clutching his musket, called out to some members of the taua that they could dig potatoes up to that line, but if they crossed it he would fire.

Soon after, HMS *Hazard* arrived from Wellington bringing some Imperial troops, with a Major Richmond in command. He and a party of officials landed and entered the taua's camp, where Richmond took a much firmer line than had been taken two years before with Taraia, Tupaea and Tohi Te Ururangi. Richmond informed Te Heuheu that if he did not return to Taupō immediately he would be regarded as an enemy of the Crown, and liable to attack by the forces on HMS *Hazard*. At this crucial moment some of the weight of the threat of Crown force was unfortunately removed by a strong offshore wind that carried the *Hazard* well out of sight for some days!

During this time, however, the Anglican Bishop Selwyn also spoke at length with Te Heuheu about the risks he was running, and in the end Te Heuheu agreed to a symbolic action to discharge the utu obligation. This involved approaching Te Ihupuku pā, firing a volley, then returning to Taupō. The bishop and Major Richmond visited Te Ihupuku and managed, after some difficulty, to get agreement there that no firing would be made in response. They also persuaded the large garrison there of about a thousand toa to lay out a supply of food for the Ngāti Tūwharetoa taua at Kai-iwi as a peace token.

Despite these good intentions, matters did not go entirely smoothly. First there was the reaction of Te Heuheu to the pathetically small pile of food left at

Kai-iwi, which was all the pā garrison felt they could give as they were already struggling to feed themselves. Te Heuheu took this as an insult and burnt the food in disgust.

The following day the bishop, Major Richmond and a few of their officials went into Te Ihupuku to persuade the pā's occupants to allow the taua to come up to the southern bank of the Waitōtara River to fire their formal volley. It took all that day and into the evening to arrange this, but then the following morning they became aware that some of the younger hotheads in the pā intended to secrete themselves in firing positions by the river banks and ambush the taua.

Selwyn and Richmond quickly crossed the river to try to persuade Te Heuheu to fire his volley from a distance. Te Heuheu expressed his appreciation for their bringing this news of the planned ambush, and agreed to fire his volley from where they were standing, about 5 kilometres from the pā. With that, a haka was vigorously performed, the volley fired, and the taua turned for home.

In that dramatic and highly symbolic manner the Musket Wars finally came to an end.

AFTERWORD

In purely factual terms the Musket Wars can be seen to have come to a conclusion in 1845 when the men of Te Heuheu's Ngāti Tūwharetoa taua fired the dramatic final salvo near Te Ihupuku pā and made their way home to Taupō. However, the consequences for Māori of these long-running, massively disruptive wars, which had spanned nearly forty years since the first use of muskets at Moremonui in 1807, were to linger well into the future. More than 150 years after the final confrontation, the significance of the Musket Wars continues to be felt.

As we have seen, the Musket Wars had a huge impact on relationships between iwi and hapū throughout the country. The outcomes of the various conflicts also had consequences in terms of customary entitlements that have impacted, and continue to impact on Treaty settlements, particularly in locations with overlapping interests. I have mentioned earlier the need for the Musket Wars to be recognised as being of major significance in the teaching of our history, and not simply treated as some minor aspect of 'initial contacts' with Pākehā. A knowledge of these events and the background to them is essential not only for all those involved in the settlement process, but for all New Zealanders who wish to understand their country and its history. Most importantly, however, these are not just events of 'historical' significance — they continue to affect our relationships, how we work together as we go forward, and how we view our country.

Connecting to these events physically by identifying and protecting locations of particular interest, making them accessible and providing information about what has occurred, is also important. As with other significant eras in our history, being able to imagine and interpret these dramatic and wide-sweeping events 'on the ground', will enable us to look at our country with fresh eyes.

GLOSSARY

Note: Translations provided in this glossary reflect usage in the text; it should be noted that many words have different meanings depending on context.

aruhe	fern, fern root
haka	war dance
hākari	feast
hapū	section of an iwi
heke	travelling party, migration
hui	meeting
iwi	tribe
kāinga/kāika	village, settlement
kaitiakitanga	guardianship
kauhoe/kaihoe	waka crew or paddlers
kaumātua	old man, elder
kō	digging stick
kōhera	bad omen
kōhuru	stratagem
kuia	old woman
kūpapa	Māori fighting in alliance with the Crown
mana	authority, influence, pride, power
manaakitanga	hospitality
māra	cultivation, garden
mau rākau	traditional Māori weapons
mere	short flat club
mōkihi	a craft or raft made of flax stalks tied in bundles
niho mangā	barracouta's tooth
ope	group; part or division of a taua or heke
pātītī	tomahawk
patu	short flat weapon, similar to a mere
patu aruhe	heavy stone tool used to beat the roots of ferns (aruhe)
pounamu	greenstone
pūkana	the grimacing often accompanying waiata, whaikōrero or haka
pūtangitangi	paradise ducklings
pūwhara	tower
rāhui	embargo, ban
rangatira	chief
raupatu	conquest
ringa kaha	force of arms
rohe	district
taiaha	short stabbing spear with a flattened end, able to be wielded like a sword
takahi	walking of the land
take	cause, motivation
takiwā	district of an iwi
tao	spear
taonga	highly prized object or natural resource
tau	a traditional form of song
taua	raiding party, raid
tikanga	customary practice
toa	warrior
tohutō	macron
tuku	formal gift
umu (hangi)	earth oven
utu	revenge, retribution
waiata	song, chant
waka	canoe
waka taua	war canoe
whaikōrero	formal speech
whānau	family
wharau	lean-to, temporary shelter
whata	very high, stage-like structure or platform

SELECT BIBLIOGRAPHY

This bibliography lists key books and theses, with a focus on recent publications in the field. A full bibliography is available in *The Musket Wars*. A massive source of materials and or iwi / hapū specific materials relevant to the effects of the Musket Wars has been created in recent decades by Waitangi Tribunal Reports, and the evidential reports prepared as part of the Record of Inquiry for each historical inquiry. The latter sources are detailed in each report. The Waitangi Tribunal webpage is the commencement point for those reports and sources.

Anderson, A. *Te Puoho's Last Raid*. Otago Heritage Books, Dunedin, 1986.

—— (ed.), Beattie, J.H. *Traditional Lifeways of the Southern Maori*. University of Otago Press, Dunedin, 1994.

—— Binney, J. & Harris A. *Tangata Whenua: An Illustrated History*. Bridget Williams Books, Wellington, 2014.

Ballara, A. *Iwi: The Dynamics of Māori Tribal Organisation from c.1769 to c.1945*. Victoria University Press, Wellington, 1998.

—— *Taua: 'Musket Wars', 'land wars' or 'tikanga'? Warfare in Māori Society in the Early Nineteenth Century*. Penguin, Auckland, 2003.

Barratt, G. *Bellingshausen: A visit to New Zealand 1820*. Dunmore Press, Palmerston North, 1979.

Barton, R.J. *Earliest New Zealand: The Journals and Correspondence of the Rev. John Butler*. Palamontain & Petherick, Masterton, 1923.

Begg, A.C. & N.C. *The World of John Boultbee*. Whitcoulls, Christchurch, 1979.

Best, E. *The Pa Maori*. Government Printer, Wellington, 1927.

—— *Tuhoe: The Children of the Mist*. A.H. & A.W. Reed, Wellington, 1925.

Binney, J. *The Legacy of Guilt: A Life of Thomas Kendall*. Bridget Williams Books, Wellington, 2005.

Brailsford, B. *The Tattooed Land: The Southern Frontiers of Pa Maori*. Reed, Wellington, 1981.

Buchanan, J.D.H. *The Maori History and Place Names of Hawke's Bay*. Reed, Wellington, 1973.

Burns, P. *Te Rauparaha: A New Perspective*. Reed, Wellington, 1980.

Carkeek, W.C. *The Kapiti Coast: Maori Tribal History and Place Names of the Paekakariki–Otaki District*. A.H. & A.W. Reed, Wellington, 1966.

Carleton, H. *The Life of Henry Williams, Archdeacon of Waimate*. 1874. Revised edition. A.H. & A.W. Reed, Wellington, 1948.

Cloher, D.U. *Hongi Hika: Warrior Chief*. Viking, Auckland, 2003.

Collins, H. *Ka Mate, Ka Ora! The Spirit of Te Rauparaha*. Steele Roberts, Wellington, 2010.

Cowan, J. *A Trader in Cannibal Land: The Life and Adventures of Captain Tapsell*. Coulls, Somerville & Wilkie, Dunedin, 1935.

Davis, C.O. *The Life and Times of Patuone*. Steam Printing Office, Auckland, 1876.

Easdale, N. *Missionary and Maori: Kerikeri 1819–1860*. Te Waihora Press, Lincoln, 1991.

Evison, H.C. *Te Waipounamu: The Greenstone Island*. Aoraki Press, Christchurch, 1993.

Grace, J. Te H. *Tuwharetoa: A History of the Maori People of the Taupo District*. A.H. & A.W. Reed, Wellington, 1959.

SELECT BIBLIOGRAPHY 195

Gudgeon, T.W. *The History and Doings of the Maori from the Year 1820 to the Signing of the Treaty of Waitangi*. H. Brett, Auckland, 1885.

Hamer, D. & Ballara, A. *The Making of Wellington 1800–1914*. Victoria University Press, Wellington, 1990.

Harcourt, M. *The Day Before Yesterday*. Reed, Wellington, 1940.

Houston, J. *Maori Life in Old Taranaki*. Reed, Wellington, 1965.

Jones, K.L. *Nga Tohuwhenua Mai Te Rangi: A New Zealand Archaeology in Aerial Photographs*. Penguin, Auckland, 2007.

Jones, P. Te H. *King Potatau*. Polynesian Society, Wellington, 1959.

Keene, F. *Tai Tokerau*. Whitcoulls, Christchurch, 1975.

Kelly, L.C. *Tainui*. Polynesian Society, Wellington, 1949.

Kereama, M. *The Tail of the Fish*. Oswald-Sealey, Auckland, 1968.

King, M. *Moriori: A People Rediscovered*. Viking, Auckland, 1989.

Lambert, T. *The Story of Old Wairoa and the East Coast*. 1925. Third edition. Reed, Auckland, 1998.

Lawson, L.B. *Wharekahika: A History of Hicks Bay*. L. Lawson, Onepoto, 1986.

Little, M. & B. Macnaught (ed.). *He Whakaputanga: Declaration of Independence 1835*. Dept of Internal Affairs, Wellington, 2017.

McConnell, B.N. *He Taonga Tuku Iho*. Reed, Auckland, 1999.

McDonald, R.A. *Te Hekenga: Early Days in Horowhenua*. G.H. Bennett, Palmerston North, 1929.

McEwen, J.M. *Rangitane: A Tribal History*. Heinemann Reed, Auckland, 1986.

Mackay, J.A. *Historic Poverty Bay and the East Coast, North Island, New Zealand*. J.G. Mackay, Gisborne, 1949.

McNab, R.M. *The Historical Records of New Zealand*. Two volumes. Government Printer, Wellington, 1908.

—— *The Old Whaling Days*. Whitcombe & Tombs, Wellington, 1913.

—— *From Tasman to Marsden*. J. Wilkie, Dunedin, 1914.

Mitchell, H. & J. *Te Tau Ihu o Te Waka: A History of Maori of Nelson and Marlborough*. Volume 1. Huia Publishers, Wellington, 2004.

Mitira, J.H. (Mitchell, J. H.). *Takitimu: A History of the Ngati Kahungunu People*. A.H. & A.W. Reed, Wellington, 1944.

Monin, P. *Waiheke Island: A History*. Dunmore Press, Palmerston North, 1992.

—— *This is My Place: Hauraki Contested 1769–1875*. Bridget Williams Books, Wellington, 2001.

Moon, P. *Fatal Frontiers: A New History of New Zealand in the Decade before the Treaty*. Penguin, Auckland, 2006.

O'Malley, V. & Armstrong, D. *The Beating Heart: A political and socio-economic history of Te Arawa*. Huia Publishers, Wellington, 2008.

Phillips, F.L. *Nga Tohu o Tainui: The Landmarks of Tainui*. Two volumes. Tohu Publishers, Onehunga, 1989, 1995.

Pool, D. Ian, *The Maori Population of New Zealand 1769–1971*. Auckland University Press, Auckland, 1979.

—— *Te Iwi Maori: A New Zealand Population, Past, Present and Projected*. Auckland University Press, Auckland, 1991.

Ramsden, E. *Marsden and the Missions: Prelude to Waitangi*. A.H. & A.W. Reed, Dunedin, 1936.

Rawson, D.H. *The Gliding Peak: More Tales of Old Taranaki*. D.H. Rawson, New Plymouth, 1990.

Richards, R. *Murihiku A revised history of the Southern New Zealand from 1804 to 1844*. Lithographic Services, Wellington, 1995.

Rogers, L.M. *The Early Journals of Henry Williams, 1826–1840*. Pegasus Press, Christchurch, 1961.
Sale, E.V. *Whangaroa*. Whangaroa Book Committee, Kaeo, 1986.
Sherrin, R.A.A. & Wallace, J. H. *Brett's Historical Series: Early History of New Zealand*. H. Brett, Auckland, 1890.
Sissons, J., Wi Hongi, W. & Hohepa, P. *Ngā Pūriri o Taiamai: A Political History of Ngapuhi in the Inland Bay of Islands*. 2nd ed. Reed, Auckland, 2001.
Smith, S.P. *Maori Wars of the Nineteenth Century*. Second edition. Whitcombe & Tombs, Christchurch, 1910.
—— *History and Traditions of the Maoris of the West Coast*. Polynesian Society, New Plymouth, 1910.
Sole, T. *Ngāti Ruanui: A History*. Huia Publishers, Wellington, 2005.
Stafford, D.M. *Te Arawa: A History of the Arawa People*. A.H. & A.W. Reed, Wellington, 1967.
—— *Landmarks of Te Arawa*. Volumes 1 and 2. Reed, Auckland, 1994.
—— *A Wild Wind from the North: Hongi Hika's 1823 Invasion of Rotorua*. Reed, Auckland, 2007.
Stone, R.C.J. *From Tamaki-Makau-Rau to Auckland*. Auckland University Press, Auckland, 2001.
Tate. H. (ed.) *Karanga Hokianga*. Motuiti Community Trust, Kohukohu, 1986.
Taylor, G. *A History of Māori from Lake Grassmere to Wharanui*. Ward Museum, Blenheim, 2014.
Vayda, D. *Maori Warfare*. A.H. & A.W. Reed, Wellington, 1960.
Vennell, C.W. *The Brown Frontier*. A.H. & A.W. Reed, Wellington, 1967.
Walker, R. *Ōpōtiki-mai-Tawhiti: Capital of Whakatōhea*. Penguin, Auckland, 2007.
Wilson, O. *From Hongi Hika to Hone Heke: A Quarter of a Century of Upheaval*. John McIndoe, Dunedin, 1985.
—— *Kororareka & Other Essays*. John McIndoe, Dunedin, 1990.
Wright, M. *Guns and Utu: A Short history of the Musket Wars*. Penguin, Auckland, 2011.
Wright, O. *New Zealand 1826–27. From the French of Dumont D'Urville*. Wingfield Press, Wellington, 1950.
The People of Many Peaks. The Maori Biographies from the Dictionary of New Zealand. Volume 1. Bridget Williams Books/Department of Internal Affairs, Wellington, 1991.

THESES

Ballara, A. *The Origins of Ngati Kahungunu*. PhD thesis, Victoria University, Wellington, 1991.
—— *Warfare and Government in Ngapuhi Tribal Society: 1814–1843*. MA thesis, University of Auckland, Auckland, 1973.
Shawcross, K. *Maoris of the Bay of Islands*. MA thesis, University of Auckland, Auckland, 1966.

ARTICLES

(*JPS: Journal of the Polynesian Society*)
Downes, T. 'History of Ngati Kahungunu: Life of Nukupewapewa.' *JPS* 25: 33 & 77.
Graham, G. 'The Fall of Mauinina and Mokoia and the death of Kaea.' *JPS* 32: 94.
Melvin, L.W. 'Te Waharoa of the Ngati Haua.' *JPS* 71: 361.
Tarakawa, T. 'The Doings of Te Wera Hauraki and Ngapuhi on the East Coast N.Z.' *JPS* 8: 183 & 242, 9: 54 & 74
Te Kahu, T.W 'The Wars of Kati Tahu with Kati Toa.' *JPS* 10: 94.
Turumeke, E. 'Narrative of the Battle of Omihi.' *JPS* 3: 107.

INDEX

Page numbers in *italics* indicate illustrations.

A

Admiralty Bay 114
Ahaura River 116
Ahoaho 157
Ahuahu 68
Akaroa Peninsula whaling 31; *see also* Horomaka
Ahuriri River 143
Akaroa 111, 112, 117, 119, *122*, 132, 140, 145
Alligator Head 108
American whalers 159
Aotea (Great Barrier island) 71, 89
Aotearoa 70, 130, 132, 183, 189
Arowhenua 142
Ashley River *see* Rakahuri
Astrolabe 66, *122*
Atkins 160, 161
Auckland *see* Tāmaki
Australia, and musket trade 30
Avon River (Marlborough) 141
Awamate pā 105
Awaroa Stream 55
Awatere River, East Coast 44

B

Bay of Islands *see* Pēwhairangi
Bay of Plenty first use 12, 13; significance of taua 20, 21; effects of taua on 23, 44, 55, 81, 89, 91; and *Venus* 32, 33, 39, 40; and Ngāpuhi taua to Rotorua 58; and East Coast 61, 64, 68, 164; and Kaiuku 158 western 168, 179, 182 eastern effects of taua and migrations involving 24; musket trade 32; and Ngarara events 163, 165
Bayley's Beach *see* Ripiro
Bellingshausen, Captain von 42
Bluff 143
Boultbee, John 135
Bream Bay 64
British 185
Brown, Alfred 182
Burns, Barnet 164
Busby, James 70

C

Cambridge *see* Maungatautari
Camp Bay *see* Pohue
Canterbury, pā in 18 central, first use 12
Cape Campbell *see* Te Karaka
Chatham Islands *see* Rēkohu
Christchurch, first settlement 13
Christianity and Christians, influence for peace 13, 62, 166, 167, 178, 180, 189, 190
Clarke, George 183
CMS (Anglican Church Missionary Society) mission station 31; taua observed by 48; and Tauranga 180
Clementson 113, 114
Cloudy Bay *see* Karauripe
Coalgate *see* Whakaepa
Cook Strait *see* Raukawa Moana
Coromandel Peninsula taua and migrations involving 24, 67, 89; *Venus* 32; *see also* Te Tara o te Ika a Māui
Crail Bay 108
Croisilles Harbour 103, 114
Crown (British) effect of British military force 13, 14; Treaty guarantees to Māori 16; obligations arising from Treaty breach 17; significance 21; comparison of casualties inflicted by 21, 22; conflict at Whanganui 26; at Heretaunga (Hutt) 27; purchases in Te Tau Ihu 27; and He Whakaputanga 70; and Ngāiterangi and Te Arawa 183; and Te Heuheu 190
Cuba 129

D

Dannevirke 149
Dargaville 34, 41
de Thierry (Baron) 47
Dunedin 145
d'Urville, Dumont 66
D'Urville Island *see* Rangitoto

E

East Bay *see* Umukuri
East Coast (and East Cape) *see* Te Tai Rāwhiti
Elaine Bay 114
Elizabeth 112–14
Ellesmere Lake *see* Waihora
Endeavour Inlet 107
England and English, and Hongi Hika 47, 48, 53, 102
Esk River *see* Waiohinganga River
Europe and Europeans, and musket trade 30, 31, 75, 90, 128, 129, 130, 131, 136, 142, 145, 162–64, 183–85, 190
Evans, Mt *see* Pohue, Mt

F

Featherston 126
Fighting Bay *see* Ōraumoa
Fiordland, sealing 31, 131
Flaxbourne River *see* Waiharakeke
Forsyth Island *see* Paruparu
Foveaux Strait 131
France (and French) 70, 129

G

Gate Pā 26
'Girls' War' 67
Gisborne *see* Tūranganui
Golden Bay *see* Mohua
Goose Bay 110
Gore 127, 143
Green Lake *see* Rotokākahi
Greymouth and Grey River *see* Māwhera
Greytown 104
Guard, Jack 139

H

Haast Pass 127, 143
Haerehuka 168, 169
Hakikino 75
Hangaroa River 154
Haowhenua (Horowhenua battles) 94, 125, 128, 141
Haowhenua (Maungatautari pā) 80, 81, 91
Harwood, Captain 28
Hastings 75
Haupapa 169, 170, 172
Hauraki Gulf or basin, musket trade 31; and *Venus* 33; taua involving 42, 48, 71
Hawea Lake 143
Haweis 160, 162
Hawke Bay *see* Hawke's Bay
Hawke's Bay first use 12; significance of taua 21; taua and migrations involving 24, 75, 149, 150, 154

198 THE FORGOTTEN WARS

Hazard, HMS 190
He Whakaputanga 70
Heberley, Worser 110
Hempleman, George 132, 145
Herald 90
Heretaunga River (Hutt River) comparison of casualties 22; taua and migrations involving 25, 26, 27, 40, 125, 127
Heretaunga (Napier area) taua and migrations involving 24, 94, 149, 150, 152, 154, 155, Herua 62
Hicks Bay see Wharekahika
Hikairo 60, 178, 180
Hikapu pā 108
Hikupoto 62
Hikurangi 62
Hikareia 170, 171
Hine-i-turama 169, 170
Hobson, Governor William 183, 184
Hokianga Harbour and musket trade 30, 31; taua involving 40
Hokio Stream 97, 98
Hokitika 116
Hokowhitu 179
Hongi Hika 48, 51; and Venus 32, 39, 40; and Moremonui 35, 36; and Kendall and England 43, 102; taua to Tāmaki and Hauraki led by 48, 53, 55; and Mātakitaki 55, 58; and Rotorua 58, 60; and Te Aupōuri 62; and Te Ika a Ranganui 64; and Pomare 65; and Ngāti Pou 65, 67; and Te Wera 151
Hopai Peninsula 108
Horeke ship building 31
Horomaka whaling 31, 140, 142, 144, 145; see also Akaroa
Horowhenua first use 12; taua and migrations involving 24, 25, 74, 80, 82, 96, 97, 100, 119, 120, 125; and Ngāti Raukawa 94; and coalition dissolution 125, 127; and Taua-nui 141; and Te Whatanui 155, 189
Horowhenua (Lake) 76, 94, 96, 97, 99
Hotuiti 99, 100
Houhora 63
Houwawe 36
Huataki pā 106
Hukatere 63, 64
Hunua effects of taua on 25
Hunuhunua 66
Hutt River see Heretaunga

I

Imperial Army (British) 185

Iwikau 149, 175; and Te Matakatea 84; and Ngāti Kahungunu 149; and Ngā Rauru and Ngāti Ruanui 185, 186, 189, 190

J

Jean Bart 129

K

Kāi Tahu first use 12; significance of taua involving 21; taua involving 27; and Tuturau 28, 127; sealers 31; and Kekerengu 104; and Ōmihi and Kaikoura 107, 108, 110–14; and northern taua to Kaiapoi and Ōnawe 116–20, 136; early sources of muskets 131, 132; Taua-iti 128, 138–42; Te Puoho 142–44; and final taua 144–46; and Waitangi Tribunal 146
Kāi Tūāhuriri 118, 132, 144
Kaiapoi significance and Kaihuanga involvment 18, 132, 135; and northern taua 111, 112, 114, 136; and siege of 114, 116, 117, 119, 140, 141, 168; and peace arrangements 144
Kaihau 82
Kahotea pā 155
Kaihu Valley 41
Kaihuanga clashes, 132–34
Kai-iwi 190, 191
Kaikōura first use 12; significance 18; and northern taua 104, 116, 117; and Taua-iti and Taua-nui 136, 140, 142
Kaingaroa (Rēkohu) 146
Kaingaroa Plains 75
Kaipaka pā 80, 81
Kaipara Harbour and area effects of Ngāpuhi taua on 22, 41, 64; and Te Amiowhenua 75
Kaitaia 63
Kaitorete Spit 135, 142
Kaiuku siege 24, 158
Kaiwaka Stream 157
Kakapo Bay 139, 140
Kakatarau 165, 166
Ka Mate 87, 92, 192
Kāpara Te Hau (Lake Grassmere) significance 18, 106, 127, 136, 138
Kaparatehau (rangatira) 26
Kāpiti Island first use 12; taua and migrations affecting 24, 73, 76, 104; whaling 31; and Te Rauparaha 40, 59, 75, 96, 124, 125; and Ngāti Raukawa 94; and Ngāti Toa 99–103; and Kekerengu and

Te Waipounamu 106–108, 111–14; and Te Maiharanui 136; and Taua-iti and Taua-nui 139, 140, 142; and aftermath of Te Puoho's taua 144, 145
Kapuni Stream 80, 84
Karaka Point 108
Karauripe (Cloudy Bay) 140
Karetai 136, 139, 140, 142, 145
Kata 169, 170, 172
Katikati 182
Kāti Māmoe sealers 31
Kāti Waewae 116
Kauhoe 144
Kawakawa Bay 61
Kawatiri (Westport) 116
Kawau Island 82
Kaweheitiki pā 81
Kawepō, Renata 157, 174
Kawhia first use 12; migrations from 23; Captain Kent 32, 79; and Tuwhare 37, 38; and Te Rauparaha 72
Kekeparoa 25, 164
Kelly 32
Kendall, Thomas musket source 31; and Hongi Hika 43, 51
Kent, Captain musket trade 32, 79, 81
Kerikeri musket sources 31; and Ngāti Whātua 41; taua involving 48, 68
Kiharoa 170
Knight, Samuel 172
Kohere, Mokena 165
Kopu 43
Korokai 171
Korokoro 39, 40, 42, 43
Kororareka 68
Korowhai 42, 46
Kōwhai pā 106, 116, 124
Kukeke 143
Kukutai 75
Kūpapa comparison of losses inflicted by 21, 22
Kurahaupō taua affecting 24, 103, 106, 107, 108, 110, 112, 141

L

Lake Forsyth see Wairewa
Lake Onoke 104
Lake Papaitonga 97
Lake Rotoehu 58, 172, 179
London 47
Lord Rodney 28, 146
Lottin Point see Wakatiri
Lyttelton Harbour see Whakaraupō

INDEX 199

M

Maewe 190
Mahia pā at 18; effects of migrations involving 24; and Ngāpuhi taua 45, 61, 62; and Nukupewapewa 126; and Te Paraihe's and Te Wera's involvement 148, 150–54; and Heretaunga clashes 155; and Kaiuku siege and aftermath 158, 159; and Ngarara events 164; Mahurangi 42, 46
Mair, Gilbert (senior) 90, 91
Makakote pā 94
Makarora 143
Maketu 175; Tapsell at 32; and Ngāti Pukenga 39; and Pomare 44; and Te Heuheu 93; and Te Arawa 169–70, 177–80
Mama 72, 78
Manaia 80
Manawatāwhi (Three Kings Islands) effects of migrations involving 25, 64
Manawatū 103; and Te Rauparaha's taua and heke 96, 97, 100, 105
Mangakahia 41
Mangamuka 66
Manganui (Port Underwood) whaling 31; taua involving 106; and Taua-iti and Taua-nui 139, 140
Mangapiko 56, 57
Mangatoa 76, 92
Mangawhai 92
Manukau Harbour 55
Manukorihi see Te Orahi
Maraenui and Venus 34, 40, 61
Marakopa Beach 77
Marfell's Beach 106
Marino 61
Marlborough Sounds 103, 131
Marsden, Samuel forbids musket trade 31; and Venus 40
Maruroa 143
Marutūahu first use 12; taua and migrations involving 24, 80, 81, 89, 158, 182; and musket trade 32
Mataipuku 172
Mātakitaki significance 18, 78, 79; losses at 21, 55, 56, 58
Matakoa Point 45
Matamata first use 13; migrations and taua involving 23, 24, 68, 80, 81; and Te Arawa taua 169–71, 177, 178, 180
Matarehua 39
Matata 170

Mataura River 143, 144
Matthews, Richard 187, 190
Mauinaina significance 18, 80; and Ngāpuhi 53, 56
Maungaharuru 160
Maungakawa 80
Maunganui, Mount taua involving 42, 46, 180
Maunganui Bluff 34, 35
Maungapōhatu 61
Maungatapu pā (Tauranga) significance 18, 68; and Ngāti Maru 90; and Te Arawa 178, 180–82
Maungatautari taua and migrations affecting 23, 24, 25, 80, 81, 94, 155
Maungawharau 149
Māwhera (Greymouth and Grey River) 116, 144
Mayor Island see Tuhua
Measley Beach outbreak of measles 14, 142
Mikotahi pā 82
Mimihau Stream 143
Moehau 67
Mohua (Te Tai Tapu or Golden Bay) first use 12; and Ngawhakawa 29; and northern taua 116; and Te Puoho 127, 144
Mokau River 82, 100
Mokoia pā (Auckland) significance 18, 80; and Ngāpuhi 53, 56
Mokoia Island (Lake Rotorua) and Ngāpuhi 29, 58, 60; and Ngāti Hauā 171
Molesworth Station 116
Montefiores 32
Moremonui 34, 35, 36, 64, 192
Morgan, John 180
Moriori first use 12; significance of taua on 21, 23, 24; and raupatu 146, 147
Mōtītī Island and Venus 33, 39; and Te Haramiti 68, 81; and Ngarara events 164
Mōtu and Venus 34, 40; and Te Wera 61; and Whakatohea 164
Motuhoa Isalnd 179
Motuhora Island 160, 162
Motunui 78
Motuopihi 76, 92, 94, 185; pā 87
Motutaiko Island 160
Motutawa 59, 82, 178
Muaūpoko migrations involving 24, 96–101; and Ngawhakawa 28; and Ngāti Raukawa 95

Murihiku (Southland) first use 12; source of muskets 27; and Tuturau 28; sealing 31; and northern taua 117, 119, 127, 136; and Kaihuanga clashes 132, 133; and Taua-nui 140, 142; and Te Puoho 143, 144; and aftermath 145
Murimotu effects of migrations involving 25, 64
Muriwai (location) 75
Muriwhenua 178, 180, 181
Murupaenga at Moremonui 34, 35; and Taiamai 41; and Te Ika a Ranganui 64

N

Nainai 169
Napier first settlement 13, 152
Navy (Royal) 190
Nelson see Whakatū
New Plymouth first settlement 13; purchase of land for 26; see also Ngāmotu
New South Wales 114, 145
New Zealander 43, 162, 163
New Zealand Company colonists 16; purchases 26, 27; and Te Kuititanga 128; and Rēkohu 129; and Te Tau Ihu 145
New Zealand Wars comparison 14, 15, 21, 23; significance 19, 26, 165
Ngā Teko pā 84
Ngāi Tahu see Kāi Tahu
Ngāiterangi first use 13; comparison of casualties 22, and NZ Wars 26, and Te Waru 28, musket trade 32; and Venus 34, 39; and Te Morenga 42; and Pomare 44; and Ngāpuhi taua to Rotorua and Bay of Plenty 58, 64, 82; and Maungatapu 68; and Te Tumu 70; and Te Waharoa 81, 91, 92; and Te Rohu 89, 90; and Haweis events 162; and conflicts with Te Arawa 168–85
Ngaki 183
Ngākuta Bay (Port Underwood) 138
Ngāmotu hapū 79, 81, 125, 126
Ngāmotu (New Plymouth) and whaling 31; and Waikato taua 82, 120, 189
Ngāpuhi first use 11, 13; early taua 20, 34, 38, 75; Waipa occupation 21; comparison of losses inflicted by 21, 22; general effects of taua 22, 24,

25, 26, 72, 89, 93, 94, 106, 148, 166; at Tauranga 28; musket trade 31; and *Venus* 32, 33, 34, 39, 40; at Moremonui 34, 35, 36; and Tareha 41; and Murupaenga 41; and Te Waru 43; and Korokoro 43; and Te Whetumatarau 45; and Ngāti Whātua 46; and taua led by Hongi Hika 47, 53, 54, 80; and Pomare 55, 65; and Mātakitaki 55–58, 78, 79; and Rotorua taua 58–60, 178, 179; and Pomare and Te Wera 61, 62, 64, 153; and Te Aupōuri 62, 63; and Te Ika a Ranganui 64, 65; and Ngāti Pou 66; and Te Wherowhero 66, 67, 69, 80, 82; and Rangitukia 67; and 'Girls' War' 67; and Maungatapu taua 68; and Te Haramiti 68, 81, 91, 92; and Titore 70; and He Whakaputanga 70; and 1837 civil conflict 71; and Aotea 71; and Te Rohu 89, 90; and Te Wera and Te Paraihe 94, 151; and Tuakiaki 154; and Heretaunga clashes 156; and Kaiuku siege 158; and *Haweis* events 162–64; and Kekeparaoa 164
Ngarara 148, 160, 162, 163
Ngāreua 179
Ngaruroro River 152
Ngatuna 129
Ngā Pōtiki hapū 164
Ngā Rauru 96; and Whanganui 120; and Ngāti Tūwharetoa 185, 186, 189, 190
Ngāi Tai 166
Ngāti Apa (Rangitikei area) effects of migrations involving 24, 96, 97, 99, 100, 103
Ngāti Apa ki te Rā Tō first use 12; effects of migrations involving 24; and Muaūpoko and Kāpiti Island 99, 100, 102, 103; and northern taua 66, 106, 107, 108, 116, 122
Ngāti Awa taua involving 24, 44, 55, 61, 64, 91, 164; musket trade 32; and *Venus* 39; and Ngarara events 148, 163; and Te Mautaranui events 152, 154; and Toka a Kuku 166
Ngāti Hauā clashes with Te Arawa 13, 14; migrations involving 24; and Te Haramiti 68; and Te Rauparaha 38, 52, 72; and Ngāti Maru and

Ngāti Paoa 80, 81, 89, 93; and alliance with Ngāiterangi 91, 92; and conflicts with Te Arawa 168–72, 177
Ngāti Hawea 152
Ngāti Hei 89
Ngāti Ira early effects 15; comparison of casualties 22; effects of taua and migrations involving 24, 26, 40, 76, 97, 99, 101, 103, 104, 108
Ngāti Kahungunu first use 13; taua and migrations involving 24, 26, 44, 45, 75, 148; musket trade 32; and Te Wera 61, 62, 64; and Ngāti Raukawa 94; and Te Rauparaha 97, 99, 101; and Ngāti Tama 104; and Te Ātiawa 125, 126; and Te Wera's protection 148; and Ngāti Tūwharetoa 149–54; and Mahia 151–54; and Pohatuoa and Heretaunga conflicts 154–57; and Kaiuku siege and aftermath, 158, 159; and Kekeparaoa 164
Ngāti Kōata and Kawhia 72; and Te Amiowhenua 77; and migration 96; and Tutepourangi 103; and Ngāti Toa taua 114; and alliance with Te Rauparaha 130; and Taua-iti 139
Ngāti Kuia first use 12; effects of migrations involving 24; and Muaūpoko and Kāpiti Island 99, 100, 102, 103; and northern taua 106, 108, 112, 114, 116
Ngāti Maniapoto and Te Rauparaha 72; and Te Amiowhenua 75, 77; and Ngāti Tama 82; and Te Arawa 169
Ngāti Maru significance of taua led by 21, 38, 40; comparison of losses inflicted by 22; taua and migrations involving 25, 26, 48, 53, 54, 55, 64, 69, 71, 89; and *Venus* 33, 34, 39, 40; and Rangitukia 67; and Ngāti Hauā 80, 81, 91; and Te Rohu 89, 90, 164; and Ngāti Tūwharetoa 92–94; and Ngāiterangi 178, 183
Ngāti Maru (Taranaki) 79, 80
Ngāti Mutunga first use 12; significance of taua and migrations involving 21, 24, 25, 26, 74; and Rēkohu 28; and migrations 96, 103, 104, 120,

127; and Ngāti Kahungunu 104, 129; and coalition dissolution 126, 128; and Ngāti Tama on Rēkohu 128, 129, 146, 147; and Taua-iti 139
Ngāti Paoa effects of taua and migrations involving Ngāpuhi 24, 25, 46, 48, 53, 55, 66, 89; and Ngāti Hauā 80
Ngāti Patutokotoko 189
Ngāti Pikiao 171, 172, 179
Ngāti Porou first use 13; musket trade 32; and *Venus* 34, 39; Ngāpuhi taua involving 44, 45, 61, 62; and Whānau a Apanui 148, 165, 166, 167; and Ngarara events 163, 164, 165; and Toka a Kuku 166, 167
Ngāti Pou 66, 68
Ngāti Pukeko 39, 55, 61
Ngāti Pukenga 39, 60, 169
Ngāti Rāhiri 37
Ngāti Ranginui 26, 180
Ngāti Rangitahi 26, 27
Ngāti Rangiwewehi and Te Aokapurangi 29, 60; and Ngāpuhi taua 69; and Ngāiterangi 169, 172; and Ngāti Hauā 178–80
Ngāti Rārua and Kawhia 72; and Te Amiowhenua 77; and migration 96; and taua to Kaiapoi 116–18; alliance with Te Rauparaha 130; and Taua-iti 139; and Te Puoho 144
Ngāti Raukawa battles involving 24; taua and migrations involving 24, 25, 94, 104, 125; losses at Te Totara 55; and Te Rauparaha 60, 103, 130; and Te Amiowhenua 76; and Ngāti Maru 92; and Te Ātiawa 95, 189; and coalition dissolution 125, 146; and Taua-iti 139; and Ngāti Kahungunu 150, 151, 154, 156; and Kaiuku siege and aftermath 158, 160
Ngāti Rēhia 73
Ngāti Rehua 71
Ngāti Ruanui 79, 82, 84, 89; and Te Rauparaha's heke 96; and Ngāti Tūwharetoa and Te Atihaunui 168, 185, 189, 190
Ngāti Tama first use 12; significance of taua and migrations involving 21, 24, 25, 26, 73, 74, 77, 82, 96, 120; and Rēkohu 28; and Ngawhakawa 28, 29; and Kāpiti Island 100, 103, 104;

INDEX

and Ngāti Kahungunu 104; and taua to Kaiapoi 116, 118; coalition dissolution 125, 126, 128; and Ngāti Mutunga on Rēkohu 128, 129, 146, 147; and Te Puoho's taua to Tuturau 143, 144
Ngāti Tamaterā 64, 81, 89, 153, 182
Ngāti Tarawhai 179
Ngāti Tauwhao 183
Ngāti Te Kohera 155, 160
Ngāti Te Upokoiri and Ngāti Raukawa 94; and Ngāti Kahungunu 151, 157
Ngāti Tipa 75
Ngāti Toa first use 12; significance of taua led by 21, 23, 25; migrations led by 23, 25, 96; battles involving 24; sales to NZ Company 27; and Tuwhare 37; and von Bellingshausen 42; and Kawhia 72; and Te Amiowhenua 75, 77; and Ngāti Raukawa 94; and Muaūpoko 97, 98, 99; and Kāpiti Island 100, 103; and Te Pehi Kupe 102; and Kaiapoi 111; and Takapuneke 113, 114; and Te Hoiere and Kaiapoi taua 114, 118, 119; and Te Ātiawa 127, 128; and customary rights 130; and Taua-iti 136, 138–40; and final Kāi Tahu taua 145
Ngāti Tūwharetoa first use 12, 13; significance of taua involving 21, 24; musket trade 32; and Te Matakatea 84; and Ngāti Maru taua 92, 93; and Ngāti Kahungunu 149–52, 155, 156; and Kaiuku siege and aftermath 158, 159; and Ngā Rauru and Ngāti Ruanui 168, 185, 186, 190, 192
Ngāti Wai 71
Ngāti Whakaue 168–69, 171, 177–79
Ngāti Whanaunga 89
Ngāti Whātua and Ngāpuhi taua 21, 34; taua and migrations involving 24, 25, 75, 78; and Moremonui 34, 35, 36; and Tuwhare 37; and Tareha 41; and Korowhai 42; and Te Ika a Ranganui 64, 65; and Ngāti Kahungunu 153
Ngāti Whatuiāpiti 149
Ngaure 163
Ngawhakawa endurance of 28, 144

Ngunuru effects of Waikato taua on 22
Niho 116, 144
Nikora 157
Nimble 183
Ninety Mile Beach *see* Te Oneroa
Nohoawatea 21, 64
North America and musket trade 30
North Cape 64
Northland 156
North Island musket effects throughout 22, 36; musket trade 32; and von Bellingshausen 42; and Hawke's Bay taua 149; *see also* Te Ika a Māui
Northern Wars comparison 22
Nuhaka River 153
Nuka 182
Nukupewapewa 104, 126
Nukutaurua effects of taua and migrations involving 24; and Te Wera and Te Paraihe 151

O

Oaro 110
Ōhau Channel 58
Ōhau River (Horowhenua) 97
Ōhauā 61
Ohinekonehu pā 157
Ōhinemutu 171–72, *176*, 177–78
Ōhiwa Harbour 90, 91, 164
Ohura River 94
Okahu pā 172
Okahukura 39
Okauwharetoa 45
Okoki pā 74, 75, 77
Okukari pā 106, 110
Okurarenga significance 18, 153, 158, 159
Omakukara pā 159, 160
Omere (Cape Terawhiti) 41
Ōmihi significance 18, 104, 108, 110, 111, 136
Omokoroa pā 180
Omuru-iti 163, 165
Onapua Bay 106
Ōnawe pā significance 18; and northern taua 111, 119, *122*, 136, 140
Ongare pā 182, 183
Ōpotiki comparison of casualties 22; effects of migrations involving 25; musket trade 32; and Pomare and Te Wera 61, 91
Opua Bay 106, 139
Opunake 80, 84
Orahiri pā 58, 79
Orangituapeka 84

Ōraumoa (Fighting Bay) 139, 140
Ōruanui 159
Otahuhu 55
Otago *see* Ōtākou
Otaka pā 81, 82
Otamarakau pā 169
Otara 61
Ōtaki first use 12; and Ngāti Raukawa 94, 95, 128; and Te Rauparaha 96, 103, 125
Ōtākou (Otago) outbreak of measles 14; whaling 31; and northern taua 117, 119, 127, 136; and musket sources and Kaihuanga clashes 131, 132, 134; and Taua-iti and Taua-nui 139, 140, 142; and Te Puoho's taua 143; and final Kāi Tahu taua 144, 145
Ōtorohanga 58
Otuihu 68, 71
Otūmoetai pā 90, 181, 182
Ouokaha Island 108

P

Paekākāriki pā 98–100
Paengaroa 60
Paewaka 152
Pakiri 46
Pakowhai 151
Pakura 165
Panmure Basin 53
Papuni Stream 155
Parahaki pā 169
Parapara 144
Parinui o Whiti 106, *124*, 141, 145
Paruparu (Forsyth Island) 108
Patangata 155
Patea (South Taranaki) 186
Patea Inland 151
Patoka pā 84, 186, 187, 189, 190
Patuki, Topi 144, 145
Patuone *41*; taua led by 40, 75, 76
Pehi Tahau 119
Pehikatea 104, 125
Pelorus Sound *see* Te Hoiere
Peraki 132, 144, 145
Petre *see* Whanganui
Pēwhairangi (Bay of Islands) and musket trade 30, 31, 32; and *Venus* 32, 39; taua involving 42, 43, 44, 45, 62, 69; and Hongi Hika 47, 48; and 'Girls' War' 67; and *Haweis* events 162, 166
Piraunui pā 186
Piripekapeka pā 93
Pirongia, pā 18; and Mātakitaki 55
Pohaturoa pā 154
Pohue (Camp Bay) 134

202 THE FORGOTTEN WARS

Pohue, Mt (Mt Evans) 134
Pōkaia 34, 36
Pomare (I) 88; Whetoi, 68; early taua led by 40, 42, 44, 45; taua after 1820 led by 48, 54, 55; and Mātakitaki 58; and Rotorua 58, 60; and Bay of Plenty and East Coast 61, 62, 64, 148, 163; and Te Rore 65, 79; and Te Mautaranui 152–54
Pomare (II) Whiria 67, 68, 71
Pomare (Ngāti Mutunga) 146
Pongakawa Stream 58, 179, 180
Ponui 182
Porangahau 149
Porirua 103, 126
Port Jackson 89
Port Underwood see Manganui
Post Settlement Governance Entities (PSGEs) 18
Potangaroa 75
Pouto 41
Pouwhakarewarewa 102, 110
Poverty Bay 45, 164
Preservation Inlet see Rakituma
Privy Council 141
Puaha, Rawiri 138
Puhirua pā 172, 178
Pukehinahina (Gate Pā) comparison of casualties 22
Pukerangi 68, 82
Pukerangiora significance 18; comparison of casualties 22; and Te Orahi 29; and Te Amiowhenua 77, 79; and Te Wherowhero 81, 120, 168
Puketapu pā 162
Pukuharuru 143
Purahotangihia pā 157
Pureko 118
Puremutahuri Stream 166
Putikiwharanui pā effects of taua involving 25, 26, 190

Q
Queen Charlotte Sound see Te Tōtaranui

R
Raglan Harbour see Whaingaroa
Raihe-poaka 77
Rakahuri (Ashley) River 116–18
Rakituma (Preservation Inlet) whaling 31, 131
Rangihoua 31
Rangihoungariri 97
Rangi-i-paea 61
Rangitaiki 39
Rangitāne Manawatū: effects of migrations involving 24, 96, 97, 99, 100, 103, 105

Te Tau Ihu: first use 12; effects of migrations involving 24; and Kāpiti Island 100, 103, 105; and Te Rauparaha's taua 106, 108, 116, 117, 136; and Taua-iti and Taua-nui 138, 141
Rangitikei 101, 103
Rangitoto (D'Urville Is) and Ngāti Kuia 99, 103; and northern taua 114, 116; and Taua-iti 139
Rangitukia pā 67, 89, 90, 94, 165
Rangiwaitatao 152
Rarangi 106
Raukawa Moana (Cook Strait) first use 12; and Te Rauparaha 41, 42, 105, 106, 112, 114; and Taua-iti and Taua-nui 139
Raukokore River 165
Raukumara Ranges 164
Rēkohu (Wharekauri or Chatham Islands) 130; first use 12; effects of era on 17; significance of taua involving 21, 23, 24, 25, 28; and raupatu 127, 128, 146–47; and fighting between Ngāti Tama and Ngāti Mutunga 128
Reretawhangawhanga 100
Rerewaka 107, 108, 110, 111, 136
Retaruke River 94
Richmond, Major 190, 191
Ripapa Island pā 132, 133, 135
Ripiro (Bayley's Beach) 34
Roimata 113, 114
Rongowhakaata and Ngāpuhi and central iwi taua 44, 45, 148, 158; and Ngarara events, 164; and Toka a Kuku 166, 167
Rotoaira 76, 92, 93
Roto-a-Tara 75, 149–51, 155, 157, 158, 160
Rotoiti North Island 58, 60
Rotokākahi (Green Lake) 59, 178
Rotorua first use 13; and Ngāpuhi taua 58–60; and Te Amiowhenua 75; and Kaiuku 158; and Ngāiterangi and Ngāti Hauā 168–72, 178, 179
Ruahine Ranges 149
Ruakituri 152, 154
Ruapuke Island source of muskets 27, 131; sealers 31; and taua to Te Tau Ihu 120, 142; and Te Puoho 143, 144; and aftermath of Te Puoho's taua 145
Ruatāhuna 55, 61, 64, 157
Ruatoki 55
Russians 42

S
Selwyn, Bishop 190, 191
Shortland, Acting Governor Willoughby 184, 185
South America 34
South Island see Te Waipounamu
Southern Alps see Te Tiritiri-o-te-moana
Southland see Murihiku
South Westland (Te Tai Poutini) sealing 31
Stewart, Captain 112, 114
Stirling, William 143
Sydney and musket trade 32, 102; and visiting rangatira 47; and Captain Stewart 113, 114; and Karetai visit 142; and Kāi Tahu visit 145

T
Taepiro pā 102
Taiamai 39, 41
Taiaroa and nothern taua 117–19; and Kaihuanga clashes 132–34; and Taua-nui 140, 141; and Te Puoho 144; and final Kāi Tahu taua 145
Tainui first use 12; significance of taua led by 21; losses inflicted on 21; taua and migrations involving 25, 26, 64, 69, 75, 80–82, 89; and Te Orahi 29; musket trade 32; and Mātakitaki 55, 56, 58, 79; and Te Rauparaha 72, 78; and north and central Taranaki taua 79; and Ngāti Raukawa 94, 130; and Ngāti Tama 100; and Te Rauparaha's allied iwi 130; and Ngāti Kahungunu 151, 154; and Kaiuku siege 158; and Te Arawa 169, 181
Taiporutu, Wetini 171
Taitai mountains 45, 62
Takarua 80, 81
Takahanga pā 116, 117
Takapuneke 112–14, 122, 132, 136, 140
Takerei 116, 144
Tamahiki 87
Tamairangi 104
Tamaiwahia 169, 172
Tāmaki (Auckland) first settlement 13; pā at 18; taua and migrations involving 24, 26, 48, 53, 66, 75, 79; musket trade 32
Tamatekapua 60
Tamiuru 180
Tānenuiarnagi pā 151

INDEX

Tangahoe River 79
Tangatahara 111, 119, 120
Tāoho 34, 35
Taotaoriri 62
Taoū 75
Tapsell, Hans trading 32; and Te Heuheu 93; and Te Arawa 169, 170, 172
Tapuika 60, 179
Taputeranga taua involving 26, 76, 103, 104
Taraia 176, 182, 183, 190
Taranaki pā at 18; significance of taua 21, 36, 80; central Taranaki 80; northTaranaki, first use 12; comparison of casualties 22; taua and migrations involving 23, 25, 26, 37, 78, 79, 100, 103, 120, 125; and Te Amiowhenua 75, 76; coalition dissolution 130; south Taranaki, first use 12; significance of taua involving 21, 37, 38, 79, 80, 96, 168, 185; and Treaty of Waitangi 189
Taranaki, iwi 37, 38, 84, 185, 187, 188; mountain 80, 84
Tararu 54
Tararua Ranges 76
Taraua 23, 128
Tarawera 156, 157, 160
Tareha early taua led by 40, 41; and Hongi Hika 53; and taua led by 68, 82
Tasman Bay 116
Tasmanian waters 32
Tataramaika 37
Taua-iti effects of 27; and Te Tau Ihu 120, 128, 136, 138, 140
Taua-nui effects of 27; and Te Tau Ihu 120, 140, 141
Tauhara 41
Taumata a Kura, Piripi 62, 166, 167
Taumatawiwi 91
Taumutu pā 132, 134, 135
Taununu and Kaihuanga clashes 132–34
Taupiri and Te Orahi 29, 77
Taupō first use 13; significance of taua and migrations involving 21, 23, 81, 93, 94; and Ngāti Kahungunu 155–57; and aftermath of Kaiuku 159, 160; and Te Herekiekie and Te Heuheu 188, 189, 190, 192
Tauranga pā at 18; comparison of casualties 22; musket trade 32; taua involving 26, 42, 68, 69, 82, 90–92; and Te Waharoa 81; and *Haweis* events 162; and Te Arawa taua

169–71, 178–79
Tautari 170–72
Tauteka 84, 185–87
Tauwharerata pā 126, 127
Tawaputa 33
Tawhe 103
Tawhitinui Reach 114
Te Ahukaramu 94, 103, 155
Te Aitanga a Hauiti impacts of taua 148; and Kekeparaoa 164
Te Aitanga a Mahaki effects of migrations involving 24; and taua impacts 148; and Kekeparaoa 164
Te Amiowhenua and Te Orahi 29; iwi involved and route followed 75–78, 79, 81, 127; and Te Wharerangi 92; and Roto a Tara 150
Te Amohau 158, 182
Te Aokapurangi and Te Wera 29, 44, 60
Te Arakai 93
Te Araroa pā at 18; and Ngāpuhi taua 44, 45, 61
Te Arawa first use 13; and Hikairo 28; and Te Aokapurangi 29, 44; musket trade 32; and Ngāpuhi 43; losses at Te Totara 55; and Ngāpuhi taua 58–60, 69; and Te Rauparaha 105; and Ngāti Kahungunu 153; and Kaiuku siege 158; and conflicts with Ngāiterangi and Ngāti Hauā 168–72, 177–79, 185
Te Arawai 149, 151, 158
Te Ata o Tu, Hakopa 118, 119
Te Ātiawa Taranaki and Horowhenua area: comparison of casualties 22; taua and migrations involving 25, 26, 27, 37, 74, 79, 81, 82, 89, 89, 96, 100, 103, 144; sales to NZ Company 27; and Te Amiowhenua 29, 76–78, 81; and Te Namu 84; and Ngāti Raukawa 95, 125, 189; and Waiorua 102; and Ngāti Kahungunu 104, 125–27; and Kaiapoi 116; and coalition dissolution 125–27; and Te Rauparaha at Te Awaiti 128; and Taua-iti and Taua-nui 139
Te Atihaunui ā Pāpārangi taua and migrations involving 25, 76, 92, 94; and Te Rauparaha's taua and heke 96, 97, 120, 125; and Kāpiti Island 100; and Ngāti Ruanui and Ngā Rauru 168, 185, 190
Te Aupōuri taua and migrations

involving 24; and *Venus* 32; and Ngāpuhi taua 63
Te Awaitaia 72, 81
Te Awaiti whaling 31, 110, 128; and Taua-iti and Taua-nui 139
Te Haereroa 182
Te Hana 148, 162, 163
Te Hanataua, Te Rei 89
Te Hapuku 152, 160, 174
Te Haramiti (cannon) 92
Te Haramiti (rangatira) 68, 81, 91
Te Haupa and *Venus* 33, 34, 39, 40
Te Hauwaho 152
Te Heke Mai i Raro 94
Te Heke o Tama te Uaua 82, 120, 125
Te Heke Tātarāmoa 96
Te Heke Whirinui 94
Te Herekiekie 185–88
Te Heuheu, Iwikau *see* Iwikau
Te Heuheu, Mananui 175; and Ngāti Maru 92, 93; and Ngāti Kahungunu 149, 150, 155, 157; and Kaiuku siege and aftermath 158–60; and Ngā Rauru and Ngāti Ruanui 185, 188–91, 192
Te Heuheu, Manuhiri 149
Te Hiakai 72, 78
Te Hiko o te Rangi 112, 113, 118, 120, 121
Te Hinaki 53
Te Hiku o Te Ika (The top of the North Island) 62, 63
Te Hoiere (Pelorus Sound) 99, 108, 110, 114, 139
Te Hotete 151
Te Houtaewa 63
Te Hunga 169, 182
Te Ihupuku pā 186, 189–91, 192
Te Ika a Māui (North Island) first use 12, 20; taua involving 26, 47, 75, 77, 101, 103, 120
Te Ika a Ranganui comparison of losses 21; and battle 64
Te Kaeaea (Taringakuri) 26; settles with Crown 27; and Ngāti Kahungunu 104
Te Kai a te Karoro 35
Te Kaitote pā 77
Te Kaha and Te Wera 61; and Ngarara events 164, 165; and Toka a Kuku siege 166, 167
Te Kahupapa 149
Te Kanawa 75, 79, 89
Te Kani a Takirau and Ngāpuhi 45; and Kaiuku siege 158; and Toka a Kuku 166, 167
Te Karaka Cape Campbell 106, 136, 138, 140

Tūranga 164
Te Kawau, Apihai 87, and Pukerangiora 29, 75, 78
Te Kekerengu 103, 104, 108
Te Kohika 156–58
Te Kooti 157
Te Kotukuraeroa 185–87
Te Koutu 171, 172
Te Kuititanga 95, 128
Te Kura Te Au (Tory Channel) 106, 110, 139, 140
Te Maiharanui and northen taua 111–14, 120; and Kaihuanga clashes 132, 134, 135; and Te Pehi Kupe 100, 136; and Tutehounuku 136
Te Manutoheroa 116, 128
Te Matakatea (Te Moki), Wiremu 80, 84, 89; and Ngāti Tūwharetoa 185–87
Te Maunu 89
Te Mautaranui and Pomare 55, 61, 64, 152–54
Te Moananui 152
Te Moki *see* Te Matakatea
Te Mokonuiarangi 158
Te Momo 155, 156, 158
Te Morenga and *Venus* 32, 33, 34, 39; taua led by 40, 42, 43, 55; and Hongi Hika 53
Te Namu pā 80, 84, 189
Te Oneroa (Ninety Mile Beach) effects of Ngāpuhi taua on 22
Te Orahi (Manukorihi) courage and endurance 29; and Te Amiowhenua 77
Te Pae o te Rangi 59
Te Pakeke pā 152, 153, 155
Te Papa (Tauranga) significance of 18; comparison of casualties 22; taua involving 26, 90, 91; and Te Arawa 179
Te Papa (Ōpōtiki) 91
Te Papuni pā 152
Te Paraihe taua and migrations involving 24, 75; and Ngāti Raukawa 94; and Tutepakihirangi 125; and Ngāti Tūwharetoa 149–53; and Heretaunga clashes 155; and Kaiuku siege and aftermath 158–60
Te Parawhau taua involving 53, 66, 79, 82
Te Paruparu 136, 138
Te Patutarakihi 180
Te Pehi Kupe and Kapiti Island 99, 102; and Te Waipounamu 106, 107, 111, 112, 119, 120
Te Pehi Turoa and Ngāti Raukawa 94; and Te

Rauparaha 120, 125; and Ngāti Tūwharetoa 189
Te Porere 157
Te Puehu 179, 180
Te Puoho and Ngawhakawa 29; and migrations 100, 103, 104, 127; and heke to Tuturau 142–44; and aftermath 145
Te Puhi 53
Te Pukuatua 178, 182
Te Puni taua involving 27
Te Puniunuku pā 125
Te Raki 143
Te Ranga comparison of casualties 22; and NZ Wars 26
Te Rangihaeata 104, *123*; and Ngāti Rangatahi 27; and Muaūpoko 97; and Waiorua 102; and Taua-iti 139
Te Rangikoeaea 92
Te Rangitake, Wiremu Kingi 89
Te Rangituke 52, 65, 66, 79
Te Rangiwaitatao 64
Te Rapa pā (Taupō) 94, 185, 186
Te Rarawa taua involving 25, 63
Te Ratu (Te Raki or Te Rato) 98, 100, 107, 116
Te Rauangaanga and Te Rauparaha 72
Te Rauparaha first use 12; *38*, 52; and Te Whakataupuka 14; early taua involving 25, 26, 27; and Tuwhare 37, 38; and taua led by Patuone and Waka Nene 40, 42; and Motutawa 59, 60; and Kawhia 72; and Kāpiti Island 75, 100–103; and Te Amiowhenua 77; and migration 78, 80; and Motuopihi 92, 185; and Ngāti Raukawa 94; and Muaūpoko 94, 97, 99; and Rangitāne in Te Tau Ihu 105–108, 135; and Te Maiharanui 110–12, 114, 136; and Te Hoiere and Kaiapoi taua 114, 116–20; and Whanganui taua 120, 125; coalition dissolution 125, 130; and Te Puoho and Te Ātiawa 127, 128; and Taua-iti 138–42; and aftermath of Te Puoho's taua 144, 145; and Ngāti Raukawa 155
Te Rauparaha, Tamihana 41, *123*, 136
Te Reinga Falls 154
Te Riupawhara 93
Te Rohu and Tauranga 69; taua involving 81, 89, 91
Ngāti Maru rangatira comparison of casualties inflicted by 22; and Rangitukia

67, 94; taua involving 26, 69, 81, 89–91, 164
Ngāti Tūwharetoa wahine 160
Te Rore 65, 79
Te Roroa and Moremonui 34, 35
Te Ruaki pā 79, 84, 89
Te Ruamaioro 94
Te Ruaoneone 105, 106
Te Tai Poutini (Westland) and Ngawhakawa 29; sealing 31; and northern taua 116; and Te Puoho 127, 142–44
Te Tai Rāwhiti (East Coast) taua involving 21, 23, 40, 42, 44, 45, 64, 149; musket trade 32; and *Venus* 34; and Ngarara 163, 164; and Toka a Kuku 166
Te Tai Tapu (Golden Bay) *see* Mohua
Te Tai Tokerau (Northland) 11, 55, 60
Te Tara o te Ika a Māui and *Venus* 33; *see also* Coromandel Peninsula
Te Tarata pā 104
Te Tau Ihu (the Top of the South Island) first use 12; effects of taua on 23, 24, 25, 27, 63; and Muaūpoko and Kāpiti Island 98, 100, 102; and northern taua 105, 107, 116, 125; and Te Puoho 127, 128; coalition dissolution 130; and Taua-iti 136, 140; and final Kāi Tahu taua 144, 145; and Waitangi Tribunal 146
Te Tawai pā 157
Te Teko 39
Te Tiritiri-o-te-moana (the Southern Alps) 116
Te Tōtara pā Thames 18, 43, 53, 56, 80
Te Tōtaranui (Queen Charlotte Sound) *see* Tōtaranui
Te Tumu pā 70, 169–72, 177, 180
Te Ua 152, 154
Te Uira 97
Te Ururangi, Tohi 171, 182–85, 190
Te Waewae bay sealers 31
Te Waharoa death 14; and Te Rauparaha 72; and Ngāti Maru 80, 81; and Tareha 82; and Te Matakatea 89; and Whakatōhea 91; and Te Arawa 169, 171, 179, 180
Te Waharoa, Tamihana Tarapipi 180
Te Waipounamu (South Island) first use 12; effects of taua on 23, 63, 100, 103, 105; and Te

INDEX

Kekerengu 104; and northern taua 107, 108, 111, 112, 114, 119, 120; and Kaihuanga clashes 132, 135; and Taua-nui aftermath 142, 146
Te Waireporepo 152, 154
Te Waru courage of 28, 46; and *Venus* 39; at Maunganui 42, 43
Te Wera Hauraki taua led by and migrations involving 24, 42, 44, 45, 55; and Te Aokapurangi and Mokoia 29, 60; and East Coast 61, 62; and Ngāti Raukawa 94; and Tutepakihirangi 125; and Whānau a Apanui 148; and Mahia 151–53; taua with Pomare to avenge Te Mautaranui 154; and Heretaunga clashes 155, 156; and Kaiuku siege and aftermath 158–60; and Ngarara events 163; and Toka a Kuku 166
Te Whakataupuka death 14; and northern taua 119; and early musket acquisition 131; and Kaihuanga clashes 132–35; and Taua-nui 140, 142
Te Whanake 182, 183
Te Wharepouri taua and heke involving 27, 79, 82; and Ngāti Kahungunu 125–27; and Ngāti Mutunga 127
Te Wharerangi 76, 87, 92–94
Te Whareumu (Ngāpuhi rangatira) 43, 46
Te Whareumu (Ngāti Kahungunu rangatira) 45, 61, 62, 148, 151, 152
Te Whatanui 92, 94, 104; and Muaūpoko 95; and Ngāti Kahungunu 150, 154, 155, 158; and Ngāti Tūwharetoa 189
Te Whe 113, 114
Te Wherowhero 88; and Te Orahi 29; and Mātakitaki 56–58, 79; and Te Rangituke 66; and taua to Te Tai Tokerau 69, 70; and Te Rauparaha 72, 78; and Te Amiowhenua 77; and taua to north Taranaki 79, 81; and Pukerangi 82, later taua to north and south Taranaki 82, 120; and Ngāti Kahungunu 152
Te Whētumatarau significance 18; and Ngāpuhi taua 45, 54
Te Whiti o Tu 151, 152
Teiteinui 178
Temuka 119, 142

Thames pā at 18; effects of taua and migrations involving 24, 43, 53, 54; musket trade 32
Thomas, Bill 144
Three Kings Islands *see* Manawatāwhi
Tiaia 114
Tiakitai 152, 154, 155
Tihoi 160
Tikitiki 165
Tikokino 151
Tiniroto Lakes 155
Tirarau 21, 68, 82
Tiria 79
Titi o Kura Saddle 152
Titia 181
Titirangi pā Marlborough Sounds pā) 108
  Wairoa area pā 64, 152, 153
Titiraupenga pā 156–58
Titoko 92
Titore 69, 67–70, 82
Tiwai Point 143
Toetoe Bay 144
Toheriri 97
Toka a Kuku 166, 167
Tokomairiro 142
Topeora 104
Tortoise, HMS 185
Tory 128
Tōtaranui 106, 108, 127, 139
Treaty of Waitangi influence for peace 14; guarantees to Māori in and effects of signing 16, 21; compensation rights for breach of significance 19, 23, 25, 26, 128; and Te Rauparaha 130; and Taua-iti and Taua-nui 141; and Kāi Tahu 145, 146; and Moriori 147; and Te Arawa and Ngāiterangi 181–83, 185; and conflict in Whanganui area 189
Tuainene 125
Tuakiaki 152, 154
Tuhawaiki and northern taua 112, 119; and Taua-nui 140, 141; and Te Puoho 144; and aftermath of Te Puoho's taua 145
Tūhoe taua and migrations involving 24, 25, 55, 61, 64; and Te Mautaranui 152, 154; and Ngāti Kahungunu 157
Tūhourangi and Ngāiterangi 59, 60; and Ngāiterangi 179, 181
Tuhua (Mayor Island) 170–72, 183
Tuhuru 116, 144
Tukitua 157
Tukituki River 155

Tukituki Patu Aruhe 106
Tukorehu and Pukerangiora 29; and Te Amiowhenua 75, 77; and north Taranaki 79; and Ngāti Ruanui 89; and Ngāti Kahungunu 149
Tupaea 170, 182–85, 190
Tūranganui (Gisborne) or Tūranga effects of migrations involving 25; and Ngāpuhi taua 44; and Ngarara events 164
Tutaakamoana 160
Tutehounuku 136, 140
Tutepakihirangi 104, 125
Tutepourangi 102, 103
Tuterangianini 81, 91, 92
Tutukaka 69, 80, 82
Tuturau 127, 143, 144
Tuwhare 37, 38, 75, 76

U
Umukuri (East Bay) 108
Urania 102
Urewera effects of taua and migrations involving 24, 39, 55, 61, 152, 157
Urenui 74
Utuhina 171

V
Venus 32, 33, 34, 39, 40
Vernon Lagoons 106
Victoria, HMS 185
Victoria, Queen 189
Volcanic Plateau musket trade 32; and Ngāti Maru taua 92, 94

W
Waiapu and Ngāpuhi taua 45; and Whānau a Apanui 165
Waiau River 64
Waiharakeke (Flaxbourne) River 136, 138
Waihau Bay (eastern Bay of Plenty) 165
Waihau pā (Tiniroto Lakes) 155
Waihi estuary (Bay of Plenty) 179, 181
Waihi pā (Taupō) and Ngāti Maru taua 92, 93; and Ngāti Kahungunu 160
Waihopai Valley (Marlborough) 141
Waihora (Lake Ellesmere) 132, 135, 142
Waihou River 54, 183
Waihuka River 164
Waikaia River 143
Waikanae 99, 100, 103, 125, 128
Waikare Lake 82

Waikato (iwi) comparison of casualties inflicted by 22; Waikato taua north 22; south 24; losses at Te Totara 55; and Mātakitaki 56–58; and Pomare 65; and Te Rangituke 66; and Te Rauparaha 72; taua involving north Taranaki 79, 82, 84; and south Taranaki 89; and Ngāti Raukawa 94; and Ngāti Kahungunu 149; and Ngāti Raukawa 150; and Ngāti Kahungunu 151, 152, 156, 160; and Te Arawa 178–80; and Ngā Rauru and Ngāti Ruanui 185, 189, 190
Waikato (rangatira) 47, 51
Waikato (River) comparison of effects 21; taua and migrations involving 24, 25, 55, 64, 65, 68, 81, 89; musket trade 32; and Te Amiowhenua 75, 77; Waikawa Stream (Horowhenua) 97; and aftermath of Kaiuku 159
Waikohu River 164
Waikouaiti 145
Waimana 61
Waimarama 149
Waimate North 68
Waimate pā 80, 84, 89, 189
Wainuioru River 75
Waioeka 61, 91
Waiohinganga (Esk) River 157
Waiorua 102–105, 107, 108, 116, 155
Waiotahi 61
Waipawa River 151
Waipa occupation of 21; taua and migrations involving 24, 64, 65, 75, 78; musket trade 32; and Mātakitaki 55, 56, 58
Waipaoa River 44, 164
Waipara River 116, 117
Waipukurau 151
Wairakei 159
Wairarapa taua and migrations involving 75, 97, 104, 125, 127; and coalition dissolution 126; and involving hapū of in aftermath of Kaiuku 159
Wairau River 124; Ngāti Toa taua involving 27, 105, 106, 108, 116, 136; and Te Rauparaha's mana 130; and Taua-iti and Taua-nui 141; and final Kāi Tahu taua 145
Wairau Incident 130
Wairewa whaling 31; and Kaihuanga clashes 132, 133, 145
Wairoa River Tauranga area 43 Wairoa area 64, 152–54

Waitakere taua involving 25
Waitaki River 143
Waitangi (Rēkohu) 128, 129, 146, 147
Waitangi Tribunal and general claims 29, 141; and Te Waipounamu claims 146
Waitapu 36
Waitara pā on river 18; Te Ātiawa 1848 return 26; and Te Rauparaha 74; and Te Amiowhenua 76, 77
Waitemata Harbour 55, 66
Waitotara River 96, 185, 186, 191
Waiuku 55
Waka Nene, Tamati taua led by 40, 51, 75, 76; and *Haweis* events 162
Wakatahuri 108
Wakatiri (Lottin Point) 45
Wakauna 156, 157
Wanaka Lake 143
Weller Brothers whaling station 132
Wellington first use 12; first settlement 13; comparison of casualties 22; and Whanganui 190
West Coast (North Island) taua involving 36
Westland or West Coast (South Island) *see* Te Tai Poutini
Westport *see* Kawatiri
Whaingaroa (Raglan Harbour) and Captain Kent 32
Whakaahurangi track 84
Whakaari (White Island) 163, 165
Whakaepa (Coalgate) 132
Whakakitenga Bay 114
Whakapuaka 112
Whakaraupō (Lyttleton Harbour) 113, 132
Whakarewa 81
Whakatane musket trade 32; and *Venus* 39; early taua involving 55; and Pomare 61; later taua involving 90; and Ngarara 148, 160, 162
Whakatara pā 92, 93
Whakatari 114
Whakatōhea migrations involving 25; musket trade 32; and Pomare and Te Wera 61, 64; taua involving 91; and Ngāti Porou 148; and Ngāti Kahungunu 153; and Ngarara events 163, 164; and Kekeparoa 164, 165; and Toka a Kuku 166
Whakatū (Nelson) first settlement 13; northern taua 112, 116

Whānau a Apanui musket trade 32; and *Venus* 34, 40, 61; and Ngāti Porou 148, 165, 166, 167; and Ngarara events 163, 164, 165; and Toka a Kuku 166, 167
Whanganui (also Petre) first use and settlement 13; purchase of 26, 190
Whanganui Inlet (South Island) taua involving 27
Whanganui River and iwi, taua and migrations involving 23, 25, 26, 36, 76, 84, 92, 94, 96, 100; and Te Rauparaha's taua 120, 168; and Ngāti Tūwharetoa 185–88, 189, 191
Whanganui a Tara first use 12, 15, 128; comparison of casualties 22; taua and migrations involving 24, 25, 28, 40, 76, 97, 103, 104, 126; and coalition dissolution 126, 130; and final Kāi Tahu taua 145
Whangaparoa Bay 61, 165
Whangape 82
Whangarei effects of Waikato taua on 22, 66, 69, 82; and *Venus* 32, 39; taua involving 42, 53, 79, 80
Whangaroa Harbour (Northland) and musket trade 30, 31; and Hongi Hika 66
Whangaroa Harbour (Rēkohu) 146
Wharekahika (Hicks Bay) and *Venus* 34, 40; and Ngarara events 163
Wharekauri *see* Rēkohu
Wharekura 61, 165
Wharepapa pā 14
Whareponga Bay 45
Wharetomokia 163
White Island *see* Whakaari
Williams, Captain Peter 131

ABOUT THE AUTHOR

Brought up and educated in Auckland, Ron Crosby pursued his legal career in Blenheim, including 30 years as a court lawyer particularly in Treaty related and Resource Management cases. He is a hearings commissioner under the Resource Management Act 1991 and was appointed to the Waitangi Tribunal in 2011.

Ron's first book, researched and written over a five-year period, was *The Musket Wars: A History of Inter-Iwi Conflict, 1806–1845* (1999), which was widely applauded as the first comprehensive account of this period. His subsequent books are *Gilbert Mair: Te Kooti's Nemesis* (2004), *Andris Apse: Odyssey and Images* (2006), *Albaneta: Lost Opportunity at Cassino* (2007), *NZSAS: The First Fifty Years* (2009), *A Desperate Dawn: The Battle for Turuturu Mokai* (2013) and *Kūpapa: The Bitter Legacy of Māori Alliances with the Crown* (2015). He retains a deep interest in New Zealand's back country and history.

His interest in te ao Māori is constantly reinforced by his whānau relationships, his wife Margy (pictured above with Ron) being of Te Rarawa and Te Aupōuri descent. They have three adult children and eight grandchildren, and live in Blenheim.

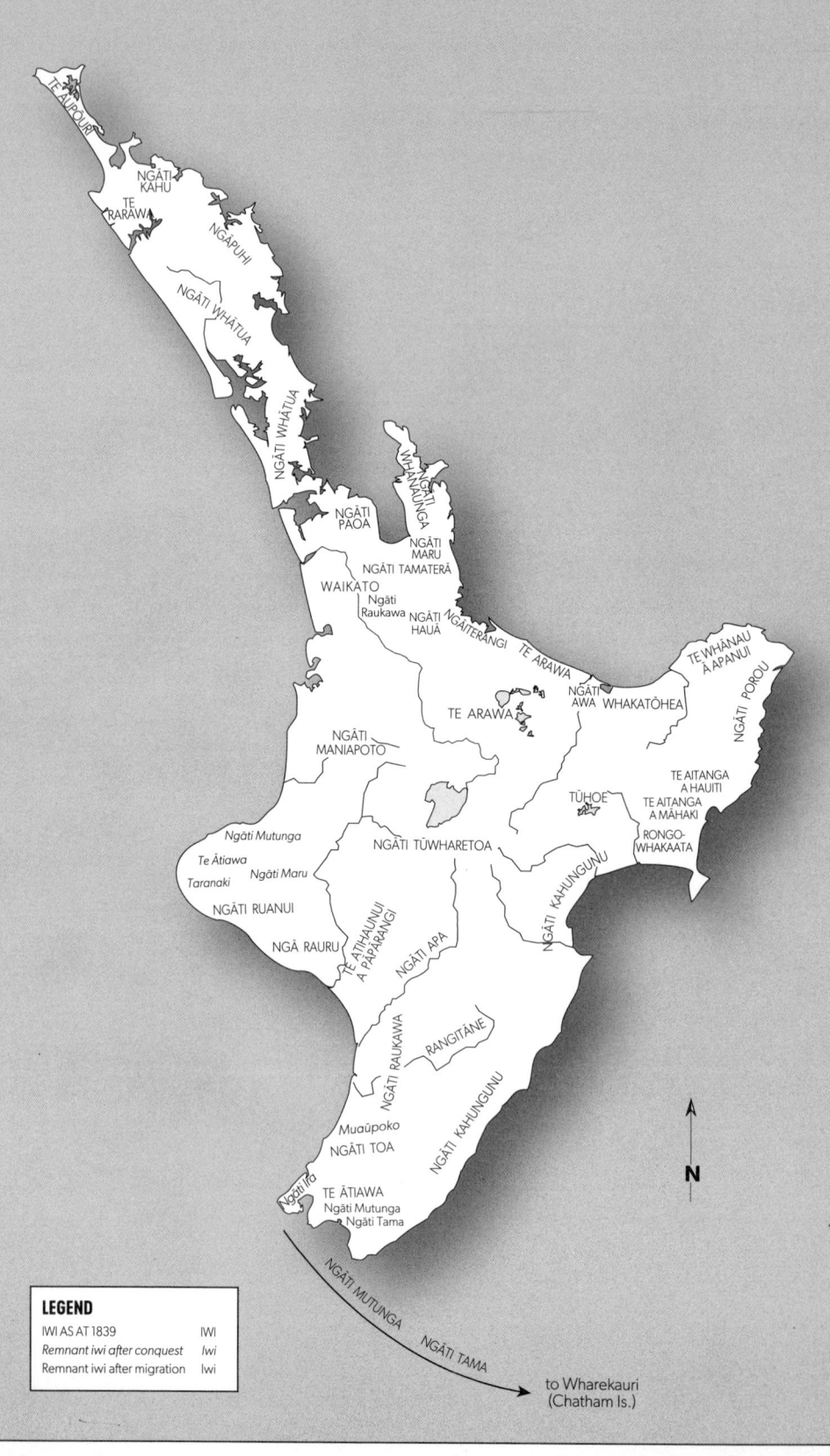